CH00970542

'This book is a profound wake up call to ⸺ and communities that will meet the trip ⸺ resource depletion and doing more with le ⸺ 'warts and all' journey of the LILAC hous ⸺ a fundamental set of ethics which provic ⸺ comprehensive and practical guidance for 1 ⸺ ᵍ ⸺⸻⸻. This book will inspire those who wish to undertake a journey of collectively building their own homes, and just as importantly, it generously explains to others involved in housing, what the secret ingredients of collective success are.'

Fionn Stevenson, Professor, School of Architecture, University of Sheffield, UK

'Almost everywhere that people are talking about radical housing solutions in Britain they are talking about LILAC. If you want to know how the world is being changed for the better, from the bottom and straw–bale up, you need to read LILAC's story.'

Danny Dorling, Halford Mackinder Professor of Geography at the University of Oxford, UK, and author of All That is Solid: The Great Housing Disaster

'An engaging account of how an affordable, low-impact cohousing scheme was conceived, negotiated (and how and with whom!), designed, financed and built in Leeds, within a discussion of what this contributes to addressing larger local, city and global social and ecological challenges.'

David Satterthwaite, Professor, International Institute for Environment and Development (IIED)

'I am convinced that living within planetary boundaries is not only possible, but that we can lead better lives by making the transition. Paul Chatterton has taken an architect's plan of this idea and made it a practical reality. His inspiring book tells the story of how to build better communities and respect the Earth they are built upon.'

Andrew Simms, author of Cancel the Apocalypse, *Fellow of nef*

'New thinking about how together we find ways to walk lightly upon the Earth and solve the growing affordable housing crisis is easy in comparison to the vision, tenacity and commitment needed to deliver innovative solutions. The LILAC members have the latter in spades. This book is an inspirational story about how a group of ordinary people transformed the way housing can work through a pioneering mutual home ownership development. It will inspire a generation.'

Cllr. David Rodgers, Deputy Cabinet Member for Housing Employment and Skills, London Borough of Ealing; former CEO of CDS Co-operatives and past President of Co-operative Housing International.

LOW IMPACT LIVING

This book is the inspirational story of one project that shows you how you can become involved in building and running your neighbourhood. The author, co-founder of Lilac (Low Impact Living Affordable Community), explains how a group of people got together to build one of the most pioneering ecological, affordable cohousing neighbourhoods in the world. The book is a story of perseverance, vision and passion, demonstrating how ordinary people can build their own affordable, ecological community.

The book starts with the clear values that motivated and guided the project's members: sustainability, cooperativism, equality, social justice and self-management. It outlines how they were driven by challenges and concerns over the need to respond to climate change and energy scarcity, the limits of the 'business as usual' model of pro-growth economics, and the need to develop resources so that communities can determine and manage their own land and resources. The author's story is interspersed with vignettes on topics such as decision making, landscaping, finance and design.

The book summarizes academic debates on the key issues that informed the project, and gives technical data on energy and land issues as well as practical 'how-to' guides on a range of topics such as designing meetings, budget planning and community agreements. *Low Impact Living* provides clear and easy to follow advice for community groups, students, practitioners, government, business and the development sector and is heavily illustrated with drawings and photographs from the project team.

Paul Chatterton is a writer, researcher and campaigner. He is Reader in 'Cities and Social Change' in the School of Geography at the University of Leeds where he cofounded the 'Cities and Social Justice' Research Cluster and the Masters programme in 'Activism and Social Change'. He has written extensively on urban issues and movements for social and ecological justice. More information on his work can be found at www.paulchatterton.com.

Earthscan Tools for Community Planning Series

There is increasing global demand for more local involvement in the planning of the environment. This is the only way that communities will get the surroundings they want and make the transition towards a sustainable future. This series of short, accessibly priced, practical books have been written by the world's leading planning professionals to provide tools to support community planning wherever it occurs. Each book is a stand -alone, but together they create a compelling resource for planning professionals, community groups, activists, planning students and anyone looking to facilitate engagement in a community context.

Low Impact Living
A field guide to ecological, affordable community building
Paul Chatterton

The Spacemaker's Guide to Big Change
Design and improvisation in development practice
Nabeel Hamdi

Community Matters
Service-learning in engaged design and planning
Edited by Mallika Bose, Cheryl Doble, Paula Horrigan and Sigmund Shipp

The Community Planning Handbook (Second Edition)
How people can shape their cities, towns and villages in any part of the world
Nick Wates

Sustainable Communities
Creating a durable local economy
Rhonda Phillips, Bruce Seifer and Ed Antczak

The Placemaker's Guide to Building Community
Nabeel Hamdi

Creative Community Planning
Wendy Sarkissian, Dianna Hurford and Christine Wenman

Kitchen Table Sustainability
Wendy Sarkissian, Nancy Hofer, Yollanda Shore, Steph Vajda and Cathy Wilkinson

The Community Planning Event Manual
Nick Wates

LOW IMPACT LIVING

A field guide to ecological, affordable community building

Paul Chatterton

Routledge
Taylor & Francis Group

LONDON AND NEW YORK

earthscan
from Routledge

First published 2015
by Routledge
2 Park Square, Milton Park, Abingdon, Oxon OX14 4RN

and by Routledge
711 Third Avenue, New York, NY 10017

Routledge is an imprint of the Taylor & Francis Group, an informa business

British Library Cataloguing-in-Publication Data
A catalogue record for this book is available from the British Library

Library of Congress Cataloging-in-Publication Data
Chatterton, Paul, 1972-
    Low impact living : a field guide to ecological, affordable community
    building / Paul Chatterton.
        pages cm. — (Earthscan tools for community planning)
    Includes bibliographical references and index.
    1. Housing, Cooperative—Great Britain—Case studies. 2. Ecological
    houses—Great Britain. 3. Common interest ownership communities
    —Great Britain. 4. Community development—Great Britain.
    5. Sustainable urban development—Great Britain. I. Title.
    HD7287.72.G7C43 2014
    334'.10941—dc23   2014003840

ISBN: 978-0-415-66160-7 (hbk)
ISBN: 978-0-415-66161-4 (pbk)
ISBN: 978-1-315-76592-1 (ebk)

Typeset in Bembo
by Keystroke, Station Road, Codsall, Wolverhampton

For Tash, Milo and Rafi, who made it all worthwhile.

CONTENTS

ILLUSTRATIONS

Figures

Tables

FOREWORD

At the time of writing, the Lilac cohousing scheme is one of a small breed of happy projects around the country that serve as exemplars of how we might build not just affordable homes but thriving, social and sustaining communities. When I visited in 2013, construction was just finishing and we planted a rowan tree to mark the beginning of ownership. The civilized aspect of ownership here is that it is shared. The allotments, community hub building and public realm are shared. The project even came about through a shared approach to finance via a groundbreaking mutual financial model.

All this is exciting, adventurous, but – in case you feel daunted by what has been achieved – hardly risky. All the ideas that Lilac brings together are proven, either in the UK or on the continent. In my own company, Hab, we adopt the same approach of bringing the best practice from other schemes and putting it together in one place. This is important because we need to demonstrate that great place making, innovative architecture and socially progressive ways of making more sustainable communities are not weird or dangerous or expensive. In fact the proof from looking around what's happening in places like Denmark, Germany and Holland is that, in the longer term, these places are more resilient, cheaper to look after, and desirable places to live.

Lilac is a British exemplar that may even prove to be a template for many more, similar schemes. There's much learning to be gleaned in these pages. It's as much a field-guide as anything else – for other practitioners and community groups wanting to go on a similar journey. If that's your great desire then I wish you every ounce of luck and energy. As to inspiration, you're holding it in your hands.

Kevin McCloud

ACKNOWLEDGEMENTS

The Lilac project would not have happened without the generous and creative input of so many groups and organizations. In alphabetical order, these include: Amazonails, Bernard Williams Associates, Camberwell Project, CDS Co-operatives, Coho Ltd, the Common Place in Leeds, Community Land and Finance, Connect Housing, Co-operatives UK, Cooperatives Yorkshire and Humber, the Department for Communities and Local Government, the Department for Energy and Climate Change, DWF LLP, Ecology Building Society, the Global Ecovillage Network, the Homes and Communities Agency, Integral Engineering Design, Leeds City Council, Leeds Ecovillage, Leeds Environmental Design Associates, Leeds Love it Share it, Lindum Group, Maldaba Ltd, Modcell, the National Self Build Association, the Permaculture Association, Progetic Energy Consultants, the School of Geography at the University of Leeds, Stroma, Synergy Housing, Triodos Bank, the Tudor Trust, the UK Cohousing Network, UnLtd, White Design Associates and Yorkshire Design Studios.

Among this huge cast of organizations, special thanks need to go to certain people: David Rodgers for his foundational work on mutual home ownership, and being a constant guide and advocate for what we were doing; Barbara Jones for giving inspirational impetus to build with straw; Jimm Reed for his dedication and direction as project manager over the years; Craig White for his role as creative architect and inventor of Modcell; and the whole team at Lindum Group, who provided such wide-ranging support throughout. In addition, there were so many people who substantially helped and supported us at Leeds City Council and the Homes and Communities Agency that it's not possible to list them, or remember them all here, but a huge thanks to you all. Certain friends also helped hugely with constant informal advice over the years. I'd like to particularly thank Martin, Roger, Olly, Irena and Andy. Thanks also to mine and Tash's parents and family, for believing in what we were doing over the years. My colleagues and students at the School of Geography at the University of Leeds also require special thanks for supporting me over the years and for allowing me to use my valuable time to develop and reflect on Lilac.

And of course, I acknowledge the foundational and inspirational role played by all the Lilac members for making this happen. In alphabetical order and at the time of writing, they include: Alan, Amanda, Amber, Andy, Avelino, Ben, Beth, Bonnie, Brenda, Celia, Clive, Eden, Edgar, Elinor, Ellie, Erica, Fra, Fran, Grace, Hannah, Jenny, Joe, Kirsty, Laura, Laurie, Lee, Lewis, Liz, Lucy, Maddi, Maria, Max, Mike, Milo, Orla, Paul, Rafi, Rick, Robin, Rosa, Samuel, Sarah, Stefan, Tash and Uddyotani. This is a truly amazing group of people who made a beautiful leap of faith to make this project happen. Thanks also to former members: Helen, Giles, Tom, Andrea and Mark. A further acknowledgement goes to the growing number of people on our waiting list who have supported us in numerous ways.

Thanks also to the team at Routledge publishing who supported this proposal and helped bring the book to publication. Particular thanks go to Alice Aldous, Siobhán Greaney and Nicki Dennis. I also must acknowledge Laurie from Lilac for editing assistance, as well as Alison Manton from the School of Geography and my friend Brian for help with redrawing figures. There are a huge amount of illustrations in this book, which I have used to try to bring the story to life. Thanks to Andy Lord, Modcell, White Design Associates and Lindum Group for permission to use great colour photographs that appear in the centre of the book (and thanks to Modcell for the use of the front cover photograph). Thanks also to the following for granting permission to use the illustrations that appear throughout the book: Modcell (Figures 3.5, 3.17, 4.17), White Design Associates (Figures 3.6, 3.13, 4.6, 4.7, 4.11, 4.12, 4.15, 4.16, 4.18, 4.20, 4.21), Lindum Group (Figure 3.14), Martin Johnson (Figure 4.2), Roger Stannard (Figure 4.4), Progetic (Figures 4.30, 4.31, 4.32, Table 4.1), Steve Wilcox and the Joseph Rowntree Foundation (Figure 5.1), Robin Lovelace (for creating Figures 5.3 and 5.4 using the free and open source graphics package ggplot2), Maldaba Ltd (Figures 5.6, 5.7), the Yorkshire Evening Post (Figure 6.6), Diana Leafe Christian (Figure 6.8, Table 6.2) and Seeds for Change (Figure 6.10). All other figures and illustrations are courtesy of Lilac.

There are so many other people, projects and places that we have learned from and been inspired by in countless small ways. Many have faded from my memory, and some may have only provided a fleeting glimpse or a passing conversation. Nevertheless, I owe a debt of gratitude to all of these moments. In some small way, they made Lilac what it is today. So, if I've ever had a conversation with you about

Lilac, I send my deepest and most sincere thanks to you. You were part of the journey and you know who you are. . . .

Finally, given that there are many references to people, places, events and facts in this book, along the way I will have inevitably made a few errors here and there. Suffice it to say that I take full responsibility for all of these errors. I would be delighted to receive feedback on anything I have misrepresented or got factually wrong. Because this book is based upon real events and people, I have anonymized facts or events to maintain confidentiality where appropriate.

1

INTRODUCTION

Building an impossible community

'You are doing what?' asked Peter, in a half-incredulous, half-disinterested tone.

He had obviously heard hundreds of people come up with similarly ambitious ideas over the years, and this was another one. Peter ran a successful eco-camping site in rural Wales, on the back of a long-standing career as an eco-builder.

'We are going to build 20 houses from strawbales in Leeds where we live. We are going to run it as a cooperative so it'll be permanently affordable. It's based on cohousing principles with a common house in the middle where we will eat and hang out together', I repeated, briefly this time as I detected he was starting to lose interest.

This was in 2007, and Tash and I were standing in the middle of a large marquee in a forest deep in west Wales at the Do Lectures, a weekend retreat showcasing radical alternatives run by the ethical clothes makers Howies. I had been invited to give a talk on my experiences in self-management and popular education in changing the world.

'Have you found some land? Have you got a project manager? Where is the money coming from? What's your loan-to-value ratio? Has your quantity surveyor done a preliminary budget?' Peter asked abruptly.

'Well err, no. We are right at the beginning, but we'll sort all that out', replied Tash authoritatively, attempting to retain some control over the conversation.

'Look, good luck with it. It sounds great. You've got a long way to go. But if you don't mind me saying you sound incredibly naive. Get some help. You've got a long way to go,' said Peter as a parting shot as he drifted off round the tent to talk to other guests. We looked at each other.

'We are building an impossible community, right?' she said.

'Yeah, probably. But it's never stopped us before.'

What's this book about?

Back then it did seem a truly ambitious idea, a dream that may or may not come to fruition. Now I live in the Lilac project. It's the first of its kind in the UK, and maybe even the world. It's certainly never been done before in the way we have done it. Lilac stands for 'Low Impact Living Affordable Community'. It is a member-controlled cohousing cooperative comprising 20 highly insulated homes built from timber and straw with a shared common house. It uses a unique fully mutual equity leasehold model that makes it affordable in perpetuity. The dream became a reality after nearly seven years of hard work. This is the book about how we made it happen; about how a group of ordinary people got together to do something quite extraordinary – to build the first cohousing project that was both affordable, low impact, cooperative and committed to building a supporting, nurturing community. And all this happened in the rather unlikely city of Leeds – a large post-industrial city in the north of England struggling to find its feet after heavy industry had long moved overseas.

Low Impact Living is a book about lots of things – cohousing, cooperative living, low carbon housing, good place making, community self-governance, and social and ecological justice are just a few of them. Specifically, it's a book about the Lilac project and how a group of people made what seemed like an impossibility into a reality; how years of dreaming, talking and planning became a pioneering reference project. It was six incredibly hard years. But of course we didn't just make Lilac happen on our own. A huge cast of people and ideas were mobilized, and our idea grew strong as we walked on the shoulders of countless other inspirational people and places. This book tells the story of what motivated us to build Lilac, how we actually made it happen, what Lilac means, its main aspects, glimpses of what it's been like living there in the first year of its life, and what lessons may be drawn from this experience.

The reasons for writing this book are numerous. There is so much to say about how Lilac came about, so many insights, lessons and potentials for the future for others to follow and learn from what we have done. I wanted to offer an honest 'warts 'n' all' account of how we did it. I wanted to show how difficult, complex, but also how amazing and exhilarating it is to believe in something that breaks through the deadlock of convention, and then find a way to turn your dream into a reality. But beyond a straightforward account, I want this book to provide some useful factual and technical information and resources for those who want to follow up the detail of what we did and how we did it. Glance through any large bookstore and you will find scores of books on eco-building, green architecture and sustainable cities. These are great, of course, and many have inspired me along the way.[1] But they lack something. With a few exceptions, they are often dry technical guides. They offer a wealth of concepts, insights and technical data, all of which are really vital. But what's missing are people. How do sustainable cities actually come about? Who is doing the ecobuilding, for what reasons, and what kinds of visions of the future do they have? What motivated them, and how did they overcome obstacles? Who is going to use these books to bring about the wide-scale and increasingly urgent social transformation in our lifetime? The underlying premise of this book is that the task is too vast and complex, too delicate and subtle, to leave it to the architectural profession, big government or big business. Sure, they have resources and answers, but they need to be seen as enablers rather than experts in charge of the process. All too often the story of our cities unfolds through the power and politics of an elite group. This kind of top-down approach, as I'll explore in this book, cannot on its own deliver the kinds of innovations needed to tackle the multiple crises ahead.

So I wanted to write a book that stands out from what already exists – a book that is based on the direct and real-time experience of a group of people. I wanted to write a book that many different people could relate to and be inspired by. The book's title *Low Impact Living* is intentionally open and questioning. It may be interpreted in many different ways. At the most basic level, low impact living evokes the daily practices of treading more lightly on the planet. This has long been a calling of the environmental movement. And of course now we can measure exactly how lightly we live on the planet through sophisticated ecological footprinting tools.[2] But beyond the ecological, what else does a low impact life mean? The Lilac model is a living experiment into the interconnected and holistic ways in which our lives can be reformulated so that they tread more lightly. Thus, low impact can refer to many areas of our lives be it social, political and economic. This raises a whole raft of challenges such as: how can we create communities that are both more inclusive and embrace difference; how can we find a deeper sense of fulfilment beyond rampant consumerism; how can we communicate in ways that are less violent; how can we move away from the brutality of top-down planning; how can we govern ourselves in less hierarchical ways; how can we control and soften the impacts of a turbo-charged casino-like global economy? A neighbourhood based upon low impact living, then, is intended to be deeply transformative, a bulwark against the status quo and a move towards a possible future that is only partially outlined but urgently needed. The subtitle '*A field guide to ecological, affordable community building*' was chosen for specific reasons. It will be great if this book is dog-eared, scrawled on, used in all sorts of contexts, and covered with tea and coffee stains. And it's about the act and art of building — not just bricks and mortar (or straw and timber), but the communities which will mobilize to shape the neighbourhoods of tomorrow.

So, you may find the book educational and challenging if you are a student or researcher in further or higher education looking to broaden your understanding of the challenges and responses that our society faces. You may find this useful if you are a teacher and looking for case study material that you want to share with others. You may find this inspiring if you are part of an emerging group looking for ideas and advice about your project and how to move forward. You may find this informative if you are a policy maker, stakeholder or part of a statutory agency and have a role in facilitating these kinds of projects. I wanted to lay down something that was a mixture of styles and narrative voices — that weaves together diverse elements such as conceptual discussion, personal story, chronological narrative, resource manual, technical guide, reference list. So in this book you will find detailed discussions of the ideas and concepts that underpin the Lilac project, a grounded chronology of events as they directly unfolded, and personal reflections woven together with technical information, guides, resources and templates that we have directly tried and tested.

This book is only my account of how we built Lilac. It is written from my perspective as the first secretary of the society and as the contact point for our team of professionals during the construction phase. But I helped build Lilac along with several other hugely dedicated co-founders. Now there are 35 adult inspirational members and 10 amazing children who all together make Lilac what it is. I see Lilac as part of an open source revolution. The creative genius of the collective exceeds any of the talents and competencies of the individual parts. At this scale of operation there is a logic, and indeed magic, to Lilac through group think, collective learning and skill sharing. Of course, now there are lots of other stories and perspectives about Lilac from the diverse membership. Each would recount the Lilac story in their own way, and from their perspective, and in the future I hope many more stories on Lilac will emerge. So mine is an initial and partial account, and I owe a debt of gratitude to the many other perspectives and ideas I have encountered along the way. This book would not have happened without them. It is a deeply individual account set in a deeply collective context.

Structure of the book

I have divided the story of Lilac into seven chapters. After this introduction, Chapter 2 deals with the context, values and challenges that underpin Lilac, and made us act. Chapter 3 presents quite a detailed chronology of the six years that represent the development journey of Lilac, as well as some reflections on the first year of living there. The next three chapters offer a detailed exploration of the main aspects of the Lilac concept – low impact living, affordability and community. Chapter 4 explores how we put low impact living into practice and looks at how we designed Lilac and conceived the overall strategy for reducing its ecological impact. Chapter 5 discusses our pioneering mutual cooperative financial model that attempts to embed economic equality. Chapter 6 explores what community means to us and how we put it into practice, especially in the context of cohousing. Lilac is about much more than these three aspects. They are deeply integrated and holistic, and together have synergistic effects, reinforcing the positive impacts of the other. Although this book discusses the three elements of Lilac in turn, this division is rather false and the real strength comes from the whole model working together. The final chapter provides some overall insights and lessons for a range of different groups (grassroots, developers, the local state) and explores the problems and pitfalls associated with projects like Lilac.

These chapters may be read in any order or indeed as stand-alone entities depending on your interests. I have kept the book as brief as possible – thus it offers an initial understanding without overwhelming one with detail. Behind almost every page there lurks another story. Clearly, I hope this book will be used to give impetus to projects around the world, but I must offer an honest disclaimer and reality check. What worked for us may not work for you. And Lilac represents the specificities of the UK, its financial, land and legal arrangements, many of which are unique and not repeatable elsewhere. I have tried to keep this in mind and give broader lessons as my hope is that this is a book that will be read and used as much outside the UK as within it. No two moments in time or place are the same. Your journey, wherever you are, will be different to ours, and necessarily so. The rest of this book is dedicated to telling the story of Lilac in some detail.

Postscript: cohousing is good for your health

On Sunday, 2 June 2013, only a couple of months after we had moved into Lilac, and only one week after the contractor finally left the site, I had a cerebrovascular accident (CVA) – more commonly known as a stroke. It was a fairly small stroke, but it was a life-changing event. I was sitting in my allotment at Lilac which is only a few metres away from the houses. I was marking some end-of-term essays (I teach geography at the University of Leeds) and doing some weeding in the sun. I was quite dehydrated from a bottle of wine that I had drunk the night before. I was chatting to Ellie who had the allotment next to mine and she went off to get us both a cup of tea as I sat there in the hot sun. I stood up to go and do some weeding and the most amazing lightheaded and out-of-body sensation engulfed me.

I started to wobble, my limbs felt heavy and I fell to the ground on all fours. I was having what the medical profession calls a 'vasovagal attack'. Then I began to vomit profusely. It was heard right across the site by people who were wandering around doing their Sunday chores. Through a cloud of mist I saw Ellie walking back towards me holding two cups of tea. I began to call her name but I couldn't form any words. When she arrived she asked me jokingly what I was doing on all fours, thinking I was messing around. But when she realized what state I was in she immediately started to help.

Luckily for me, Ellie is a paramedic and remained calm. She shouted for help and a bunch of Lilac residents came running. I was hyperventilating. They calmed me down and gave me some water. I was totally out of control and couldn't speak or move my body as I slumped to the floor wondering what the hell had happened to me. After about five minutes they decided to try to get me inside. They found a wheelbarrow on the allotment, lifted me up and put me in it, and began to wheel me back towards my house. At the front door, they lifted me out and I started to crawl on all fours into the hallway. I again attempted to talk to them but couldn't. It took me about 20 minutes to reach the sofa and I lay there lifelessly into the evening. For the next two days I stayed in bed recovering.

I only found out eight days later that I had had a stroke. Throughout the whole of that week, I thought I was recovering from a nasty virus. Although they now know it was an ischemic stroke, they never found a cause. It's what they call cryptogenic. Their best guess is that a small blood clot may have formed from an arterial dissection in my neck. The clot then broke off and created a blockage. Dehydration may also have played a part. The block restricted the flow of blood and oxygen to my brain which led to three small lesions where brain tissue had died (or infarcts as they are called) in my cerebellum and mid-brain. It is terrifying to think that this is like a game of Russian roulette. The block could have affected other parts of my brain, and more important functions. Luckily, the parts that it affected related to coordination, and specifically fine motor skills in my right hand. The damage was not severe and new neural pathways opened up around the dead cells within a few months.

This all happened in the middle of writing this book. The second half of it has been written with me slowly punching individual keys like a school kid learning to use a keyboard for the first time. I then acquired some dictation software to speed things up. Living in a cohousing community was an amazingly lucky break to deal with an event like this. Everyone knew what had happened, and everyone was eager to help. Normally, it's great having one neighbour who can help you out. But I had dozens of people checking in, making food and doing little chores for me to make my recovery period easier.

Did the stress of building Lilac play a part? We will never know. One person's stress is another person's pleasure. And the medical profession cannot offer any definitive evidence linking stress and stoke events. Certainly the six years of building Lilac taxed me heavily. There are lessons to make sure the big workloads are shared early and evenly as the size of a project develops. What happened on that Sunday in June was a huge shock to my body. There were probably countless warning signs building up to this point which I had ignored as I was too busy frantically helping to finish Lilac and keep up with my day job. But after the day of my stroke there was no doubt that things had to change. I am now a lot slower and do less. I spend more time pottering around Lilac with my family. My body is more in control, and I'm listening to it every day.

I always wonder what would have happened if I had collapsed in a quiet corner of my house or in an empty allotment far from my house where nobody would have found me for hours, possibly days. But thankfully I was surrounded by fellow cohousers, with a strong sense of togetherness. People often say that one of the great benefits of a cohousing community is the natural surveillance it offers to check in on people's well-being and health. That day I knew exactly what that meant. On 2 June 2013, cohousing could possibly have saved my life.

Notes

1   There are many great books out there, and too numerous to mention. A selection include the following: Satterthwaite (1999), Newman (2008), Newman *et al.* (2009), Rydin (2010), Anderson (2006), Bicknell *et al.* (2009), Phillips *et al.* (2013), Hamdi (2004, 2010), Bulkeley *et al.* (2010), Williams (2012), Lerch (2007), Peters *et al.* (2010), Pullen (2011), Santini and Zilafro (2009), Cook (2011), Desai (2009), Hall (2013), Johnston *et al.* (2013), Anderson (2009), Calthorpe (2013) and Register (2006).

2   The concept and tools of ecological footprinting are now well developed. See e.g. Wackernagel *et al.* (2006), and see the very useful and comprehensive website http://www.footprintnetwork.org/en/index.php/GFN/. One Planet Living (http://www.oneplanetliving.org) and the Living Building Challenge (http://living-future.org/lbc) are also useful frameworks to assess the broader ecological and social impacts of a community.

2

CONTEXT, VALUES AND CHALLENGES

In this chapter I want to take a step back from the Lilac project. I want to put the idea in its wider context in a number of ways. First, I'll explore what I see as Lilac's broader context which has offered inspiration. Second, there's a range of motivations and values that have driven the people behind the project. These make Lilac what it is and include environmental sustainability, self-reliance, grassroots, learning, equality, well-being, diversity and ethics. Finally, each of the three elements of the Lilac concept (low impact, affordable, community) relate to some of the interconnected challenges of our age. This chapter outlines these challenges as they give the project its substance. Lilac is not just a great place to live. It's a direct response to climate change, financial turmoil and social breakdown.[1] Figure 2.1 shows the interrelations between the values and the challenges.

Lilac's wider context

Lilac's desire to build a pioneering, affordable, low impact cohousing community has deep roots. We have learned from many others, past and present, and continue to do so. There is a kinship with groups daring to be different, rejecting convention, and the 'business as usual' approach to their lives, from around the world and different periods in time. Examples abound: the land occupations of South America and Africa where people have claimed a historic right to land and strive for greater autonomy and self-management, such as the Movemento Sem Terra in Brazil, the Ejército Zapatista de Liberación Nacional (EZLN) in southern Mexico, and the shack dwellers' movement in South Africa; the Diggers during the English Civil

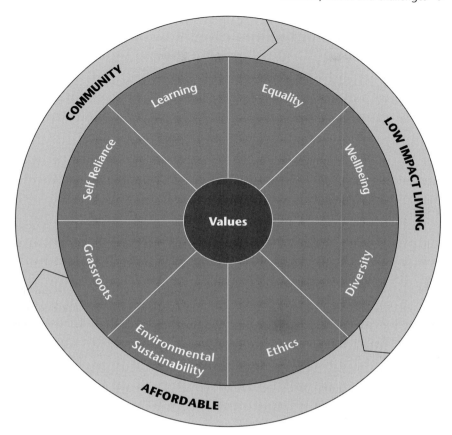

FIGURE 2.1 Lilac's three aspects and its values

Source: Lilac.

War who claimed that land was a common treasury for all; networks like Radical Routes who support self-managed housing cooperatives; the European social centres movement where groups rent or occupy buildings to challenge property speculation and provide free entertainment, language classes, workshops and libraries; pioneering self-builders who have built eco-villages, low impact dwellings and earthships using novel and recycled materials often defying planning regulations; and cooperatives such as Mondragon which continue to uphold international values of solidarity and mutualism. More recently, we have seen a new global movement seeking greater justice and equality and a historic rebalancing of power. Encampments spread out across the world from Zuccotti Park in New York and gave birth to the Occupy

Movement and groups such as Los Indignados in Spain. 'We are the 99 per cent' became a call to arms to challenge the dizzying imbalance of power and wealth in our contemporary society.[2] What these examples share is a desire to hold land, resources and wealth in common. The commons is a powerful idea, representing both the ancient commons worked by the commoners but also a clear roadmap for how greater common ownership can manage international resources and provide a remedy for the growing social, economic and ecological injustices that define our world.[3]

In terms of housing, Lilac is part of a broader and now well-established community-led and self-build movement which is pretty diverse and difficult to characterise. Self-builders represent a long-standing desire to establish more self-managed ways of living, and a desire to create places that reflect the needs and desires of residents. Some have sought to opt completely out of conventional structures, building temporary and low impact dwellings in rural areas such as yurts, benders, roundhouses and earthships. A whole 'back to the land' movement has sought greater self-sufficiency, trying to reverse the onslaught of industrial urbanization.[4] Many of these have used natural materials such as timber, hemp and straw to self-build housing at very affordable levels. They stand in complete opposition to conventional planning which seeks to centralize and control where housing and communities are built. Eco-villages have also flourished where groups have built communities on intentional values. These now represent a worldwide movement.[5] Similarly, cohousing communities have emerged where groups have sought to co-locate housing to design in strong bonds of togetherness, and to develop a clear and often intentional community identity. This cohousing movement has spread globally in very different ways, as Chapter 6 explores. Over the past decade, Community Land Trusts have provided a new mechanism for the community control of land and housing. They have flourished in Scotland where rural communities have used new legislation to acquire land in perpetuity for the local community, and are now growing in other parts of the world. Where Lilac emerged in the UK, there has been a community-led housing renaissance as groups use new funding streams and policy mechanisms to become co-producers in their own housing. These 'custom builders', as they are called, conceive, design and manage their own housing, procuring the services of others to construct it.

None of these examples implies a particular form of tenure or ownership. These vary and may include houses for sale, lease or rent, shared or limited equity schemes, condominiums, tenant management organizations, rental or equity-based cooperatives, or indeed a mixture of these. Levels of self-governance can also vary significantly, from very high levels of collectivity in shared income communities where wealth is held in common, to simple management companies which run housing with the input of private tenants or owners. Lilac represents a blend of these trends, as a cohousing community drawing on a form of cooperative tenure where members acquire an equity share, and acting as custom builders who co-produce their project with a team of professionals.

Motivations and values

Low Impact Living is not just a book [...] o build an ecologically minded, affordable co [...] bout the values and motivations that allowed [...] rpin any project are crucial. We live in an age [...] ity and equality are thoroughly overused. T [...] over. Given this fuzziness over their actual [...] become [...] empty containers, reloaded with meaning, for good or fo [...] ever is using them. Values are living entities. They are mutable and dynamic. They are debated and contested, over long email exchanges, in meetings, policy reports, around camp fires or in corridors. Such debate has to be embraced. This is the life-blood of any healthy community. As it grows and changes, its values and vision also change. It is important, then, that groups are upfront about their values, what they aim to achieve through them and what kind of vision they are offering to others for the future.

One of the challenges we are facing is when groups emerge too quickly, or are forced to act or form through policy or funding opportunities without enough consideration of what is motivating them to act. Sure, things can turn out all right, but fractures and fault lines can quickly emerge over issues that were not explored or discussed sufficiently beforehand. If values and visions are laid down at an early stage, then day-to-day decision making becomes so much easier. Good decisions naturally flow from clear values. They can be referred back to. Put simply, being values-led gives a project strength, confidence and durability. So what were the values that motivated Lilac?

Environmental sustainability

With such an eco-minded project in an age preoccupied with climate change, concerns of environmental sustainability are always going to be paramount. Living sustainably, as we have learned from the pioneering work from the UN's Commission on Sustainable Development and its Earth Summits, means balancing the economic, social and ecological, not just for current but also for future generations. This starting point is central to allow us to rethink our patterns of living in a broad, holistic way. It allowed us to open up the scope of the project from the outset and to reflect on how sustainability is achieved through our patterns of work, consumption, travel, eating, play and community life. What quickly becomes clear in any effort to seek greater sustainability is that it is a deeply interconnected and holistic undertaking. Something as straightforward as a housing project is actually a complex metabolism. There are inputs, outputs and flows. It works like an organic whole with attention needed for all the parts. There are co-dependent systems operating, including finance, governance, energy, water, food, work and leisure. All of these issues need addressing.[6]

We have to guard against uses of sustainability which reduce its potency and drain its meaning. It is so often used to give a green gloss to the business-as-usual model of economic growth. In fact, at the heart of the sustainability debate are some huge tensions over meaning and direction. On the one hand, weaker or shallow versions of sustainability are seen as technocratic or managerial endeavours which treat the environment in an instrumental way as something which is external to human nature and from which profit may be extracted. At its crudest level, sustainability is stripped of its environmental origins and is used to refer to the need to merely sustain activity, especially economic activity. On the other hand, stronger or deeper sustainability regards the environment as a co-dependent part of human society, and thus something that needs valuing for its intrinsic worth.[7] These debates won't be reconciled anytime soon, but the key point is that these differences actively shape contemporary policy and action. The modern global economy and its institutions pay scant attention to what it would actually mean to reconcile environmental, economic and social objectives. We need to be alive to these differences and how they unfold on our patch.

Self-reliance

A second core value is self-reliance. This is both a simple yet deeply profound concept. In our increasingly globalized world, meeting as many of our needs for daily life from within our local community makes intuitive sense. Supply chains are shortened, carbon footprints reduced, dependency on large multinationals decreased and local re-spending is increased. Self-reliance needs to be fairly pragmatic. The aim is not complete self-sufficiency. Very few localities can be completely self-sustaining. Market mechanisms which are controlled and based on equality may be used to trade goods and services between localities. Problems may also emerge when localities wall themselves off from the world, limiting the flows of knowledge and people that can enrich our lives and make us more thoughtful and tolerant of difference. Further, self-reliance as a concept needs to be understood broadly. It's about food and energy, the areas where we can really reduce our carbon use. But it's also about work, neighbourly ties and emotional support, for example. There is little point in growing your own food if you fly away on foreign holidays twice a year and make all your money from globalized hedge-fund dealing. The idea of bioregions is useful here too, to seek as many connections as possible within coherent regions that are more naturally defined. Common sense is needed about which flows are beneficial to communities and which are less so. Ultimately, flows of people and culture enrich localities whereas fast-paced flows of goods and capital can cause turbulence and undermine the potential for local livelihoods.

Importantly, self-reliance is also about governance: how we make our decisions and who makes them for us. In the face of increasingly unaccountable and unresponsive governments at many different levels, groups are exploring new ways to make decisions for themselves. There is plenty of information in this book about community self-management, and it's really central to the Lilac idea. Many of my influences have been with groups which have been seeking greater autonomy. 'Autonomy' is of Greek origin (auto-nomos), literally meaning to self-govern. But this is not the autonomy of an individual to do whatsoever they please – the classic entrepreneur or bullish leader. All of us as individuals are placed in dense networks of co-dependent relations with those around us. At its heart, then, autonomy is a collective impulse. Our ability to flourish as human beings depends so much on the quality and extent of these relations. This is a central idea for good place making.

What autonomy rejects are more top-down and overly bureaucratic ways of making decisions and governing localities. These come in many different forms in different parts of the world and are so entrenched that we often don't recognize them – the town hall, local political party, workplaces, schools and even family relations. Deeper levels of creativity and innovation emerge from less hierarchical and more networked governance forms. In an era of globalization, the centralized power of nation-states has diminished or a least been partly transferred upward to supranational organizations and downward to cities and subnational organizations. Among all this restructuring, we can begin to recognize the diverse and far-reaching networks that make these things we experience as communities function.[8] Beyond the centralized and top-down forms of governance associated with the nation-state are more horizontal or direct forms of democracy, or what Ben Barber called 'strong democracy'.[9] Tools such as consensus decision making are a key part of this push towards more direct forms of democracy. There will be more on this subject in Chapter 6.

Grassroots

What leads naturally from self-reliance is valuing the grassroots. This is a tricky term that is worth exploring to give it clearer meaning. Grassroots projects are self-initiated and people-led. Their main feature is that they are healthily removed from the influence and motives of governments, large institutions or big business. Many grassroots groups may be more agitational towards the big state and market capitalism. In this sense, they are more like social movements seeking paradigmatic shifts to overturn the status quo and usher in a radically different social deal. Some are more reformist, seeking incremental change within the world as it is. Others are more utopian, trying to opt out completely and creating radically different examples of how the future might be. But whatever the stance, there are pragmatic moments when all projects have to deal with policy, red tape, bureaucracy and regulations. Many others face repression, infiltration and surveillance by the state or its agents. There is, then, an important balancing act at the grassroots where groups agitate against the world as it is try to prefigure the future world they hope for, and simply deal with the realpolitik of the world in which they find themselves.

The grassroots is a particularly fertile area for innovation.[10] But innovation requires certain ingredients and capacities: key individuals who have deep and varied access to contacts and knowledge and who are prepared to share these; plausible narratives of the future that sound feasible and can demonstrate why it is better than what we have now; enabling institutions that are keen to take and back risks and relinquish control; and a generally supportive social context where ideas will be accepted or at least not blocked. For projects to succeed, and succeed quickly, many of these aspects need to be co-present.

Learning

Learning seems an odd value. Who doesn't learn? But beyond the daily act of learning new skills, projects need to become perpetual places of learning. This is in terms of ongoing educational work but also in terms of training in a range of skills from construction to cooking and facilitation. Learning is crucial because it allows projects to act as wider inspirational resources for other groups. So much learning becomes embedded in individuals in projects that quite a lot of effort is needed to break this out and lay it down so that others may access it. This book is part of this. One important aspect of project learning is to promote a commons approach to knowledge where information and knowledge is shared openly between non-commercial groups to ensure replicability is enhanced. Creative commons licensing (non-commercial, attribute, share-alike) is used widely here to ensure that grassroots innovation is not locked behind corporate firewalls. Co-creation and co-production are vital components which allow us to start to dramatically change the way we think and act. Wider groups of stakeholders come together in a shared process of learning and problem solving.[11]

Equality

Equality is one of those values that is overused and stripped of substance. Equality, and its inverse inequality, comes in many different guises – social, cultural, political.

To say we don't live in an equal world is obvious but what do we do about it? What actually generates inequality?[12] Inequality becomes ingrained through economic and political institutions as well as historical patterns of uneven development, colonialism and imperialism, between different places and countries. Clearly these are issues that are far too big for an individual project to take on. But the important issue here is that as projects develop they need to learn from the past and embed more equal ways of operating that will last.

Equality may be embedded through a whole range of policies on equal opportunities that do not tolerate any form of discrimination on grounds of race, sex, disability, belief, religion, sexuality, age, social group or health condition. These are key principles that also uphold the functioning of cooperative entities throughout the world. Economic equality is also crucial for community-led projects. This may be embedded through clear procedures that limit fast capital flows and speculation, decommodify assets and attempts to rebalance wealth and income diversities within a community setting. These aspects can be very personally challenging, especially for those who have individually gained and prospered from the inequality of others and the status quo. But unless projects commit to at least experimenting with a more equal and just world, they will do little more than simply reproduce inequality and injustice for future generations. We also need to think in terms of intra-generational and inter-generational equality – equality not just between people in the here and now, but also equality for the next generation yet to be born. One of our deep responsibilities is to bequeath to future generations a more equal society.

Creating a more just world sits alongside equality. David Schlosberg conceives of three ways of thinking about justice: as the unequal distribution of impacts and responsibilities; as unequal recognition in terms of disrespect, insult and degradation that devalue some people and some place identities in comparison to others; and injustice in terms of participation and procedure regarding access to information, fair process and regulation.[13] We can also think about the need for many kinds of justice: social, political and ecological. It is all these combined that makes the search for justice so important and so elusive. We are actually seeking more just relations and outcomes between people, places, and also between the human and natural world. A central part of equality and justice, then, is a commitment to responsibility towards each other as well as towards our environment and community.[14] Fostering a sense of equality between individuals is crucial. Much of this means stripping away status and prestige that gets attributed to us in other work and professional contexts, and being prepared to meet others as equals in a community setting. Tools and techniques such as consensus and non-violent communication are used here, and are explored in Chapter 6.

Well-being

Our health and well-being are more important to us than most other aspects of our lives. So much of this derives from the quantity and quality of the relations around us in our immediate communities. Without realizing it, how the daily lives of projects operate greatly affect the well-being and health of its members and participants. Creating places that are healthy and safe is far from straightforward. Part of it is down to good design – homes with high levels of comfort in terms of heat, noise and air quality, as well as designing in beauty, natural features and useful amenities. Much also derives from processes that protect and nourish community members, be it clear and fair policies and procedures on respect, disputes and decision making, or more informal moments of listening and sharing. Feeling healthy can come down to such simple things as neighbourliness, timely advice, others knowing your needs, or just people who watch out for you. Seeing your neighbours on a daily basis at the kitchen window, in the post room, bike shed, car park, refuse deposit area or communal compost facilities allows regular feedback on their well-being. It may be nothing more than a glance or a lifted eyebrow. It may be a brief word that leads to a deep conversation. But they are all essential check-ins that add up to a constant invisible web of well-being monitoring. So much contributes to our overall sense of well-being that it has to be an evolving and highly responsive undertaking. What I will explore in this book is how Lilac's cohousing model and design principles attempt to intentionally increase well-being.

Diversity

Similarly, diversity is a broad and catch-all value. It's fairly commonplace to want to seek diverse communities. But these can easily become over-prescriptive as projects seek, often too artificially, to rebalance what they see as a lack of diversity around them. Clearly, allowing projects to become dominated by sectarian or partisan interests may reduce the attractiveness of them to others as well as increase the very real chance of squabbles over details and doctrines. A more productive route to diversity is simply to be open to the various flows around you. A project can, and should, accommodate a diversity of people and value difference, but it can cause problems to seek it out and engineer it. Trying to strive for a perfect balance of different identities and values within a project is rather like chasing clouds. Being part of a diverse community also means looking beyond the internal confines of the project. A commitment to reaching out and being a 'community within a wider community' is really important. This involves reaching out to share values, respecting the values of others, while also being open to the possibility of being influenced by other – often very different – values around you.

Part of embracing diversity is to establish robust ways to acknowledge and deal with the differences people already represent and the conflict that can arise from this. Conflict is actually a really normal and healthy outcome of a diverse community. Moments of conflict are intense periods of learning if handled in the right way. When somebody says to you 'I don't agree with that', this should actually be received as a gift rather than a threat! That sounds difficult to appreciate at first. But, in fact, the times where we have learnt most are the times we have been pushed outside our comfort zones – and outside the realms of what we think is possible.

Handling ethics

One of the things we did together early on was to create an ethical policy to guide our interactions with other groups and organizations. Many organizations pay lip-service to ethics through their corporate social responsibility agenda, but what we did was at a much more profound level. We attempted to write a policy which reflected the kind of world we believed in – 'be the change you want to see' as Gandhi said. The ethical policy took a considerable amount of time to write, especially since we had to reflect on some really deep and complex political and social issues relating to animal rights, militarism, climate change and the free movement of people.

We haven't used the policy very much but it has been useful when we have encountered ethical dilemmas. For example, we were approached by an architectural firm to enter a competition. One of our members found out that among a whole range of very exciting sustainability initiatives this firm also designed military bases and weapons stores. Having an ethical policy allowed us to state politely and clearly that we could not work with them and the reasons why not. In the long term, a statement of ethics is helpful for organizations to reflect on their own practices and what they are trying to achieve.

Our agenda for change

By now, it's probably clear that Lilac is much more than a place to live. It's much more than a housing project. It's a living laboratory of how the world could be different. It was brought to life by a desire to address some of the grand challenges of our age. Responding to these challenges has been central to shaping the idea of Lilac and motivating the members into action. The first challenge asks how we can establish ways of living that have a much lower impact on the environment, result in far less greenhouse gases and adapt to a changing climate. The second challenge asks how we can do this in a way that is affordable, more equitable and accessible. The third challenge asks how we can do this in a way that radically changes how

TABLE 2.1 Lilac's ethical policy

In all our involvements/interactions with external institutions, companies, banks, etc., including:

- investments
- trading
- financial activities
- acceptance of loans, grants and donations
- employing contractors
- hiring services

1   We will endeavour to work with companies and trading partners who share our values.
2   We will not support or benefit from:

- manufacture or trade of military equipment
- involvement in the nuclear power industry
- manufacture or involvement in animal testing of cosmetic, household products or ingredients
- involvement in the animal fur trade
- involvement in blood sports

3   We will try to avoid and minimize our trading with companies that benefit from:

- extraction and production of fossil fuels
- manufacture of polluting chemicals
- involvement in unsustainable forestry and timber trade
- manufacture of tobacco products
- involvement in animal farming
- involvement in genetic modification
- involvement in animal testing for medical purposes
- involvement in exploitative pornography
- involvement in any form of environmental degradation
- exploitative working conditions

4   In assessing our business activities we will uphold human rights of all and we will only work and trade with organizations and individuals which are tolerant and accepting of all regardless of: gender, sexual orientation, race, disability, class, age.

Source: Lilac.

we relate to the people around us and increase a sense of community, respect and understanding. This is profound stuff. These are huge transformational challenges. What they actually add up to is a significant challenge to the status quo. They are anti-paradigmatic, even anti-capitalist. They represent a growing force for change that is persuasive and powerful. They would, as Eduardo Galliano stresses, turn the world upside-down.[15] Together these challenges led us to create a project around three central concepts: low impact living, affordable and community. The challenges were laid down. Lilac was born. All that was left to do was to step into the unknown.

The challenge of low impact living: changing our buildings and behaviour

The first challenge, which is probably the overriding one, is how to create ways of living that have a lower impact. This could seem rather broad. How low is low enough? What kind of impact? Impact upon whom? What areas of living? While much could be said here, this section will focus on the low impact challenge as an environmental one. How to reduce the ecological footprint of humanity is now essential, given that we have exceeded the carrying capacity of the global biosphere in terms of greenhouse gas emissions. In 2013, the Intergovernmental Panel on Climate Change (IPCC) laid down the challenge in uncompromising terms regarding global carbon budgets. Humanity can only emit between 800 billion and 1200 billion more tonnes of carbon if it wants to stay within safe limits of increases of global surface temperatures. At a rate of 50 billion tonnes of carbon emissions per year that gives us around 25 years, or one generation, for decisive action.

Our generation has been shaped by the prospect of rising emissions from carbon dioxide and other greenhouse gases, the prospect of rapid global warming, the irresponsible use of fossil fuels and the perilous dependency upon energy-dense lifestyles, the potential impacts of ecocide and the damaging effects on the global biosphere. Momentum has been gathering for the great task of tackling climate change for decades. The 1960s and 1970s brought crisis in the post-war economy and a growing awareness that something was deeply flawed, with the model of high growth being pushed by the advanced economies of the West. Rachel Carson's book *Silent Spring*, the 1972 report by the Club of Rome, *Limits to Growth*, and the UN Conference on Human Environment more familiarly known as 'the Stockholm Conference' in the same year were landmark events. The UN Environment Programme which came shortly after became a key institution for change, founding the Intergovernmental Panel on Climate Change (IPCC) in 1988.

The 1980s became a decade preoccupied with sustainable development. How could all this rapid growth going on in the global economy be handled in a way that would balance social and ecological needs? The Brundtland Commission's report in 1987, *Our Common Future*, paved the way for the UN Conference on Environment and Development in 1992, or as it is now known, the Earth Summit in Rio de Janeiro. This was a landmark event – a long-awaited moment that could potentially be a watershed for the world. One aspect that came out of it was 'Local Agenda 21', an attempt to instil sustainable development into the heart of every municipality in the world. More significantly, the UN Framework Convention on Climate Change was established in 1994 which ratified the first global agreement to reduce greenhouse gases from 1998, the Kyoto Protocol. The UNFCCC meets annually through the COP process, where progress is monitored and further declarations and action are taken.

With such a tremendous amount of activity, the prospect of taking on and defeating the generational challenge seems good. But the balance sheet is mixed. There have been two more World Summits on Sustainable Development since 1992, and the COP continues to meet with ever more depressing prognoses on the state of the global biosphere. It has often been stated that this is our last chance to take decisive action to broker a global climate deal. That chance continues to slip by. Action is simply not keeping up with the scale of the challenge. There is no let-up in the global demand for fossil fuels. Pristine environments in the polar regions continue to be opened up for further exploitation of hydrocarbons, and new reserves locked up in tar sands and extracted through so-called 'fracking' are extending the potential fossil fuel bonanza well into the twenty-first century. In addition, the IPCC reports a continued increase in the accumulation of greenhouse gases in the atmosphere. In May 2013, the Mauna Loa Observatory in Hawaii, which measures atmospheric concentrations of carbon dioxide, showed that it exceeded 400 parts per million. The scientific case for action on reducing greenhouse gases is now largely undisputed. What the scientific community clearly states is that concentrations of greenhouse gas (GHG) emissions urgently need to be brought within safe limits of 350 parts per million (ppm), compared to the current level of 400ppm and rising. Without a real breakthrough moment, current policy is setting the world on a course to levels of concentrations of 450ppm or above and this will take global warming beyond the critical level of +2 degrees Celsius.[16] Above this level, a whole host of interconnected threats unfold around, for example, biodiversity and habitat loss, food scarcity, loss of land, mass migrations, the spread of diseases, extreme weather patterns and sea-level rises.[17]

So what is needed? It is recognized that we need to do two things at the same time. The first involves mitigation strategies which could reverse and ultimately halt processes of global warming. What this means is a huge effort to decarbonize our global society. Practically, carbon reduction roadmaps are required which will reduce CO_2 emissions by 80 to 95 per cent by 2050 (relative to 1990 baselines) to get us back to near the 350ppm level and avoid dangerous levels of warming. The EU and the UK has adopted these kinds of targets, and the post-Kyoto agreement brokered in Durban and Qatar could offer global cuts in GHGs. However, it's still really unclear what needs to be done to create these reductions, and indeed whether they go far enough. Decarbonizing our societies is a huge task. It involves longer term and structural changes which will be a fundamental challenge to the way we live our lives. The Post Carbon Institute in the USA has been one of the leading think-tanks outlining how our societies could make this power-down transition away from our fossil fuel dependence on high carbon lifestyles.[18]

The second involves more immediate adaptation strategies to reduce the vulnerability of places in the face of a changing climate. This involves a whole raft of infrastructure changes to deal with a rapidly changing climate. More extreme weather patterns, as well as coastal and river flooding, are now becoming regular occurrences. We are seeing dramatic negative consequences from these events such as displacement, the loss of livelihoods, power shortages, the spread of diseases, social unrest and crop failure. Urgent attention is needed to reduce the vulnerability of our societies and create what is being called more 'climate-robust' places.[19]

Interestingly, in the face of these challenges, some of the most innovative action is emerging at the city and neighbourhood level.[20] This is mainly due to the real lack of decisive national and international policy making and action. At the city level, innovation is not quite so restrained by the huge task of agreements between diverse interests, parties and nations. The bullying and lobbying of powerful nations is not as prevalent. On one level, the task in cities is clearer. Over 50 per cent of the world's population live in urban areas and some 70 per cent of GHGs come from them. Cities, especially coastal ones, are feeling the immediate effects of a changing climate. Thus they are the perfect place for decisive action and innovation. This is where projects like Lilac come in. What we are seeing is a proliferation of examples at the community level, where people are taking back control and seizing the initiative. Not prepared to wait for big government or big industry to act, urban community groups are rising to the challenge of low impact living.

So what exactly does this low impact challenge mean for community groups? The route to creating a society that is less dependent on fossil fuel resources and which radically decarbonizes the way it operates entails quite a complex set of activities. Institutional change and technological innovation are only part of the story. The decarbonization of energy supplies, cradle-to-cradle reuse of resources, the electrification of transport, and mass insulation of homes all need to happen and are well within our grasp. But beyond these measures, what is needed is broader value change which begins to affect all areas of our lives. Governments can only do so much here, beholden as they are to short-term electoral cycles and intense lobbying from corporate cronies. To tackle fossil fuel dependency and climate change in cities requires some really novel forms of innovation and governance, and we are only just beginning to see the beginnings of this.[21]

Translating low impact living from an idea to a reality is such a challenge and so elusive because it involves not just technological change but also value, cultural, behavioural and institutional change as well as redefining relationships between individuals, communities, states and markets. Reductions in GHGs and energy use will only be achieved through developing a radically different and more collective sense of what it means to be a citizen, and not confusing this with being a consumer.[22] Living lightly on the planet raises complex ethical choices that have implications for how we design and run social and political systems. These choices make us think about many of the values discussed earlier in this chapter. What is really important to take on board is the nature of our pro-growth economy. As long as we continue to be connected to the idea that prosperity can only be achieved through high levels of economic output, the low impact challenge will remain elusive. A flourishing de-growth or steady-state economy movement has highlighted how increasing levels of income and economic growth do not increase well-being or happiness.[23] In fact, as well as making us no happier, higher levels of consumerism are rapidly increasing levels of production and GHG emissions, not to mention debt.

The way we build, and indeed retrofit, housing plays a crucial role in this low impact challenge. There is an urgent need to reduce carbon emission rates from our homes, and there are technical, behavioural and cultural aspects to this. The figures are staggering. In 2010 domestic energy consumption was 32 per cent of total UK final energy consumption, with space heating accounting for 58 per cent of this usage alone.[24] For a while, the UK government set ambitious sustainability targets for all new homes, although these were downgraded and tailed off due to industry reluctance. An undervalued aspect of this low carbon housing revolution is the shift to natural building materials such as hemp, straw and timber. As I explore in Chapter 4, these are abundantly available and excellent insulators, and their use can radically reduce the amount of GHGs from both the materials our homes are built from and also the amount of energy needed to heat them over their lifetime. But of course, its construction is only a small part of the story of the use of carbon over the life of a home. How it is used and lived in is the largely unexplored aspect of the low impact challenge. As the rest of this book explores, creating new patterns of intentional design, co-living arrangements, group learning, shared resources and neighbourliness can begin to radically reduce the environmental footprint of a community, far beyond those that could be currently envisaged by large parts of the mainstream construction industry.

The affordability challenge: a green housing revolution for all

Affordability is the second challenge. Again this is a broad area for action. It isn't really about being able to afford all the things you would like to buy as a consumer. This affordability challenge is about the broader historical struggle for economic equality and justice, and greater control of our lives. One of the ways this is acutely felt in our contemporary society is through housing. But where we live and what we live in seem such basic issues that they are very rarely questioned or interrogated. We all live somewhere, and probably feel an attachment to a place, be it a house, street or neighbourhood. We know our local park, where the convenience store is, who is friendly and not so friendly around our neighbourhood, or where to get the bus. But how many of us can actually say we are in control of our housing situation, or have a dense social network to call upon? Sure, you may own your own house, and you may have actually paid for it all. But owner-occupied houses are either dependent on easy credit, largely owned by the bank, subject to changes in interest rates that affect the cost of borrowing, or fuelling housing asset bubbles.[25] Selling is also at the whim of fickle market values and the buoyancy of the economy. Getting on to the housing ladder is also a huge problem. Private renting is little better. Residents are at the whim of private landlords, and without national controls rent may be set at levels beyond the reach of modest wages. In most countries, the state has also given up on providing affordable homes for rent at sub-market levels. The need for social housing for those with low or no incomes is a parallel struggle which must not be ignored.

At its heart then is the problem of the commodification of housing and land. Homes are considered a commodity to be bought and sold, or rented, to the highest bidder. As long as homes are so embedded in a commodity market any significant progress towards a more egalitarian society will be thwarted. Given that housing is such a central determinant of well-being and prosperity, there is a need to challenge the unsustainability of the current housing model and develop a radical alternative. Changes in housing markets over the past 20 years have become a particular barrier to greater social equality. Access to easy credit has led to a huge credit-fuelled housing bubble and an over-inflated housing market. The 2008 financial crisis highlighted the unsustainability of high levels of lending and the toxic debts which resulted from this. House prices were entirely decoupled from average incomes as people desperately scrambled to get a foot on the housing market ladder and the illusion of cashing in on housing as an asset. Such indebtedness put the commercial mortgage lenders in the driving seat and created a whole generation of home owners who are facing lifetime debt. The 2008 financial crisis cooled things slightly but the majority of people face the reality of a housing affordability crisis. Over the past few decades the gap between earnings and house prices has widened to a chasm. For example, in the UK, the average house price-to-earnings ratio doubled, from just 2.7 to 1 in 1995 to 5.4 to 1 in 2005.[26] The actual prospect of gaining access to an over-inflated housing market for a whole generation of young people who have seen employment conditions and wage levels flat line is now dire. The hallmark for many has become temporary work contracts along with insecure, high-cost and short-term rental contracts.

A further concern is that the new emphasis towards low or zero carbon housing may actually increase the affordability crisis. Distinctive self-build and eco-minded housing attracts high house price premiums and actually creates new opportunities for speculative activity and new asset bubbles. There is nothing inherently affordable about self-build and green housing. How to make housing that is both low carbon and affordable, then, is the heart of the challenge that this book addresses. What is actually happening in housing markets is that building to novel, unfamiliar and exacting lower carbon standards attracts a higher cost premium linked to greater perceived risks compared to average build costs and methods. But these increases in cost are not recognized by conventional lenders. An eco-development is valued by the bank in money terms much the same as a conventional development. This in turn creates loan-to-value ratios which are not sufficient to finance the full build cost without additional gap funding. Groups will be halted in their attempts to build affordable, green housing.

In practice, then, what we are seeing is highly uneven development in terms of affordability and equality. What is of real concern is the trend towards new green gated communities that are exclusive and private. Cities are already blighted by gated communities as wealthier groups opt out of the morass of social problems around them, walling themselves into islands of prosperity. These kinds of green developments become part of the problem, as they fail to address wider issues of growing affluence and urban sprawl.[27] The situation is ripe for a whole-scale rethink to break the market deadlock on how we build places. In his book *When we Build Again,* the late inspirational anarchist writer and social commentator Colin Ward offered many insights into how a radically different approach to housing can rebuild community. One of the wonderful sentiments in it, which has lived with me for many years, was: 'When we build again, we need not a plan for housing, but an attitude that will enable millions of people to make their own plans.'[28]

Of course, things were never always this way, and things are not the same everywhere. In large parts of the world, homes are not treated as commodities. Social housing run by the state is an important part of the equation in Scandinavia and large parts of Northern Europe. They are not seen as last resorts or stigmatized as benefit ghettos. In the UK, France, Finland and Sweden, social housing accounts for almost 20 per cent of housing stock and in the Netherlands it accounts for over 30 per cent. More interesting, there is a long history of experiments with housing projects that are less commodified and more self-managed by the people who live in them. Mutual and cooperative housing solutions have attempted to rethink housing, including tenant management organizations, shared and part equity schemes, community gateway projects, community land trusts, and short-life and fully mutual housing cooperatives. However, the existence of cooperative housing is very patchy across the EU. For example, in Sweden, the Czech Republic and Poland it accounts for around 20 per cent of housing and almost 10 per cent in Denmark. However, in most other EU countries it accounts for a tiny or negligible amount.[29] What is clear is that there is a huge potential for the growth of mutual and self-managed housing.

As I explain in Chapter 5 in more detail, Lilac addresses these issues through an innovative form of cooperative tenure called a Mutual Home Ownership Society (MHOS). Mutual home ownership is a direct challenge to the private and individual ownership of homes. It provides homes which stay at the same level of affordability from one generation to the next, and gives residents a greater say in the self-management of their neighbourhoods. In addition, it's a way we can begin to challenge the increased levels of commodification and speculation which are creating huge turbulence and disconnection in our communities.

The challenge of community: cooperativism and the mutual living revolution

The final challenge is that of community. Again community is one of those words that is overused and overflowing with meaning. We all feel associated with some kind of community, be it geographical, political, online, or related to some sport, hobby or pastime. But communities do not simply appear. They are built patiently and slowly and through much deliberation and negotiation. Rarely are they peaceful entities. Communities draw on difference and division that is ever present. To do otherwise is to exclude, silence and marginalize. There are tensions between being open, forgiving, inclusive and diverse with those towards being closed, intolerant, prejudicial and exclusive. As Zygmunt Bauman, the inspirational sociologist who has lived and worked in my hometown Leeds for many years, explores in one of his many books, *Community, Seeking Safety in an Insecure World*, the idea of a community will always generate tensions between group security on the one hand and individual freedom on the other.[30]

One of the real challenges of our age is actually to foster interactions among communities, as much as within them. Rather than a bounded sense of belonging, home or community set in isolation from each other, a greater sense of interconnection encourages us to develop broader ethical concerns for those who are not directly present in our daily lives, but nonetheless which we depend on and are affected by our actions. Think, for example, about the Bolivian tin miner, the Thai seamstress or the Congolese coffee farmer. We depend upon somebody, somewhere, for most things, and it is this recognition that can allow us to build meaningful relationships between communities based upon mutual respect and gratitude.

One of the most deleterious uses of community has been its colonization by consumerism, and especially the homogenizing effects of global branded retail. Active citizenship and relations built on deeper values of compassion, trust and beauty continue to be hollowed out as the values of the marketplace penetrate our everyday lives. Shopping malls, big box retail parks and supermarkets increasingly provide the places of encounter and meeting. Loyalty is more often defined through affiliations with consumer brands. Suburban and car-dominated urban layouts further erode opportunities for the rich street life of community interaction.[31] Gathering places and melting pots allow a rich fermentation of ideas that can lead to change. It is important that these areas are not just spaces of consumerism. They need to be open, free, independent, grassroots and responsive to local needs.

Communities are often more about process than an actual place. Community building is an art, not something that can be pulled off the shelf and put into practice immediately. There is an art to becoming a community, and communities are always in the process of being made, reforming and reshaping. The most durable communities are those that are dynamic and responsive to changes around them. This does not mean losing sight of core values or direction which give them a deep groundedness. Every community needs a clear rationale for its existence. This is often told through myths and stories, or enacted through rituals and events as time progresses. It is the deep connections that form in communities which provide the seed-beds for creativity and change.

One of the central threads of this book is that of mutualism and cooperativism as routes to community building. Mutualism is a rich historical tradition enmeshed in the nineteenth-century philosophical and practical traditions of anarchism and socialism. It simply states that the association that emerges from interdependence can be beneficial and increase well-being. As a doctrine, it outlines how people can conduct relationships based on free and equal contracts of reciprocal exchange. It advocates voluntary cooperation based on open agreements between free individuals. It is based on a passionate desire for people to govern themselves and not have authority imposed upon them, and a belief in federalism – how relationships can be facilitated among groups from the bottom up. From the nineteenth century onwards, mutualism provided a strong intellectual bulwark against the rampant individualism of the fast-expanding free-market capitalist economy. The anarchist Prince, biologist and writer Peter Kropotkin was at pains to dispute and dispel what he believed to be some of the corrosive elements of 'social Darwinism' around ideas of the survival of the fittest. Instead, he patiently outlined how the dominant tendency in human relations and evolutionary processes was cooperation and mutual aid rather than competition. Kropotkin was a great chronicler of the numerous examples of collective organization of industry, agriculture and community life, all of which have been used successfully over the centuries to allow human beings to flourish.[32]

Similarly, cooperativism is a close ally of mutualism. At its most basic level, a cooperative is an autonomous association of persons who voluntarily cooperate for their mutual, social, economic and cultural benefit. At their heart, cooperatives value direct democracy through the principle of one-member-one-vote, and the democratic control of organizations by the people they serve. The origins of the cooperative movement are commonly understood as emerging from the early decades of the Industrial Revolution in the UK where workers were keen to associate and organize for their common good. The first cooperative is usually claimed to be the Rochdale Society of Equitable Pioneers, founded among the weavers and artisans of Lancashire in 1844. The second half of the nineteenth century saw the cooperative movement flourish through the growth of friendly societies and consumer cooperatives. From these humble and radical origins, the cooperative sector now forms a fairly significant part of the economy. For example, there are more than one billion members of cooperatives worldwide, which employ over 100 million people and have a turnover of US$1.1 trillion. In the UK alone, cooperatives have a combined turnover of over £35.6 billion, and are owned by 13.5 million people.[33]

As I explore in Chapter 6, a cohousing approach has become a central part of building and designing strong communities and useful for building on the historic strengths of the cooperative tradition. It is a perfect methodology for designing highly interactive and interconnected housing neighbourhoods, and transforming interactions at the community level. It is also a perfect route for embedding mutualism, the deep associations and interconnections that can allow strong communities to emerge.

This is the context, values and challenges through which Lilac travels. Interventions on the future of housing and place making need to put these at their heart. Stated simply, Lilac was clear about the values that guided it, which emerged from the rich historical context we listened to and engaged with. Starting out from a profound set of values we were able to build a project that patiently and intentionally tackled the significant challenges of our age. The next chapter steps away from these ideas and concepts, and takes us through the twists and turns of a six-year journey of how these ideas were put into practice.

Notes

1 See Homer-Dixon (2006) and Kunstler (2006) for excellent outlines of the interconnected challenges of our age.
2 See Solnit (2004), Mertes (2004), Notes from Nowhere (2003), Hawken (2007), Featherstone (2008) and Mason (2012).
3 There is a growing amount of work on the idea of the commons. See e.g. De Angelis (2007), Hardt and Negri (2009) and Linebaugh (2008).
4 See Fairlie (2009) and The Land is Ours website (http://www.tlio.org.uk).
5 The Global Ecovillage network's website (http://gen.ecovillage.org/) provides a portal into the huge array of projects, and useful introductory books include Dawson (2006).

6   The idea of urban metabolism is a useful one to frame the challenges that cities face. See Kennedy *et al.* (2007).

7   See Chatterton (2002); also Plumwood (2002).

8   There is a growing literature on distributed, networked forms of governance. See e.g. Kahler (2009).

9   See Barber (1984).

10   There is a growing body of work that looks at the role of grassroots initiatives in establishing low carbon communities. See Middlemiss and Parrish (2010), Seyfang and Smith (2007), Seyfang (2009), Heiskanen *et al.* (2010), Manzi (2010), Mulugetta *et al.* (2010), Hopkins (2013).

11   See Egan and Marlow (2013).

12   Dorling (2011) has provided some useful insights here.

13   See Schlosberg (2007) and also Bond (2010).

14   See Agyeman (2005).

15   See Galeano (2001).

16   See Hansen *et al.* (2008).

17   See Lynas (2007), Pearce (2006), and the Global Humanitarian Forum (2009).

18   See Heinberg (2004, 2005) and Heinberg and Lerch (2010), as well as Condon (2010).

19   See IPCC (2012).

20   See Kellogg (2008), Bulkeley *et al.* (2010), Evans (2011), Peters *et al.* (2010), Phillips *et al.* (2013), Pickerill and Maxey (2009) and Rydin (2010). Transition towns have also become a global movement for tackling climate change and energy dependency on a neighbourhood scale. See Hopkins (2008), Chamberlin (2009), Murphy (2008), North (2010) and Spratt and Simms (2009).

21   See While *et al.* (2010) and Jonas *et al.* (2011), who point to a new era of political governance for cities in which there is a greater focus on policies to control carbon emissions.

22   See Dobson (2003) and Littler (2009).

23   See e.g. Douthwaite (1999), Martinez-Alier (2009), Victor (2008), the New Economics Foundation (2010), Simms *et al.*, (2010), Wilkinson and Pickett (2009), O'Neill (2012), and Thorpe (2012), as well as the website http://www.degrowth.eu.

24   See the Department for Energy and Climate Change (2010).

25   See Smith *et al.* (2009).

26   See Wilcox (2006).

27   See Hodson and Marvin (2009, 2010, 2011).

28   See Ward (1985, p. 120), and also Neustatter (2012) who presents a wonderful approach to reconceptualizing a home.

29   Pittini and Laino (2012).

30   See Bauman (2001).

31   See Gehl (2010) and Jacobs (1961).

32   See Kropotkin (1972, 1987). Such traditions have been kept alive up until the present day through radicals such as Patrick Geddes, Ebenezer Howard, Lewis Mumford, Murray Bookchin and Colin Ward in their ideas for self-regulating federations of communities. Excellent reviews of these thinkers may be found in Joll (1979) and Marshall (1992).

33   See Co-operatives UK (2012).

3
MAKING IT HAPPEN

So where do you even start to build a low impact neighbourhood? How do a group of people get together to conceive, agree and implement a plan? How do you attract members? How exactly do you find land, what happens when the lawyers get involved, and how do you persuade the bank to lend you a lot of money? How do you get a scheme through planning that practically breaks all the rules? How do you find and work with a contractor to build your dream?

This chapter will try to answer some of these questions by offering a snapshot of the six-year development journey that led to the creation of a pioneering low impact, affordable cohousing project. In largely chronological order, I want to lay out how we negotiated the difficult parts of the project in its development phase such as land, finance, planning and legal issues (Table 3.3 at the end of this chapter offers a timeline of the main events between 2006 and 2013). This section is a very honest account of the many problems and sticking points of what we went through to get these essential elements in place to move from a group of people with a great idea to a professional outfit that developers, local authorities and funders took seriously. It gives an insider's view of what to do when things go wrong, slow down, get stuck or seem to go into reverse, how to keep going when you feel over-whelmed, how to handle meetings and broker deals and, importantly, how to recognize your limits, keep a group together, and seek professional help at the right time, as well as keep them in check.

It's a very difficult task to sum up in words such a long and complex journey. One way that people have recounted such events in the past is by using Bruce Tuckman's model of small group development: Forming – Storming – Norming –

Performing – Adjourning.[1] This model is great but it is used a lot. Thus, in this chapter I want to build on this approach and present a slightly different way to tell my story. In the following pages, I divide up our journey into stages that happened at different times, had a different feeling and involved different people. So I use the following stages: Emerging – Exploring – Defining – Convincing – Building – Moving. I've done it this way as I also want to provide a means to break down the detail of what we did so that others can reflect and learn, and so that we can share our highs and lows, mistakes and successes.

Emerging: Harnessing and nurturing the idea

All good ideas start from a deep passion for change. This is a difficult thing to put into words. It is a calling to act and intervene in the world, based on deep experiences and connections with life around you. It is usually a push to bring something alive that is bigger than the individual, and a pull towards a future that you dream about. It may exist beyond words, at a very emotional level. One person may find some words to articulate this, which can help a group getting together to give shape and meaning to this passion. It is from here that others can connect.

For Lilac, the idea dated back to 2006 when a group of friends got together one New Year's Eve in December 2006. We chatted about our hopes and fears for the future and how we might find ways to live together, and bring up our children, more collectively. It was a special moment where a few of us decided that this really must happen, and we really committed our time and energy to making it happen. This meant putting aside other things in our busy lives. Of course that wasn't the real beginning. Ideas surface as part of a complex flow of life, where people and events coincide. We had been friends for years, and had been involved in all sorts of organizing and activities for the past ten years. Some of us had met through Tyneside Action for People and Planet, a direct action group that stopped cars in city centres, pulled up genetically modified crops and organized squatted social centres. We had all lived or worked in collective settings before. Some of us had founded a housing cooperative in Leeds called Xanadu, set up popular education collectives, conducted anti-poverty and anti-animal cruelty campaigning, spent time in the global South doing volunteer work, been involved in the anti-globalization and anti-capitalist movement, especially against the Group of 8 (G8) Nations, as well as Earth First! We were a fairly active bunch. We all passionately believed that our lives, our society and the places where we lived could be better, more equal and humane.

As 2007 began, we started to chat more formally. The initial group involved a number of couples who lived in different cities around the UK. Tash and I lived in Leeds, Alan and Kirsty lived in Newcastle, Christo and Holly lived in a rural community north of Newcastle, and Sim and Vicky lived in Oxford. We had a skype chat in April 2007 where we all drew pictures of our ideal community to give each other a sense of the kind of project we dreamed about. Here are some descriptions that we offered to each other:

> The community is built around a converted old building which is the communal area with kitchen eating space, hanging out space and space for use by the wider community and then there are allotments, outside tables, green space and kids playing hunt, the houses are all different sizes with their own bits of green space too.
> . . . outside there are lots of children playing – hop scotch!!!! there's a pond close by with frogs (yes, that's a frog!) and frog spawn. I wanted to get across that there is a city/big town in the distance, but that there is also access to the country. There's a bus reflecting my need for good transport links. Someone on a bike with a trailer going to visit someone elsewhere!

We visited a few projects around the UK to get some ideas. At that time, Springhill Cohousing had just opened in Stroud, and Lancaster had identified a site and were laying down clear ideas. We also visited Hockerton Housing, which although quite rural gave us an idea about how to build low impact dwellings.[2] These became long weekends so that we could get a feel of what it was like to live together, and explore ideas and chat into the evenings. What became apparent was that some of us wanted to start a more rural project and some a more urban one. As a result, people left the group, and in October 2007 we started to call ourselves 'DIY Cohousing Group' and put out a leaflet to attract other interested people. One of the difficulties though was that we didn't all live in the same city; so for the big dream to work some of us would have to move. Ultimately, we realized that this phase was coming to an end, but we all felt that it had been an incredibly valuable period for all of us, as it allowed us to explore and establish what we really wanted.

Exploring: Gathering information and assessing options

At the same time, Tash and I had been involved in parallel discussions in Leeds with a group of other people who were exploring similar ideas through a group called Leeds Ecovillage. They were exploring the idea of an eco-village in the city after a lecture was organized on eco-villages by Ezio Manzini, an Italian Professor of Industrial Design. We started going to these meetings which were held once a month at a social centre called the Common Place in Leeds city centre on a Tuesday evening. We would invite guests, discuss ideas, work through parameters and aspects of the idea, watch videos, and do anything we could to get more information to help shape options. These meetings were productive and fun, but every week different people would attend, and ideas kept expanding. Tash and I proposed that we really needed to have a clear focus so that people coming to the meetings knew what the project was about. In July 2007 we set an aim for the group to help shape a focus. It read: 'We aspire to build an eco-village community in Leeds based on the principles of ecological sustainability, cooperation and inclusivity.' Based on this aim I helped draft a discussion document to help move the project forward.

FOR DISCUSSION. A DOCUMENT TO MOVE FORWARD TO OUTLINING KEY ASPECTS OF LEEDS ECO-VILLAGE

This document builds upon previous discussions and documents produced by those interested in taking forward the idea of the Leeds eco-village. The intention of this document is to be in a position where we can give to Leeds City Council a baseline document of what we would expect of an eco-village development – and hence so that Leeds City Council know what our expectations are. This needs to be done by the end of July.

There are five (or more) key areas which the Leeds Eco-village project has identified as key requirements. These requirements act as principles which will inform (a) the members and (b) other groups such as Leeds City Council and developers, about what the minimum expectations of the Leeds eco-village group are in order for it to develop as a project.

1 Decision making and group structure

- Consensus decision making is the preferred option for making decisions. Group members will be asked to learn and use these techniques.
- Non-hierarchy, defined here as an equality of participation between members and a respect of their basic rights, is a core principle.
- Working groups will be used, wherever possible, to take forward areas of work. These groups will have a high level of autonomy to carry out their agreed remit, but will be ultimately answerable to the whole group via regular all-group meetings.
- Involvement and participation of all members will be at all times prioritized and maximized.
- Regular all-group meetings will act as the main decision-making bodies, where working groups and individuals are nominated with any tasks.

- There will be clear roles and responsibilities and terms of reference at all times in terms of decision making.

2 Commitment and values

- There will be a number of core values which members need to agree upon. These are to be finalized but will prioritize affordability, low impact living, low carbon outputs, low car use, ecological sustainability, cooperation, conflict, interaction, community building, resolution, respect, inclusivity, etc.
- There will be a clear joining process for all prospective members which will set out these values.
- There will be a required set of commitments required from members – this will include both set-up and living stages.

3 Financial and legal issues

- 100 per cent of the properties will be affordable.
- A mixture of rental and for sale properties will be built.
- Affordable will not be defined as a certain percentage below market rate but as affordable as possible with no profit component added to the sale value
- The group will look into cooperative ownership and financial structures for managing the project. These may include existing structures such as Community Interest Companies (CICs), Community Land Trusts (CLTs) or cooperative companies.
- Articles and Memorandums of association will clearly outline the values of the project.
- A number of funding sources will be considered – independent, sweat equity, loans, grants, individual mortgages.
- Over-reliance on one large source, developer or funder will be avoided.
- Resale values of properties will be limited to reduce market inflation to undermine the values of the project.

4 Design and development

- Participation and inclusivity will be maximized at both planning/design and implementation stage.
- An independent project manager will oversee the design and build phases.

- Community involvement and working with local partners will be maximized.
- Self-build will be promoted as much as possible. Local skills capacity building will be used as much as possible to facilitate this.
- Employment and skills generation is a core value of the design and development phase. The project is geared towards generating the necessary skills so that people can maximize input into the construction phase.
- It is hoped that this may lead to generating further employment among project members rather than relying on external contractors.
- Design components will maximize values of human scale, sustainability, legibility, ecological sustainability, community interaction, etc.

5 Project components

- Numerous components are integral to the project, such as:

  - Shared facilities (laundry, health, cooking, transport, etc.)
  - Green space.
  - Food-growing areas.
  - Small work spaces for employment generation.
  - Educational aspects, including site visits and workshops.
  - Public and private spaces.
  - Cohousing design principles and layout.
  - A minimization of space for car use.

Thus, even at this early stage, we laid down really clear parameters to work within. This proved essential. Throughout late 2007, the Leeds eco-village idea started to gather momentum. We met monthly at the Common Place and had a regular Sunday social to attract new people. We kept meeting to develop and refine our thinking on land, legal and finance issues. In the meantime, we drafted a constitution and set up an email list, and established working groups to devolve some of the tasks we needed to do. These included land, legal and finance, workshops, publicity, membership and process. We started to meet solicitors, local bankers, architects and housing providers to tell them about the idea and to obtain information about how we could take the idea forward.

In November 2007, we held a launch event which was a real success. We invited Jonathan Dawson, President of the Global Eco-Village (GEN) network who lived at the Findhorn Eco-village in northern Scotland. We showed a video and held a discussion event the following day to try to shape the idea. As a result of the launch event, we had a first and very positive article in the local newspaper, and, as a result, the local Green Party leader got in touch to find out more and how he could support us. He brokered a meeting with the leader of the Council at that time which really started to get us to meet contacts in the City Council. He seemed to love the idea and identified for us a lead councillor and officer to help us take the idea forward. We met Leeds City Council's climate change officer and Delton Jackson, a design officer who had done a Master's thesis on cohousing in the USA. He became a key supporter of our project over the years. From that point, we started to have real momentum and a clearer identity.

Defining: Setting parameters and laying down the basics

At this stage, there was still a broad range of opinions and preferences as to what the idea might eventually be in reality. What we realized was that an eco-village and a cohousing project can actually be quite different, and it was time to explore these differences and really define what we were doing. At the same time, we started to explore the Community Land Trust (CLT) model which we felt would be a useful legal framework for us. Throughout 2008, the CLT movement was expanding in anticipation of the 2008 Housing Act, including a legal definition of CLTs for the first time in English law. It was during this period that we started to have conversations with a local solicitor who was acting on behalf of Community Land Trusts as well as the Development Trust Association. Increasingly, it was becoming clear that we wanted to adopt a cooperative and mutual organizational model that locked in the development to the local community. I drew up a table to help clarify what I thought were the different routes we could take.

	Cohousing project	*Eco-village*
Landownership	Freehold private – householders lease from company	Community Land Trust (projects lease from the CLT)
Land sourcing	Private purchase – divided equally between number of homes	Public gifting or discounted regeneration land
Management	Through resident-based company	Multi-group partnership board
Build type	Based on decision of project members and available funds	Depends on type of agreement made
Tenure	Private and additional housing cooperative to provide cheaper rented homes	Mixed: social landlord, private, housing cooperative

	Cohousing project	*Eco-village*
Legal framework	Simple limited company or cooperative	CLT framework with additional legal structure such as CIC or limited company with charitable status
Initial investment	£5000 membership, then individual contributions to cost of land, house and common house	None or low
Size	Around 20	Depends on site but may be 100
Financial sources	Individual mortgages and private capital (supplemented by possible grants to build a few homes for rent)	Mixed: grants, mortgages, in kind (gifted), private
Density	Depends on money available	Likely to be high to meet government targets

In March 2008, we brought all this together on an options day. We used a simple PowerPoint to outline and then make decisions on the legal entity, the size and preferred location. We distilled this into a Project Outline document which laid down for the first time what Leeds Eco-village was. The basic parameters were that we decided upon an urban location with 20 homes. The entity would be a fully mutual housing cooperative and members would have to put in £5000 at risk to join. This money would provide the organization with some working financial resources. We were still exploring options in terms of whether the homes would be for sale or rent, or mutually owned by a cooperative.

It wasn't until April 2008 that we came across the Mutual Home Ownership Society (MHOS) model. I attended the annual Community Land Trust (CLT) conference in London. This was an important time for the CLT movement as it was about to be formally defined in law. David Rodgers, then chief executive of CDS Co-operatives, and someone who became a close friend and mentor for the project, outlined how the MHOS model could act as the mutual body that owned the houses on land owned by the CLT. We were captivated by the model. It seemed to embody everything we wanted – equality, mutualism and cooperation. I'll explain much more about the MHOS model in later chapters, but this was the moment that we really found a focus for the project. We met David again in the summer over a good bottle of wine in a restaurant in Manchester. Coming out of the restaurant we were buzzing with ideas, and possibly the wine! Over lunch, we had all our questions answered and were fully inspired by the MHOS approach. We were going to be the first in the UK, and with economic equality at its heart we felt that this was the right thing to do. We had found our focus to make this the pioneering project we had hoped for.

The project was becoming fairly formalized throughout 2008. We launched our membership for the first time which included Fran, Mark, Lou, Gary, Cristina, Andy, Tash and myself. Only three of us now live in Lilac, but the initial support of the others was crucial. We organized monthly socials, met in each other's houses and kept up with the formal monthly meetings. It was a busy and exhilarating time. We had no idea how long we had to go, or how much we had to do.

The summer of 2008 represented a change in momentum. We seemed to step up a gear now that we had people who were formally members and we had a document which we could show to people. We wrote our first formal business plan and sent it to senior officers at Leeds City Council, which included a request to transfer a piece of land for free to a CLT which we aimed to set up. We were heartened that we actually got to meet some quite senior-level policy makers to discuss this option. However, with hindsight, it was understandable that our plan was met with a polite but ultimately unsuccessful response. While they liked the idea, they wanted to see much more work on what it all meant. We were perhaps naive and got carried away with all the talk at the time about asset transfer to community groups.

The setback seemed huge at the time, but it was actually a crucial first step to test the idea and make contacts. I remember going for a cup of tea afterwards with Fran and Tash. We stared into out drinks, not able to talk. We had assumed they would meet our requests enthusiastically. But it felt like coming out of the headmaster's office. Nice attempt, but this was a D minus. Go away and do lots more homework. The thought on all our minds was 'How dare they, don't they realize we are trying to tackle climate change and the affordability housing crisis?' Was this the end? What do we do next?

We regrouped and continued to explore and give the idea more detail and precision. We needed better financial projections and some real idea of scheme costs. And, most of all, we needed a piece of land. We continued to scour the region for available sites, and to talk to anyone who was interested. We looked at derelict and decommissioned churches, abandoned pubs and we even talked to a local developer who, prior to the 2008 crash, offered us a piece of land for £1 million as part of his dream for a 20-acre eco-town on the edge of Leeds! He disappeared in the recession, and now clusters of faceless townhouses cover the site.

Over the summer of 2008, I also applied for and won a small grant from a social enterprise charity called Unltd. This allowed us to make our first move towards being an actual legal entity rather than an informal group. It was only a small amount but it allowed us to set up essential infrastructure; we paid for the incorporation of our Society rules, set up a website, prepared a leaflet and bought a banner. In late 2008, Alan and Kirsty also moved from Newcastle to Leeds to join the project. This was a decisive moment. We had developed the idea with them back in 2006 and they helped us really drive forward the idea. Some of the other founders – Christine, Andy and Gary – shifted away from the project as their priorities and life circumstances changed. We were left with a really focused and committed group of six: me, Tash, Fran, Mark, Alan and Kirsty. It really felt like this was an idea that would happen now, no matter how long it would take.

We thought long and hard about how we would build the project and what we would build our homes from. Early on, we made a commitment to using natural materials, especially straw and timber, as it offered benefits in terms of cost and resident involvement in the actual construction. We had early conversations with some really impressive and community-minded strawbale builders based in the Yorkshire region about how we could build with strawbales. They were called Amazonails and were an outfit run by two women who focused on promoting much-needed gender equality in the construction industry. We first met them in the Ecology Building Society's meeting room, a strawbale roundhouse that Amazonails had built. We explored some initial costings and design work with them, and the grant I received from Unltd paid for a brief feasibility study that gave us a very rough idea of project costs. This was the first time we seriously started to think about what materials we would use and how much it would cost. We visited the Building Research Establishment (BRE) in Watford to gather ideas and wandered around a surreal demonstration eco-park with half a dozen zero carbon houses built by various corporate builders. We saturated ourselves with facts on passivehaus standards, mechanical ventilation with heat recovery (MVHR), solar pumps, thermal mass, u-values and airtightness measures, and came away wondering how we would ever choose. We also visited an inspirational small housing cooperative near Cambridge who had built their homes entirely from hempcrete – a super-insulating and carbon neutral alternative to concrete.

By autumn 2008, it was about time for a name change. The eco-village label is fine, but we had realized that what we were doing was not really just a village, nor just eco. Our vision was based in a city, and we wanted to have a social, ecological and economic impact. Naming projects and groups is really difficult. We didn't want to be cornered into stereotypes about communes, hippies or environmentalists. The name came to Tash and I on my uncle's sixtieth birthday walk. Uncle John had just finished walking 5000 miles round the coastline of Britain. We were trekking along the cliffs of the southwest coastal path towards Lands End, chatting, as we always did, about the eco-village. We were playing a word game to see what name we could come up with.

FIGURE 3.1 Ecohouse at the Building Research Establishment, Watford

Source: Lilac.

FIGURE 3.2 Hempcrete houses near Cambridge

Source: Lilac.

'It's low impact, right?' I said.

Yes, and what else?' replied Tash.

'Eco, affordable, community, cooperative, mutual. . .' I started to recount a long stream of buzz-words that had been going round in my head for weeks.

'LILY? Low Impact Living?' said Tash.

'And what's the 'Y'?

'Oh yeah, erm I'm not sure. Yurt?' she replied.

'Very funny. Anything serious? Look, let's take this back to basics. It's Low Impact, right?' I said.

'And it's affordable and we are building houses. No. Actually we are building a community aren't we, a community of people?'

'Low Impact affordable, community isn't it? LIAC? No. LIAD? LAD? LID? No that's silly. LIAH? No that doesn't work.'

'Wait on, what about LILAC? Low Impact Living Affordable Community', Tash said.

FIGURE 3.3 The Lilac logo

Source: Lilac.

> 'Yeah brilliant. Lilac. Lilac! I hate that colour', I replied.
> Don't worry. We don't have to use the colour.'

And so Lilac was born. We got a friend of ours to make us a logo which has been with us ever since. It depicts a wind turbine next to a cityscape set in a cloud. It was a jolly little picture that thankfully is not often reproduced in the colour lilac. By autumn 2008, we started to call our project Lilac. Over the winter of 2008, we started to look over rules from CDS Co-operatives based in London to become a Mutual Home Ownership Society. By the next spring Lilac was registered as an Industrial and Provident Society under English law. It was signed by five founder members – by that time Mark had dropped out – all of whom paid their £5000 joining fee. This gave us important development finance, but at this early stage it was at risk for those who paid it.

SO WHAT IS AN INDUSTRIAL AND PROVIDENT SOCIETY?

UK cooperative law is fairly underdeveloped and relies on arcane nineteenth-century legislation. The Industrial and Provident Societies Act of 1893 (updated in 1965) provided the legal origins. These Acts allow for the creation of two broad categories of cooperatives. Bona fide cooperatives trade for the mutual benefit of their members, while societies for the benefit of the community (bencoms as they are called) trade to benefit the broader community. All sorts of entities choose these routes: consumer, agricultural and housing cooperatives, working men's clubs and allotments, friendly societies and social enterprises. What sets cooperatives apart from limited companies is that they are set up on a not-for-profit basis, with all assets held in common by the membership and shareholdings limited, which prohibits individual profit. There are now a growing number of legal forms that undertake similar functions, such as Community Interest Companies and Development Trusts.

Convincing: Making the case and getting land and finance

By 2009, we had all the main elements in place: an identity and vision, a first business plan, a legally incorporated entity, a small, committed group, a website, and a clear idea of the kind of place we wanted to be. We now turned to convincing the world, or at least the City Council, about the need to support us and make Lilac happen. We discussed in some detail available land with Leeds City Council. During the freezing January, we were shown several sites and visited them all. Many were very unappealing cleared bits of land on the edge of the city or recently demolished inner-city housing. We narrowed it down to three: a park near an old mill which was earmarked for redevelopment, a site in Pudsey on the edge of Leeds, and an old school site in Bramley called Wyther Park about three miles from the city centre. It was this last one that really caught our imagination. We drew up a list of criteria and scored all the sites we came across (see Table 3.1). In April, we had a meeting to choose one, and the old Wyther Park site was the clear winner. Figure 3.4 shows the piles of coins we used to rank the different criteria so that we could see the results in a highly visual way. It had great transport links, was easily accessible to the rest of the city, was in the middle of an existing community, and had a good south-facing aspect for natural solar gain. The site had a development brief drawn up for it which marked it out for housing. We were amazed that a large housing provider had not snapped it up. But usefully, at least for us, the global financial crisis was unfolding around us and new developments had tailed off.

Once we had committed to this site, the task now was to go after it and enter into detailed negotiations with the local authority. One of the most challenging aspects for any community group is how to develop a negotiating approach with your local authority. There are so many diverse departments and people that a group will encounter. Profiling them and understanding their roles and requirements is vital to navigate the expansive waters of a large urban authority. Local officials and politicians who are encountered all have different roles, priorities and understandings of what you can achieve, their own local authority's aims and opinions on the likely success of your project. A clear pecking order became apparent to us. Those in the

TABLE 3.1 Our criteria used to rank shortlisted sites

Criteria	Quantitative measure	Source
Financial cost		
Guide price	price per acre	seller
Local land prices	price per acre	Land Registry
House prices in area	price for 1-bed / 3-bed	online property search
Other interested parties	number	seller
Physical environment		
Quality of drinking water	hardness of water	Yorkshire Water
Aspect (south facing?)	degrees south	map
Amount of light (shaded?)	%	
Flood risk	% risk	Environment Agency
Rainfall (or even stream)	inches per year	Met Office
Adjacent buildings	y/n	map
Adjacent trees or green space	y/n	map + visit
Adjacent empty sites	y/n	map + visit
Previous industrial use	y/n	seller
Recent demolitions	y/n	seller + locals
Smoke control area	y/n	LCC
Local facilities		
Supermarket/retail park	distance	google + phone book
Pub (with beer)	distance	streetmap website
Bank	distance	visit
Primary school	distance	Leeds City Council
Post office	distance	map + Post Office website
Community centre	distance	Leeds City Council www
GP	distance	NHS choices
Library	distance	Leeds City Council www
Swimming pool	distance	Leeds City Council www
Restaurant	distance	visit + phone book
NHS dentist	distance	NHS choices
Hardware store	distance	internet
Laundrette	distance	phone directory
Park	distance	Leeds City Council www
Secondary school	distance	Leeds City Council
Local residents' association	distance	current information
Allotments	distance	Leeds City Council www
Recycling facilities	distance	Leeds City Council www
Youth groups	distance	Leeds City Council www
Café	distance	visit

TABLE 3.1 continued

Criteria	Quantitative measure	Source
Fresh vegetables	distance	visit
Play park	distance	Leeds City Council www
Ethnic food store	distance	visit + phone book
Transport		
Nearest train station	distance in km	map
Distance to Leeds railway station	distance in miles	viamichelin.co.uk
Bus frequency to city centre	buses per hour	Metro website
Level of car ownership in area	proportionate who don't have a car	neighbourhood.statistics.gov.uk (Cars or Vans)
Level of cycle use	number of journeys by bike	neighbourhood.statistics.gov.uk – Travel to Work
Cycle-only route to city centre	% dedicated cycle way	Leeds cycle map
Socio-economic indicators		
Ethnic mix	% white	neighbourhood.statistics.gov.uk
Age ranges	% 0–17 years	neighbourhood.statistics.gov.uk
Educational (primary)	aggregate of test	Leeds City Council
Educational (secondary)	% achieving Level 2	Leeds City Council
Retired	%	neighbourhood.statistics.gov.uk
Economically inactive	%	neighbourhood.statistics.gov.uk
Level of home ownership	% (outright or mortgage)	neighbourhood.statistics.gov.uk
Life expectancy	years	neighbourhood.statistics.gov.uk
Average weekly Income	average	neighbourhood.statistics.gov.uk
Index of multiple deprivation	number per year	neighbourhood.statistics.gov.uk
Community safety		
Burglary	per 1000 households each year	beatcrime.info
Antisocial behaviour	per 1000 households each year	beatcrime.info
Violent crime	per 1000 households each year	beatcrime.info
Criminal damage	per 1000 households each year	beatcrime.info
Racist attacks	number per year	Neighbourhood police team
Drug crime	number per year	Neighbourhood police team
Gun crime	number per year	Neighbourhood police team
Sexual attacks	number per year	Neighbourhood police team
Noise pollution	number per year	environmental health

FIGURE 3.4 Ranking our selection criteria with piles of coins

Source: Lilac.

design department were some of the most interesting and were always willing to listen to and explore your ideas, and would be crucial in the planning stage. But ultimately they didn't hold power or influence on costs and land acquisition. Those in planning would be central, but only at the right time. So you had to make sure you pre-empted their needs and responded to them at the right time when you submitted planning. Highways are extremely crucial. They are perhaps the most orthodox group and the most challenging to work with innovation. Arguments have to be made slowly and carefully, with close reference to local and national policy, as well as workable examples, to give them confidence that they can move in new directions. Those in asset management, essentially those responsible for managing the city's finances, are firmly in control. Whatever they said overruled anyone else. They see themselves, rightly, as guardians of the city's public finances, and they are inherently sceptical of the intentions of other groups.

On top of all this, you have to deal with the difference between officers and elected councillors. In theory the former just do the bidding of the latter. But, increasingly, the officers make policy and get the councillors to rubber-stamp it. The more active and experienced councillors are more engaged and relationships need to be built up with them, especially if they are your local councillor. Finally, community groups have to be very shrewd at appealing to the incumbent party but not being seen as too party political or connected to one party in case the overall control of the municipality changes during the development phase. Community projects need to have cross-party support to have longevity. You could be dead in the water after an election if you are seen to be the outgrowth of a defeated political party.

Due to the persistent level of communication we had opened up with the local authority we were given a meeting with asset transfer to discuss potential ways forward for buying the Wyther Park site. We met a senior asset management officer called Ben Middleton from the Council who had a genuine interest in helping us. The first part of our negotiations involved a letter to Ben in April 2008 offering Leeds City Council £80,000 for the site and including some financial projections which showed that our model was affordable at this level. Looking back, it was a rather forthright letter, as you can see from this extract:

Dear Ben Middleton,

We are writing following extensive consultation and meetings about our project with Leeds City Council officers, elected members, and local statutory and voluntary groups. We copy some of them in here to keep them up to date on the progress of this project. Our company LILAC (formerly Leeds Eco-Village) is now in a position to make a formal offer, subject to securing planning permission, on the former Wyther Park Primary School site

(Victoria Park Avenue, Kirkstall) of £80,000. We refer to the shaded grey area on the map prepared by Sue Halliday dated 14/3/08 (Plan 9771/D). We believe this is a reasonable offer given the additional benefits our project will deliver for Leeds City Council. In sum, LILAC will not only provide Leeds City Council with a capital receipt but also a range of activities which will be significantly beneficial to the city in the coming years.

We received a reply about a month later. While it was a rejection, its tone was helpful:

> Thank you for your letter dated 21 April 2009 submitting an offer of £80,000 for the above site. As you are aware this site has been withdrawn from the market due to the depressed current economic climate. The Council have budgeted to receive a sum in excess of this . . . when the market recovers.

They were clearly interested and intrigued by us, if not a little cautious. In his letter Ben continued: 'What guarantee does the Council have of what you are providing and how can the Council ensure that LILAC cannot profit from such an acquisition, i.e. sell on at a profit in five years' time?' Understandably, they were wary that the whole trend for asset transfer from central government at that time might lead to the disposal of public assets to groups who might turn out to be unscrupulous and financially gain from them. This was one of our challenges – to convince them of the worth and intention of who we were – that our cooperative model sought to bring wider community benefits and not private gain. This would simply take time.

We had another meeting with Ben to follow up on his letter. He was clear in stating that Leeds didn't want to sell the site until market conditions improved. The site had been issued a development brief for housing for sale back in 2006 when the old primary school had been demolished, but, with no buyer and the coming of the global financial crisis, the land was taken off the market. They were clear in their approach – to borrow cheap money from the financial markets due to historically low interest rates to cover their debts rather than sell off public assets at a discount or loss. Any hope of a discounted or 'free' asset transfer faded. Ben did suggest that if we wanted any below-market value purchase price this would need approval from one of the divisional heads at Leeds Council.

We were determined to pursue that site and our next step during this period was to write our Project Development Plan over the summer of 2009 and use this as the next step to strengthen our case and take it to the divisional heads. It took at least three months to write and ran to over 50 pages. It laid down the key aspects of the project in terms of policy background, membership and environmental credentials, and as much on costs and financial planning as we could determine at this time. This was essentially our detailed business case. It was a document that we wrote entirely on our own and it was a significant achievement.

In July we sent this plan to the Council, making them a higher offer, but this time asking for a deferred or split payment for the site – half on purchase, half on completion of the scheme. Here's an extract:

> Given the financial constraints that we face as a small organisation, we would like to see if it is possible to acquire the site through a phased purchase (subject to planning permission). Through our business model as outlined in the enclosed document we may be able to offer Leeds City Council an amount in the region of £500,000, an amount which we understand would satisfy a best value price. We envisage this amount would be paid through an initial down payment to purchase a building licence, followed by one subsequent and one final payment on completion of the project.

We sent this to the divisional heads at Leeds for Housing and Regeneration and Sustainable Development to seek their sponsorship of our idea. Things began to shift. The Head of Regeneration, Stephen Boyle, wrote back suggesting that there should be a meeting with the affordable housing team to discuss the plan further. New doors were opened up. We then met Ernie Grey, Lois Pickering, John Ramsden and Liz Cook from housing in the autumn to discuss affordable housing issues relating to Lilac. New challenges emerged. Our ideas and model were so new that they had great difficulty assessing what we were. From the outset they were very sceptical that our model was providing affordable housing. For them the definition of affordable housing was very closely related to social rented housing for the most needy. In contrast, we were a housing cooperative whose members did not seem to represent the greatest need, and hence did not justify any public support. This was a fair point. But we needed to stress the wider benefits of mutual housing and the fact that it was a tiny part of the current housing situation. And we certainly did not want to encroach on social housing or de-emphasize its importance.

We sent them a huge amount of information on the Mutual Home Ownership model and met a few more times. What we agreed with them as a way forward was that if they could not support us as an official affordable housing tenure type, they could offer us support to explore the potential replicability of our model. This was on the condition that we bought it at open market value and enlisted professional support to take the project forward. John Ramsden, an executive manager in the Strategic Asset Management Department, was really helpful and became key to the negotiations. We received a decisive email from him towards the end of September 2009. Tash and I were just about to set off on a late summer holiday, cycling in

Wales, and I was just checking my email (again!) when his email arrived. Here is an extract:

> Further to our recent meeting, I felt it was important that you have professional advisors on board who can help you project manage and develop realistic costings for the scheme because in policy terms the Council would want to support the development of sustainable housing which could be replicated elsewhere. . . . To that end I confirm that, subject to the principle that the site sale must be at market value, I am prepared to recommend that the Council commits some further officer time with you to test whether you can bring forward a sustainable housing model in both the environmental and financial senses, which can be replicated. The Wyther site at Bramley is still available and I understand that, subject to agreement of price, LILAC would still like to proceed with it. Following our last conversation, I can confirm that an acceptable basis in principle would be a two year building agreement, within which the development would be completed and the land paid for in stages, followed by freehold transfer of the land. Your proposal to pay the agreed market value in three equal tranches: initially on commencement of the building agreement; then at month 12 and finally at month 24, is also acceptable. Hopefully in this way we can assist you to develop a sustainable housing model which can be taken elsewhere without subsidy.

We read it. Then we reread it. Then we jumped for joy around the living room. This was the breakthrough moment. After two years of hard negotiating and persistence Leeds had finally recognized us. It seemed a small victory. But actually it was a monumental one. Their commitment to a development agreement to exclusively negotiate with us and to lend officer time was actually worth more than a cash discount on the land. We left for our holiday full of joy and wonder that we had come this far and that we were really going to achieve our dream. Again, little did we realize how much there was still left to do.

The next step was to seek out that formal professional support. You tend to find things when you look for them at the right time. I often chatted with Martin, a friend of mine who was an architectural technologist, who gave me his worldly advice as an insider. He recommended a great bunch of project managers who we first met for a coffee in October. I will never forget Martin's wise words: 'You guys are great. You are visionaries. But you need a project manager to get any further.' He was right, and we got one. This is when Jimm Reed from CoHo Ltd, a firm specializing in project and housing management, came into our lives and became the bedrock of support for us over four long years. Jimm started to advise us straight away, on an hourly basis initially before we formally passed the feasibility stage. After that we paid him a percentage of project costs. He opened doors to us, as he knew many people at Leeds City Council and in the local development profession. He was trusted and it made people regard us with a new, more confident perspective. You could just see them thinking, 'these guys have now got a project manager. They mean real business.' And the best thing was that we could now turn to Jimm to explain things to us and guide us through what had become very, very deep waters.

Jimm started to help with a range of tasks. We had to meet senior officers in Leeds' Housing Department to discuss our financial model. Their initial reaction was mixed, as they just could not understand what we were. We were not offering houses for rent or for sale; we were a leasehold cooperative offering members an equity stake in their homes and, for them, they could not see the potential of this delivering affordable housing. However, all was not lost as we laid out our model in great detail. Jimm worked hard in supporting us to explain the potential behind shared equity housing in a language they could relate to. Ultimately, given they were not offering us any cash support, Leeds City Council ended up being interested enough in what we were proposing to support it. They actually came back with a purchase price that was far higher than we could afford. Jimm reassured us that this was just a starting figure and in any case a professional valuer would help determine this price and negotiate the final market value. We put this aside to worry about at a later date. We had enough to deal with!

The exclusivity agreement was a real landmark. It laid out that the City Council would only negotiate with us for an initial period of six months in order to give us time to get together our finances and membership. This agreement was renewed for a further six months. It offered us the potential to buy the land in two segments with 50 per cent paid on the purchase date and the other 50 per cent on practical completion. This was very useful for us, as it gave us some room in our cash flow. However, in the end, given that the bank was willing to lend us enough money, and the fact that the land was not too expensive, this split payment was not a deal breaker. Jimm formally hooked us up with a local solicitor at Cobbetts LLP, now DWF, called Ian Moran. I had met Ian before as he worked in social housing law and was active in supporting Community Land Trusts as a legal framework. Ian's first task for us was to scrutinize, amend and finalize the exclusivity agreement. It was a great relief to actually have a solicitor acting for us and giving us his opinion on legal documents that were partially unfathomable to us. Ian's ability for legal speak over the years became legendary. We were all resigned to only partly understanding, safe in the knowledge that if the solicitor thinks it's all right, it probably is all right.

While all this was happening, we were putting some serious thinking into how we wanted to build our houses. This is covered in more detail in Chapter 4. But for the purposes of this part of the story, Jimm started to help us weigh up the options. As well as our conversations with Amazonails we started to talk to Stroma Design, where my friend Martin worked, about how we might build. It seemed like an interesting partnership to explore. Both firms were really interesting and had a huge amount to offer in terms of sustainable design and construction. We held a launch with them in November 2009 where we set out our Business Plan and membership scheme, and got Stroma, Amazonails and Jimm to say a few words to show the audience that we were getting a team together. Eighty people turned up, including the local MP. It felt great and there was a real buzz about the event. From this we got our first real members after the founder members: Elinor and Jenny. They were enthusiastic about strawbale building, loved the idea of cooperatives and wanted to find a strong community to live in. They were the first people beyond the founders who were prepared to believe in us and to put their money in at risk. It was another real milestone.

But there were so many questions left unanswered. Could we build so many houses using load-bearing strawbale? Was the engineering evidence base there? Would the bank lend against this product? What would it actually cost and how much could we actually build ourselves? I knew we had taken an important step forward, but this wasn't the final cast who would build Lilac. We had become so committed to building with straw that in November, the founding members, along with various friends of Lilac, took a weekend break to a strawbale holiday home built by innovative strawbale builder Carol Atkinson. Over several bottles of wine, we enjoyed our first night in a strawbale house and tried to finalize how we would build our houses. The general feeling was that we just didn't yet know. We had seen so many options. But it was such a big decision and we wanted more evidence.

We were all intensively seeking out options, and by chance one option I followed up was ModCell. My old housemate Toby just happened to send round a weblink to a building Modcell had built called BaleHaus. What caught our eye was that it was built from straw and timber, but it used a prefabricated and highly engineered technique which offered cost certainty and an engineering evidence base. I decided to follow it up and jumped on a train to Bath University to meet Modcell inventor Craig White and the research team at Bath University led by Peter Walker who were monitoring the BaleHaus which had been relocated to the University campus. In its previous life, BaleHaus had been located on London Docklands next to the Expo Centre when Kevin McCloud, TV presenter of *Grand Designs*, had reviewed it, and then slept in it.

This was the first time we encountered Craig White who became the architectural creator of Lilac. Craig was part inventor, part businessman. He was knowledgeable and passionate about how to build low carbon housing and was refreshingly knowledgeable about cohousing. But they had never built houses using

FIGURE 3.5 The first Modcell BaleHaus

Source: Modcell.

Modcell, and ultimately this became one of the major reasons why what we did became so complex. It was difficult to get accurate figures. But the initial ones he did give us estimated the build cost at a little over £1000 per square metre. This was far more than we thought we could afford, so as much as we liked Modcell, we declined. That was the last we thought we would hear from Craig White.

However, out of the blue, just after Christmas 2009, Craig emailed me, excited about the opportunity of a grant from the UK's Department of Energy and Climate Change and Home and Communities Agency (HCA) which aimed to get fledgling supply chains off the ground specializing in natural materials. Modcell had been designated one of the materials, with a grant of £20,000 per home available. That was worth £400,000 to us – and this would be a welcome contribution towards a final multi-million-pound project cost. We quickly started to scope out this option as the money had to be allocated by the end of the financial year in March. What this grant opportunity meant in practice was to commit to Modcell as a procurement route, and Craig as the architect, before a builder was even chosen and before a very thorough feasibility assessment had been carried out. We had a very frank conversation about this with Jimm, who pointed out the risks, but we had become quite good at taking risk by now. We were very different to his usual risk-averse housing association clients. Things were moving swiftly and there seemed several insurmountable hurdles to achieving the grant. It had to be passed on to a registered housing provider, and the houses had to be built by 2011. Jimm teamed us up with Synergy Housing who were able to receive and hold the grant on our behalf, and the HCA were so keen to see this project happen that they took a gamble on whether we could actually complete it or not by 2011. We got Craig to Leeds to do some detailed figures. Jimm put us in touch with a quantity surveyor called Andrew Gaunt from Bernard Williams Associates who prepared our first project budget estimate. He did this for free on the basis that he would charge us for the work if we went to the next stage with him. This was a wake-up call for us. The initial cost estimate of just over £1 million doubled. We started to understand the actual cost of building a project of this scale.

In the end, for a variety of reasons we chose Modcell as a route to build our homes. The grant really helped, and it was the largest grant with the smallest number of conditions I will ever be part of! We had to commit to using Modcell and monitor our energy. The grant letter was signed on the last day of March 2010. It was so close to call. I had sleepless nights, but suddenly we received a cheque in the post. Again, another huge step had been taken forward.

Over the spring we began work on another area – planning. We met with planners at Leeds in the spring of 2010 and the first meeting was a real challenge. We put forward an outline sketch of how we saw the neighbourhood laid out on the site. We were met by half a dozen stern faces, who proceeded to rip apart almost every aspect of what we had put in front of them. They had not really heard of cohousing. We received a barrage of questions – where was the adopted highway, why didn't the homes front on to the street, why were they arranged in a horseshoe shape, why were the private gardens so small, and there was so much shared space which looked difficult to manage. In sum, what we were proposing overturned much planning orthodoxy. We began a faltering set of answers, but Jimm Reed sensed that this was not the time to take on such a battle.

'I know a lot of this seems new to you,' began Jimm diplomatically, 'and much of it goes against what you guys are used to. Cohousing is very different, so I think it might be useful if we came back and did a presentation about the principles of cohousing and how these can be used to help design strong communities.'

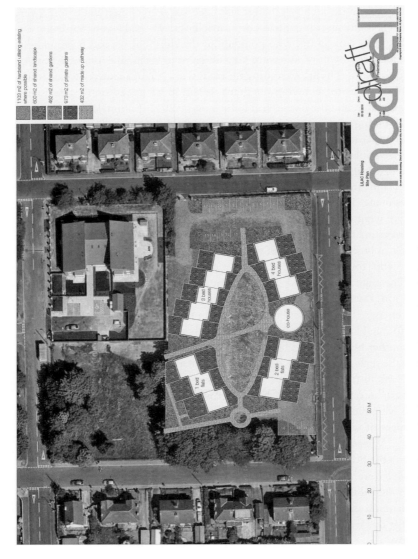

FIGURE 3.6 The first draft Lilac site plan discussed with the planners

Source: White Design Associates.

'I think that would be useful', said one of the planners.

As we filed out of the room, we all looked pretty glum.

'That actually went ok', said Craig.

'What?' said Fran. 'They practically threw us out of the room.'

'No, not at all, they have just got some natural concerns because it's so new. We can lay it all out in a more detailed meeting', he confidently retorted.

We met them again in August 2010, and gave a PowerPoint presentation on cohousing. It was very slick and informative, and was a real opportunity to step back from the issues around the site and to discuss openly with the planners the principles of cohousing. It was an illuminating event where we all talked freely about the constraints of urban planning, how to tackle climate change and what makes good places. Naz Parker, a regional director from the Homes and Communities Agency, had heard about Lilac and turned up to find out more. His presence there made Leeds Council take note. One of the most significant concerns related to the level of car ownership. We were very keen on delivering only 10 car spaces for 20 homes. The planners simply did not believe this was feasible, even when we told them that most of us cycled or took the bus. The approach of the planners was for us to provide the level of car parking that reflected car ownership in the local area. So we undertook our own traffic survey. As Figure 3.7 illustrates, we found really low levels of car ownership on our nearest street, Victoria Park Avenue. We found that car ownership in all the surrounding streets was pretty low. We took the average

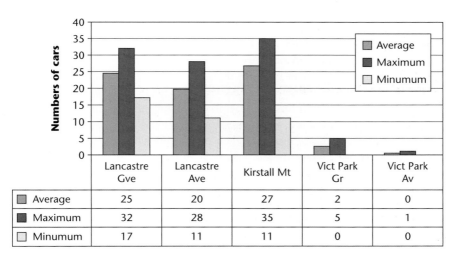

	Lancastre Gve	Lancastre Ave	Kirstall Mt	Vict Park Gr	Vict Park Av
◨ Average	25	20	27	2	0
■ Maximum	32	28	35	5	1
☐ Minumum	17	11	11	0	0

FIGURE 3.7 Data on local car ownership presented to Leeds City Council

Source: Lilac.

number of cars we could see during different hours and a range of days, and divided this by the number of homes. This showed around 0.7 cars per home. The planners wanted us to stick with one car parking space per home, but we stuck hard to a target of 0.5 cars per home. We tested this through the planning process, and we succeeded.

As summer 2010 approached, the project started to seem more and more real. We appointed Jimm Reed on a percentage of project costs rather than on an hourly rate, we appointed Ian Moran formally as our solicitor, and Andrew Gaunt of BWA became our quantity surveyor. I had a friend, Jim Clay, who worked for an engineering firm in London. It's probably clear by now that a large part of making a project happen relies on calling in favours from friends and acquaintances. Jim was an old university pal; I had known him for 20 years and we had chatted for a long time about Lilac. He felt part of it and was really pleased to contribute. He produced for us what is called a Phase One Desk Study – a report which compiles much existing information on a site such as land quality, geological profile, remediation risks, contamination and flooding. This is a really important piece of work, as it highlights if there are any big issues that might stop the development in its tracks such as high risk of flood or contamination. Nothing drastic showed up, although there was evidence of some low-level contamination from polyhydrocarbons – basically a buildup of soot and ash in the soil from centuries of industrialization around Yorkshire (something that people in this region had been eating in their food since the 1760s, I thought). However, this did come back as an issue we had to resolve; more on that later.

Over the summer of 2010, Jimm Reed put us in touch with the Homes and Communities Agency which had become interested in what we were doing, especially now that they were officially part financial backers of our project through their Low Carbon Investment Fund. In the wake of the new coalition government in the UK (the marriage of convenience between the Lib Dems and the Conservatives in 2010), the Prime Minister David Cameron was pushing the idea of the Big Society as a positive veneer for a new era of austerity politics and bank bailouts. Let communities take on the risk of managing their own affairs while the state retreats and looks after the private sector! In a strange twist of fate this actually benefited us, as Cameron sent out his minions to find community groups who were the embodiment of the localism in the Big Society. Self-build and community-led housing trusts seemed a good bet, and our model of mutual home ownership seemed to fit this perfectly. We met with Luke McDonald, a policy adviser at the HCA, to explain our financial model. This was the bit they were really interested in, as they were looking for ideas to promote innovative new housing tenure types.

We had some detailed conversations with the HCA about how they could support us further, as they wanted to see Lilac happen as quickly as possible to give momentum to the idea that the Big Society was actually generating results on the ground. One route they found to help us immediately was a small enabling grant to get us through planning. This paid for a range of consultant professionals to provide the services we needed at this point. We spent this grant on various professional fees up to planning stage such as project manager, quantity surveyor, architect, engineer, the planning application fee, and various mandatory surveys covering land, ecology and trees. The HCA sat down with us and engaged us in some very close scrutiny of our figures. They were keen to make sure that our model was sound and then they would be more confident that they could advocate for it. We had a completely open book session with them and they thoroughly investigated our economic viability. It's called due diligence.

In September 2010, we held a two-day community consultation in the buildup to our planning submission. The event was really enjoyable and we took over a nearby pocket park that had been built by the local neighbourhood watch group. With the architect we erected a small marquee and put up some display boards. Over the two days we chatted to about 40 of our neighbours-to-be and received

FIGURE 3.8 The marquee we set up for our community consultation day

Source: Lilac.

FIGURE 3.9 Lilac members explain our plans to the public

Source: Lilac.

some good press coverage. Most people were intrigued by the contemporary feel of the design-and-build method. What surprised us was an occasional hostile reaction to our affordable focus which raised concerns among locals of social rented council housing and possibly less desirable neighbours! Pitching yourself as affordable is indeed a double-edged sword.

We had also been doing our financial homework. Tash and I met with Steve Bendle, a freelance housing finance consultant from Community Land and Finance Ltd, who had been involved in trying to get the first MHOS off the ground in Stroud, but which for various reasons had failed. He did some long-term financial modelling for us to stress test our figures. His input was key and he helped us clarify how the whole MHOS was going to be financed, and importantly refinanced, over its lifetime. One of the premises of the model was a turnover of households on an average of 12 years. If this were the case, then Lilac would be able to refinance itself entirely through the reserves in its surplus equity fund (there is more on this in Chapter 5). At the same time, Tash and I took a day out of our holiday in the southwest in 2010 to meet a manager at Triodos Bank (Triodos is a small ethical

Dutch operation with headquarters in Bristol). We gave him a six-page financial summary and our meeting with them was incredibly positive. They were willing to lend in principle and gave us the green light. This was a huge relief, as other funding sources had not worked out. The Co-operative Bank, the natural lenders of the project, had rejected us for reasons we never actually got to the bottom of. The Charity Bank would love to lend to us but could not due to conflict of interest relating to lending to residents who also manage their own housing. Finally, several smaller building societies would have lent to us but could not offer enough due to lending limits.

By the autumn we began to look for a commercial valuer. They would provide an open land value to finalize the purchase price of the land from the local authority, as well as the gross market value of the project which would be used to determine how much the bank would lend us. We then received a real blow, as the detailed land survey found that the contamination was widespread and would need a complete scrape and refill of the top 600mm of the site which would incur a huge cost. This became a significant part of the negotiations with the local authority, as we now used this cost to negotiate down the sale price of the land. In fact, what we realized was that the land would have a negative value – it was effectively worthless in its current polluted state. Moreover, it had a large sewer running through the site dating from the Victorian era, rendering a small but not insignificant part of it undevelopable and making it unattractive to volume builders. The HCA became aware of this dilemma and began negotiations to release some money to Leeds City Council to decontaminate the site to enable Leeds to realize the full value of the site – and importantly a value in the black and not in the red.

The HCA found a route to do this. The HCA paid Leeds City Council to decontaminate the land on condition that they would sell the site to us. The last days of March 2011 were perhaps the most fraught of the whole development journey. Luke McDonald from the HCA was designated to help sort out the remediation grant and liaise with the Council. We had frantic conversations on the phone and spent a whole nerve-wracking day on 30 March as we finalized the grant agreement with the City Council. When Luke rang to inform me of the outcome. I was nervous to say the least. I was already sleep deprived from our first son Milo who had been born six months earlier. I paced around our attic office in between popping into the bedroom to check on our sleeping son. All I could think about was how five years of work could disappear in a second as the whole project got lost in bureaucracy. But the grant was signed and we survived another perseverance test. Luke rang me to give me the good news. I'll never forget the support and determination he showed us.

Over the winter of 2010 we enlisted a firm to value the site and negotiate the value of the land. The valuer took into consideration the contamination and, after some impressive hard negotiating with Leeds, a final price was agreed that we could afford. This was still full open market cost but it was much less than the original price of £500,000 that Leeds had stated. This is a real lesson in terms of digging deeper into land values as it is an incredibly complex area. A lot of it depends on how much the site could offer a developer in terms of aggregate commercial development yield per hectare. What our valuation report showed was that the numbers just wouldn't stack up for a commercial developer as they could not yield enough value (or profit above the build cost) from the site. This was great for us as we were not seeking to make a profit from the site or sell the homes, so it meant that we would not be competing with profit-hungry developers. In fact, the actual build cost for us was slightly more than the valuation. This wasn't an insurmountable problem, as part of the scheme was grant funded and the value would soon increase above the actual build cost with time. Enough members had also put enough money up front to mean that we could meet the full build cost comfortably. People were prepared to put in spare capital, as they wanted Lilac to happen.

However, the mortgage valuation was much more complex. We needed this value to determine how much the bank would lend us, and how much the entire project was worth in cash terms in case we went bust and the whole thing had to be disposed of on the market. The bank would essentially lend us up to 70 per cent of the mortgage valuation as determined by the valuer. It was a rocky road, as there seemed to be real confusion as to how to value our scheme, since it was a unique tenure type and had social and ecological aspects in it that a valuer did not recognize as yielding a high monetary value. What we valued, such as the communal facilities, shared open areas, cohousing design, high ecological standards, were not normally the things a buyer would pay for if the project had to be sold in the event of liquidation and bankruptcy. We were essentially building a pioneering product that the development markets would not really understand as a product. This was eye-opening stuff. There was actually a financial penalty to us for building and designing in social and ecological features, as the valuer would not recognize these in the gross development value.

What also became apparent were different ways to value projects. One is called market value with vacant possession (MV-VP) and another is market value subject to tenancies (MVSTT). The former is normally higher than the latter and the difference comes down to the fact that houses that come with incumbent tenants may be worth less if the houses have to be resold on the open market. We needed a value that was adequately high, as the bank would lend us 70 per cent of this. The lower the mortgage value, the bigger the gap between value and cost. And yes, that's right – the larger the margin of negative equity for us. After several discussions with our valuer they fully understood what Lilac represented, and eventually a mortgage value of £2.4 million was agreed.

Loanstock offer

LILAC Mutual Home Ownership Society Ltd

An ethical lending opportunity in a pioneering co-operative cohousing project – where your money will grow too!

Your financial support will help demonstrate that building an affordable low impact neighbourhood in Leeds is possible.

For more information or an **application form** see our website, email **finance@lilac.coop** or write to The Treasurer

www.lilac.coop

FIGURE 3.10 Lilac's loanstock investment flyer

Source: Lilac.

In June 2011, Triodos Bank's credit committee considered our application and, on the basis of the mortgage value, they were able to offer us a loan equivalent to 70 per cent of the mortgage valuation. This was a little more than we needed which was a great result. In the end, we borrowed around £1.5 million from Triodos Bank at a rate of 4.4 per cent over 25 years. We also considered trying to raise some capital through what is known as loanstock – basically an unsecured interest-bearing investment that non-members could make in Lilac. We held an investors' evening in 2011 and we raised a few thousand pounds. This was a small but useful amount. We couldn't depend on it as part of our cash flow, but it did help us grow a wider support base for the project.

Building: Constructing our homes

Formal project team meetings began in the summer of 2010 and this marked a period when we believed we were actually getting close to thinking about building our community on site. This was the beginning of the professionally led meetings which took the actual construction phase of the project forward. Project team meetings are fairly standard and formal affairs. They tend to be chaired by the quantity surveyor (QS) or project manager, and include the architect, engineers, client and, when appointed, the main contractor. We met monthly at the quantity surveyor's offices in Leeds' docklands. They were enlightening affairs. Joe and Fran and I, and later on Andy and Ellie, attended as Lilac representatives and tried to follow the constant conversational ping-pong between the project team, decipher the acronyms and make notes to feed back to the members. It was a frustrating year, as we seemed to have so many issues to sort out and we were no closer to appointing a builder or getting on site. Most of the discussions revolved around site issues, project costs and then the planning submission.

Our QS did a further project budget estimate now that he had all the professional team around the table. This came out considerably higher than the first estimate of just over £2 million! We began a rather depressing process of value engineering, where you basically identify elements of the project that you can tolerably delete. At this stage we lost roof gardens, balconies on the houses and decided to do the landscaping ourselves. The QS began a long process of reconciling Modcell's figures on the cost of building the homes with what he thought was realistic. This was a painful process and led to some large increases in costs.

Over the winter of 2010 the project team worked to finalize all the information for the tender documents to send out to prospective contractors. The QS led on getting together what is known as the Employer's Requirements which extended to three volumes and would become the bible for the build phase. I don't think we realized how important this would be – they would build to the instructions in this document down to the last screw and any deviation in it would be charged. There was so much information to compile for this and feedback to the members that many issues were left undecided. We took the decision that we would give the winning contractor scope to help us finalize these issues just so that we could move forward. In retrospect, this was probably not a wise idea, as it often stored up significant issues to be resolved later and led to rushed decision making and occasional misunderstandings between us and the contractor.

In February 2011, we met informally with three building contractors to interview them and explain our project. They were all very positive and boasted about how they could work with community groups and wanted to see community-led housing flourish. In terms of match with our values they were all quite equal and so the final choice came down to cost. It was a rather awkward beauty contest and it was the beginning of our realization that, as much as private developers wanted to work with the cohousing sector, there was a significant knowledge gap.

In the early part of 2011, the architects White Design were working hard getting all the planning documents ready. Since the application would be so novel and different we were advised by a senior officer at Leeds City Council to do a pre-presentation to the plans panel who would consider our application. Jimm Reed and I attended, focusing on why our scheme was affordable and what cohousing meant. The response was a complete surprise. Jimm and I were pretty nervous, worried about concerns at this stage that might prove to be unsurmountable. But instead, we held a cross-party committee of councillors captivated as we outlined Lilac and talked about the housing crisis, cooperatives and climate change. I can only assume that they were used to wealthy developers trying to get one over on them to make a fast buck and that we were a refreshing change. We had councillors from different political parties offering gestures of support for us and a small delegation followed us out, asking us to get in touch about future projects in their area. The big potential pinch point that we were concerned about was whether they would see us as affordable housing – and whether we would be forced to build low-cost houses for rent as part of the scheme to meet affordable housing targets. But these issues didn't really arise during the presentation. The councillors were just as interested in how our communal laundry would work and how young people these days had managed to hold on to such high ideals. 'It's like the good old days and the future rolled into one', quipped one councillor.

Our planning application was submitted in the last week of February 2011. This date had been delayed by several months and so the final submission was rushed. There were a number of design decisions outstanding, but given how long this had taken we decided to get it in. In the week before the application I received a bombardment of drawings from the architects for approval by our members on hard landscaping, bin stores, cycle sheds and roof parapets. I started to lose concentration

FIGURE 3.11 Lilac members celebrate the granting of planning permission

Source: Lilac.

as we desperately tried to assess them and hope they were acceptable, knowing that any major revisions would hold back our planning application again. It was a long three months' waiting, but on 25 May 2011 we received formal planning consent. No complaints, no extra conditions, no changes. We were all thrilled. We went to the planning hearing, and gave a loud cheer when they passed our application. The chair of the Committee wished us well as we filed out of the room.

We had hoped to get the tender documents out for consideration to the contractors whom we had met back in February while the planning application was being considered, but there was simply too much detail to pull together for them to be able to price the project. In the end, it felt safer to wait until we had a decision on planning before sending it out. It wasn't until June 2011 that the tender documents were sent. A further seven amendments were sent out as things just kept changing. With such a complex and new-build process, it was almost impossible to keep an overall picture of how everything fitted together, and all the requirements, changes and decisions we had made as a community.

Two months later the contractors sent their returns back. I found the whole tendering process fascinating. The QS estimates the cost of everything you ask for based on their experience. This is never disclosed to the contractors bidding for the tender. Then the contractors who bid for it cost it based on the same information and their own experience. Normally (and hopefully!), the numbers are relatively close. But what if they were not? What if all the contractors thought our QS had woefully under-costed the scheme and couldn't offer to build it for what he had estimated? Another cause for concern, and sleepless nights. The solution to a mismatch, as Jimm Reed pointed out (there was always a solution), was another more or less painful process of value engineering. Value engineering is a wonderful term for basically taking a hatchet to elements of your project that you could least tolerate being lost.

Lindum Construction Group, based in Lincoln, was a slight winner on cost. We had liked them when we met. They were an impressive mid-sized construction company with an established track record based in Lincolnshire. They fitted well with us, especially since they were an employee-owned firm. Over the year or so of the actual build phase they offered us a huge amount of support, above and beyond what a construction firm is obliged to do. For small and pioneering groups like ours this is essential. Their price exceeded the price that our QS had estimated, but not intolerably so. We drew up a shortlist of all the items we could tolerate losing so that we could get down to Lindum's price. At our August General Meeting in 2011 we drew up what we called our 'chopping board' list and considered which items to axe. We colour coded each item as follows:

Green = Go ahead with decision to omit this item to save money.
Amber = Not sure/no strong feelings either way.
Red = Do not chop this, we want to keep it!

Some savings just weren't tolerable and these included balconies on the flats, the cycle shelters and the decking over the pond. There were also potential saving areas where we could opt to do things ourselves but we decided not to go with any of these, as the actual logistics of doing them ourselves seemed horrendous. We could all imagine horror scenarios of moving into half-finished homes. There was an endless back and forth between items for a couple of weeks as we tried to finalize what we could exactly afford. Items were deleted and then added back in as we received feedback from the members. At the last minute we retained composite aluminium windows due to the lifetime savings they would offer in terms of maintenance. In retrospect, I also wish we had made the same decision on the aluminium rainwater goods, which we switched to U-PVC.

Tash did some financial modelling based on contract costs of £2.3 million, £2.4 million or £2.5 million. We found out that we could allocate £2.4 million of equity shares across the members and not exceed anyone's ability to pay to live in the

TABLE 3.2 Minimum net incomes needed at different contract costs

			Net household income required							
			1-bed		2-bed		3-bed		4-bed	
Contract cost	Build cost	Total cost	from	to	from	to	from	to	from	to
£2,300,000	£2,189,052	£3,005,266	£14,879	£20,375	£22,830	£29,914	£33,123	£41,381	£39,399	£48,547
£2,400,000	£2,289,034	£3,117,197	£15,476	£21,213	£23,749	£31,145	£34,468	£43,090	£40,999	£50,550
£2,500,000	£2,389,032	£3,229,147	£16,073	£22,052	£24,668	£32,376	£35,814	£44,799	£42,599	£52,553

Source: Lilac.

scheme. As the project grew more expensive, the minimum net incomes needed to live in the project rose. As always, Tash drew up an amazing little table (Table 3.2).

What it showed was that we could afford a contract cost of just over £2.4 million. This was great news as it meant that we didn't have to go so far in terms of the deductions we had to make. As a result, the items we finally deleted totalled over £100,000, and included the following:

Window shutters	£42,275
Mirrors to bathrooms	£743
Copper piping instead of HEP2O	£4425
Towel rail in lieu of radiators	£1600
Omit recessed spotlights to bathrooms and kitchens and add back pendants	£8727
Turf retaining wall to rear of apartments 7 and 8 and leave existing gradients	£795
uPVC rainwater goods in lieu of aluminium	£2600
Timber construction to the Common House rather than brick	£10,227
Omit private decking to front of dwellings, extend footpath	£4518
NHBC insolvency cover in lieu of Performance Guarantee Bond	£2211
Omit contingency	£50,000
Omit requirement for defects insurance	£2000
Omit Cat5 cabling add in normal connection	£1791
Omit solar thermal to Common House	£1600

The interesting point about the project cash flow was that the closer we got to the final spending and certainty that our reserves would be unspent, the more we decided to add items back into the project or consider little extras. This was a constant headache to our QS who issued over 20 contract variation instructions over the year or so of the build phase. Constant opportunities arose to add elements to the scheme, rethink design features and respond to opportunities as they arose as well as remembering items we had totally forgotten about. The list of extras we instructed came to around £80,000 and included the following:

Solar thermal units for houses	£33,000
Common House PhotoVoltaic panels 4kw	£8650
Additional PV panels for homes – 6kw in total	£7540
Tiling extra for increased choice	£5153
Extras for Common House kitchen (worktop, magic corners, pull-out cupboard, cooker, fridge)	£5000
Common House decorating	£3532
Additional kitchen unit provision for houses	£3300
Extra tiles in bathroom	£1980

Extra electrical items (sockets, switches, etc.)	£1500
Upgrade to brick wall for Common House lean-to	£1500
Obscure glazing to flat bathroom doors	£1470
Common House burner	£1455
Uplighters to houses on stairs	£1088
Common House floor upgrade wood	£1009
Waterless urinal in Common House	£650
Guttering on bike sheds	£525
Humidistat to MVHR units	£520
Worktop extension for tea-making facilities	£515
Under-cupboard lighting for extra kitchen cabinets	£456
Wall/ceiling insulation to laundry	£378
Floor insulation to lean-to slab	£360
Worktop in Common House workshop	£255
Spray tap in Common House	165
Common House external tap	£94
Common House floor upgrade vinyl	£93
Double swing door for Common House kitchen	£79

We made major additional spending decisions where we believed they met our core values and where they would yield financial savings in the long run. Thus we took opportunities to upgrade the amount of solar PV to 1.25kw peak per home and also added in solar thermal water heating to the homes. This latter option came out of the blue when we realized that the houses came with system boilers anyway due to capacity issues for hot water demand, and so we would only have to buy the actual roof panels and pipe-work. We also paid extra to give members more choice to personalize their homes from a wider range of floor tiling and kitchen cupboards. What we learned is that it's always cheaper to add items at the build stage rather than doing it later, especially since you don't pay value-added tax in the UK on new-build construction.

Based on these deductions and additions we reached a final contract price of just under £2.5 million with Lindum. This sum included a decent-sized contingency for unexpected costs. Even though it was a design-and-build contract there was a lot that could still go wrong and we needed a buffer for unforeseen costs and problems. With everything else factored in (such as the cost of the land as well as professional, planning and legal fees), the total project cost came in at around £3 million. Figure 3.12 shows the approximate areas of expenditure. You can see from this that we were fortunate that our land was relatively affordable. Even though it was bought at open market value, the land was not in the most desirable location, and we bought it immediately after the global recession of 2008. Figure 3.12 also shows our income sources. You can see that over half came from the bank, with a

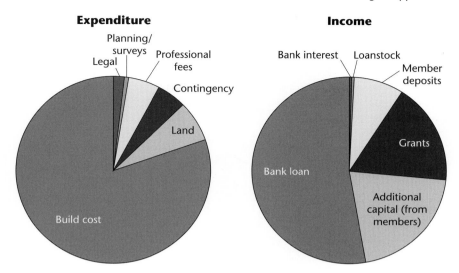

FIGURE 3.12 Approximate income and expenditure sources for Lilac

Source: Lilac.

sizeable portion coming from members who paid their 10 per cent deposits and those who voluntarily put in additional capital to buy their equity shares up front (more on this in Chapter 5). We were also fortunate to have secured a large grant as part of our income which allowed us to experiment with the relatively new and pioneering Modcell system.

As Figure 3.13 shows, the overall costs of the scheme were quite encouraging. We built 1692m² in total over 0.77 ha with a density of 29 units/hectare. With a gross development cost of around £3 million, the gross cost per square metre worked out at about £1744. If we consider the cost of constructing the homes on their own, the total project construction cost was just over £1.8 million, giving a construction cost per square metre of £1081. If we want to think about it in terms of average house prices, the average Lilac home cost £140,000, while the average for Leeds in 2013 was a great deal higher, at around £170,000. The encouraging sign is that the gross development costs at Lilac include so much more than the homes – and certainly much more than a householder would get in a regular development. It includes significant amounts of shared landscaped areas, allotments, the Common House, car parks and a public park – not to mention access to a thriving, nourishing community. In addition, these kinds of costs help prove the financial case for building with natural materials like straw, timber and lime over traditional routes that rely on cement and masonry. And we did particularly well given that

(all £ rounded to nearest £1,000)	Number	m²	Total m²	Gross cost per unit	Total gross costs	Gross Cost m²	Construction cost per unit	Total construction costs	Construction cost m²
1 bedroom apartments	6	48	286	£ 84,000	£ 502,000	£ 1,744	£ 50,000	£ 302,000	£ 1,047
2 bedroom apartments	6	71	426	£ 124,000	£ 743,000	£ 1,743	£ 74,000	£ 447,000	£ 1,047
3 bedroom houses	6	95	576	£ 166,000	£ 994,000	£ 1,743	£ 102,000	£ 615,000	£ 1,078
4 bedroom houses	2	111	222	£ 193,000	£ 387,000	£ 1,743	£ 133,000	£ 265,000	£ 1,195
Common House	1	186	186	£ 324,000	£ 324,000	£ 1,744	£ 203,000	£ 203,000	£ 1,090
Total Development Costs	**21**		**1692**		**£ 2,950,000**			**£ 1,830,000**	
Total excluding Common House					£ 2,626,000			£ 1,628,000	
Average construction cost per m²						£ 1,744			£ 1,081
Average construction cost per sqf						£ 162			£ 100
Average house price Leeds	£170,000 Source Land Registry of England & Wales April – June 2013								
Average House price LILAC	£140,000								
Percentage reduction	0.18								

FIGURE 3.13 Lilac project costs

Source: Lilac and White Design Associates.

pioneering projects like Lilac will always include additional costs in terms of extra R&D time and problem solving. Once new techniques and approaches become more mainstream, costs will hopefully come down even further.

Long, protracted negotiations stopped us getting on to site for several months. Many issues came up, all revolving around the complexity behind the contract and subcontractual relationships. We had chosen a design–and–build contractual route to fix the price and increase cost certainty. What this meant was that even though we had chosen Modcell as a build route more than a year previously they would now be 'novated' or transferred as a subcontractor under the employ of Lindum Group. The same applied for the architect and engineer. Everyone would now work for Lindum. They sensed how complex this could possibly be and started to do some very detailed financial and legal checking. They sat us and Modcell down and gave us a thorough check. From their perspective they were about to partner with two small entities to build a project which was using an approach and a financial model that had never been used before in this combination or scale.

Further complexity was added as there were several solicitors involved, each trying to protect the interests of their clients rather than the project as a whole. Contract documents were scrutinised from different perspectives which brought new complications and delays as different parties try to satisfy themselves that risks were sufficiently dealt with. On several occasions, we made our own representations to try and get them to take a more constructive approach. But it proved difficult to encourage solicitors to see the wider interests and issues at stake

Several issues went back and forth for weeks, such as how to deal with retention monies, defects insurance and what kind of building insurance we would finally use. It emerged that Modcell was still finalizing eligibility for insurance certification by the National House Building Council (NHBC) in the UK. We had to seek a third party to offer this cover but none would. In the end we had to rely on the architect's own Insurance Certificate. Over the winter of 2011 we stood on the sidelines as a bewildering array of solicitors racked up an inordinate amount of money discussing (but not resolving) a staggering amount of detail. In the end a solicitor's summit had to be called in February 2012 to find a way through all the issues that had become stuck. Until this happened the project was simply not going to break ground. Each party was trying to minimize its own risk and not take ownership or responsibility for the outstanding items. Jimm Reed bore the brunt of much of this, and showed amazing patience and diplomacy in the face of quite unbelievable legal obstacles. At one point the bank's solicitor insisted that he was reappointed as project manager using their own template, a process that was largely redundant but cost us several hundred pounds. On the day of the solicitors' summit I decided to leave Jimm to it. It was a teleconference and listening in would only increase my already high stress levels. So I took a walk over Ilkley Moor, crossing from the Wharf to the Aire

Valley. Jimm texted me when I was half-way round: 'Agreement reached, loose ends to tie up, but way forward found. Speak Monday.' I stood there on the high point of the Moor looking down at Leeds in the distance. How strange to think that a tiny dot on that urban landscape could cause so much complexity. How were cities ever built? How are we going to shift urban society towards greater social and economic sustainability in a generation? I pondered. As always, a partial victory. We had survived another challenge and on to the next.

Over the winter of 2011, work started on site as the local authority used the HCA grant to completely clear the site and replace it with uncontaminated fresh topsoil. It was amazing to see this work start after nearly three years of negotiations on this site. But we didn't actually break ground till 26 March 2012. Lindum went out of the starting blocks like a hare out of a trap, promising us a nine-month build phase and a move-in date of 19 November 2012. This all sounded fantastic to us. Lindum had said there was no reason this project should be late and this was a relatively simple job. A building project finishing on time and on cost? Would that really happen? Most people we told looked at us with a knowing smile. We should

FIGURE 3.14 Conditions on site early in the build phase were sodden

Source: Lindum Group.

have realized how much longer we needed given the pioneering nature of the project. The initial pace was dramatic. Excavations were dug. Block and beam foundations went down. But then in early summer things ground to a halt.

The weather played a significant role: 2012 was dreadful. It was the second wettest year on record since records began in the UK in 1910. The site was a quagmire and work was halted for several weeks. But it didn't stop there. Both ourselves and Modcell were underprepared for such a tight time-scale. There were simply so many items still to be finalized. Everything down to the placement of the last electrical socket had to be complete before the wood order went into the Austrian sawmill for the glulam wood. Given how pioneering Lilac is, its build duration could simply not be considered using the typical time-scales of a normal project. It wasn't until June that all the drawings were finalized and the wood cutting began. There was a six-week lead-in time for its arrival at the flying factory.

Lilac members had been trying to book time off so that we could take part in building our homes at this off-site mobile production known as the flying factory. When it finally happened in late August 2012, the flying factory took place in a large agricultural shed on a farm between Batley and Dewsbury. Sykes Farm, as it was known, was part of the Lilac story for about six weeks and it was there that all the Modcell panels were built. Over that time around 20 Lilac members and friends lent a hand bolting together glulam panels, stacking straw and inserting hazel poles. Peter Homer, Modcell's construction coordinator, worked patiently and diligently building each panel. It was an amazing experience for us to see our walls emerge. At the end of a hard day, volunteers would send texts telling the rest of us that they had built a living room wall for Number 12, or a kitchen window for Number 16. The whole process wasn't without its hiccups. None of us were experienced builders and we helped where we could. But it was a great bonding experience.

The autumn brought with it many frustrations, new challenges and delays. We knew the November deadline would not be met. We stared through the railings at our half-built homes wondering how they would be finished in only three months. More bad weather was mixed with more contractual headaches, financial uncertainties and supply chain problems. By this time I was becoming immune to bad news. We had come this far and survived so many near misses and eleventh-hour calamities that all we had to do was sit tight, surely? This was partly true but I do not think we were prepared for some of the breakdown in communication and understanding between the contractor and some of the subcontractors. At various points we, as the client, were asked to intervene and see if we could smooth things over, especially since we had previous working relations with some of those involved.

As the homes emerged, we realized how many aspects were still being worked through. How would the floor cassettes actually connect? What would the finishes,

FIGURE 3.15(a), (b) Volunteers at the Modcell flying factory

Source: Lilac.

architraves and skirting detail look like? What should be the spacing between the cedar cladding? How deep should the balconies be? A constant flow of questions emerged to resolve these final details. We didn't have a clear view on many of them and at times felt overwhelmed by the level of technical knowledge we had to adopt to answer them.

And then the checking, and the mistakes, began. We had to check everything. These were, after all, our homes, and we would have to live with it if a mistake was down to us. Hundreds of drawings were sent for our approval. Window and door placements, stud wall drawings, radiator placements, kitchen layouts, electrical plans, hard landscaping plans, bin stores, cycle sheds, external elevations. We found plenty of small errors – windows, TV aerials, radiators and sockets in the wrong place. The professional team, Lilac's working group to coordinate the design between members and the project team, checked everything. We spent long evenings looking at elevations, comparing electrical against mechanical layouts, choosing tiles and adjusting kitchen layouts.

Tash and I had to keep a constant watch on the project cash flow, vetting every new legal cost and item of expenditure to make sure it didn't exceed available project spend. This was far from straightforward, especially since the contractor, the QS as well as ourselves all used slightly different financial accounting techniques and we constantly had to reconcile and cross-check them. Tash and I would get frustrated with each other at the sheer stress and time taken trying to remember all the things we had to update each other on after a full day at work and after putting Milo to bed. We worked so hard over that year and it placed a huge strain on our normally healthy and fun relationship.

Moving: Snagging and problem solving

The move was far from smooth and it was as far from what we expected as could be possible. Christmas came and went and at least in the New Year of 2013 we knew at some point that year we would move into our homes! A January deadline passed, as did a February one. The situation was getting frustrating. It wasn't until 8 February that the contractor finally gave us confirmation of a move-in date. Again, it was difficult to count on it. It was such an upheaval to get 20 households moved into Lilac. We had all started to live round packing cases. The final news was mixed – a phased hand-over where 11 homes could move in on 28 March and the rest on 19 April. People were clearly desperate to move in after waiting for several years in some cases. But we all really wanted to move in together. For us, the big joint move-in was always part of building a cohousing community. We all had visions of carrying boxes together, helping each other out, running around the site and hugging each other in joy as the site was passed over to us fully finished. This was a really big decision for us and we had to call a special general meeting to consider the options. And moving in phases could create divisions and ways of living that could become ingrained, and move us apart rather than bring us together.

At the meeting legitimate concerns were raised about unintended divisions and further delays. In the end, we took a pragmatic approach and agreed to a phased hand-over, but on condition that the contractor guaranteed move-in dates for both phases. The phased move also meant that those moving in early would pay some rent, which would be ring-fenced for extra spending. Eleven households moved in on 28 March, but the 19 April date was missed. Some unexpected snow played a role. Another six homes were ready on 3 May with the final three moving in on 10 May 2013.

The first phase move-in on 28 March 2013 coincided with the visit of TV *Grand Designs* presenter Kevin McCloud and the, then, UK Housing Minister Mark Prisk. Coincidentally they had asked to visit us on that day to launch a multi-million-pound fund to help other projects like Lilac get off the ground. We couldn't say no. But it would make for a busy day. The morning visit went well but the after-noon hand-over was one of the most stressful and bizarre events of my life. It had snowed heavily the weekend before and various contractors could not make it. Patches of snow still covered the site. Despite good intentions, a few items were not totally finished, but it was too late to pull out. We got the keys at about 4 p.m. The situation was tinged with comedy. The team of cleaners who had been busily removing months of construction grime from the interior of the homes had gone home, a couple of rooms had no carpets, and some doors didn't lock and boilers didn't work. The site team from Lindum saw the look on our faces as they started to lock up for the Bank Holiday and leave the site for four days.

'But you can't leave!' I stammered. 'We can't move into these houses.'

Their response was amazing. The construction director, design coordinator and quantity surveyor went to the local supermarket, bought mops and hoovers, and stayed until 7 p.m., cleaning, fixing and finishing. They also forced the carpet con-tractors to go and buy more carpet rather than leaving early to enjoy the Bank Holiday. At 7 p.m. they finally left and for the first time some of us stood in the middle of the site without Lindum. It was no longer a construction site. It was our new homes. Through the exhaustion and adrenaline of the day, it felt exhilarating. But we had moved in too much of a rush. Further problems lay ahead.

I knew there would be some snagging. All new things have snags. But we encountered quite a few. The main area was the heating and plumbing, with quite a few leaks and adjustments to deal with. We also underestimated the amount of understanding and attention the mechanical ventilation with heat recovery (MVHR) units needed. We found that many installers have little knowledge of these items. They just follow the installation manuals. Therefore, you, the active client,

Initial snagging form

House Number: Date: 10th May 2013

Name:

Contact phone number:

Phase 2

Problem categories
1) Urgent. Problems with electrics, plumbing, MVHR unit etc.
2) Incorrect specification or unfinished work
3) Minor problems with finish or cosmetic problems

Category	Problem Description	Complete?
1	Bathroom window doesn't shut at all. Security issue. Also says Made in China on it! Can this be cleaned?	
1	Bedroom radiator in wrong place – doesn't allow bed to be against interior wall, unlike in upper floor one beds, and is not as per spec.	
2	3 shelves missing in kitchen (top left, to right of oven and under sink). Also tea towel rack.	
2	Water stop cover not attached under sink.	
3	Random bit of mdf in boiler cupboard	
3	Spare kitchen shelf	
3	Numerous chips, edges rubbed off kitchen units e.g. bottom edge of cupboard next to fridge	
3	Small gap in work surface below boiler	
3	Black smudgy mark on laminate next to kitchen	
2	Kitchen patio door reveal very poor finish esp. bottom left patched with unsanded different colour wood, opposite side has holes, filler and unsanded areas	
2	Wood next to sink in kitchen not varnished	

FIGURE 3.16 The snag list

Source: Lilac.

need to do your own homework and be satisfied that you understand your system, and that it's working and installed correctly.

To deal with the amount of items we had to respond to, we made our own snagging lists for each home and categorized them in terms of immediate, mistakes and cosmetic. Our maintenance task team distributed them to each household and they were diligently filled in. Figure 3.16 shows an example of snags that one home had.

The first few weeks were a blur of to-do lists and quick-fire conversations with the on-site construction team still building phase two. Here is a glimpse of one of my daily to-do lists so that you can see the range of issues we were dealing with:

- Change address on bank account.
- Get suited keys for Common House.
- Phone stamp duty office – get SDLT forms.
- Get better bolt for bike shed.
- Fence off grass area.
- Ring Jimm about external wall repairs.
- Talk to MVHR commissioner – rebalance at lower fan speed.
- Organize member meeting for energy chat.
- Ask landscape contractor about patio.
- Get health and safety file.

Residents would direct frequent and often tense requests at Fran, Joe, Andy and I whenever we left home. 'My heating isn't working'; 'I can't close my window'; 'my flooring is not flat'. The requests went on and on. Various contractors rushed around the site solving problems. Moving into a housing project where one half was still unfinished was a unique situation. Given the type of client group we were, there was an element of enjoying the daily interaction with the builders. After all, we did want to help build our own community. The stress fell heavily on the site manager Matt and his main operations manager Bob (Bob the builder was a name not lost on the children). Throughout the whole process they were impressive and professional. I once caught a view of Matt's to-do list. It ran to six pages and he had to take the brunt of workpeople failing to turn up and explain to us that once again the hand-over of our homes would be delayed. Every morning I would leave my

FIGURE 3.17
Lilac: part home,
part building site

Source: Modcell.

front door and get ready to take Milo to the nursery. I would be confronted with electricians, joiners, heating engineers and the usual daily round of questions and plans from the contractors about what would happen next. Routes round the site had to be closed as balconies went up, the drainage pond was finished, diggers moved gravel and lighting cable was laid. Our gang of toddlers who scooted around the site in a pack found it great fun, as they could watch diggers move gravel.

My lasting impression is that the sensible course of action is to wait until everything is completely finished and checked before moving in. But on reflection I'm not sure how it could have been different. After six years, we were desperate to move in. Our homes were also so different that you actually had to live in them to discover many of the problems and snags. We also wanted to move in to commence the financial mutual model that governed the homes to balance our cash flow and debt repayments.

Lindum Construction eventually left the site on 24 May 2013, one year and two months after they had begun. It had felt like an eternity, but on reflection it wasn't that long. Lindum had shown tenacity, skill and determination, and ultimately had successfully built an impressively innovative cohousing community. Of course that wasn't the end of it. Snags remained. There was also the 12-month defect period when Lindum and Modcell diligently came back and attended to the remaining items. The whole build process had lacked the big bang of moving into a completed and fully working project. We had crawled over the finish line, slightly battered and bruised. But the key thing is that 33 adults and nine children had made their dream come true. Beyond all the snags, frustrations, leaks, arguments and misunderstandings, we had actually achieved what we had set out to achieve. Six and a half years after a drunken conversation one New Year's Eve, we had actually managed to build the first affordable, low impact cooperative cohousing project of its kind.

TABLE 3.3 Lilac project timeline, 2006–2013

- December 2006. First chat among some friends about co-housing.
- 2007. Idea of 'DIY co-housing project' emerges among friends in Leeds, Oxford and Newcastle.
- 2007 to 2009. Parallel conversations about an eco-village in Leeds.
- November 2007. Weekend gathering to take forward idea of Leeds Ecovillage.
- 2008. Leeds Ecovillage has meetings with councillors, funders, landowners.
- Summer 2008. Leeds Ecovillage Business Plan discussed with Leeds City Council.
- July 2008. UnLtd grant awarded for website, legal documents, logo.
- September 2008. Name change to Lilac (Low Impact Living Affordable Community).
- January 2009. Sites discussed with Leeds City Council.
- May 2009. Lilac Mutual Home Ownership Society Ltd legally incorporated with five founding members.
- Summer 2009. Lilac approach Leeds City Council about buying Wyther Park site.
- September 2009. Leeds City Council offer support and exclusivity agreement.
- October 2009. Project manager appointed.
- November 2009. Lilac Project Development Plan launched.
- February 2010. First members join.
- Early 2010. White Design Associates appointed as architect.
- Spring 2010. HCA/DECC grant awarded to use Modcell as construction route.
- Spring 2010. Quantity surveyor and solicitor appointed.
- Summer 2010. Resident-led design workshops with architect.
- September 2010. Community consultation for planning application.
- February 2011. Planning application submitted.
- May 2011. Planning permission granted.
- Summer 2011. Tender documents sent to three potential contractors.
- Late 2011. Lindum Group appointed as main contractor.
- Early 2012. Last of 20 homes allocated.
- March 2012. Work starts on site.
- Summer 2012. Flying factory 'community build' takes place.
- March to May 2013. Residents move in.

Source: Lilac.

Notes

1 See Tuckman (2001).
2 See http://www.hockertonhousingproject.org.uk and http://www.therightplace.net/coco/public.

4

LOW IMPACT LIVING: DESIGNING AND BUILDING OUR HOMES

This chapter deals with the first of Lilac's three elements: the challenge of how we actually conceived, designed and built a low impact community. Being low impact was so essential to us that it is a central part of the name Lilac. Living lightly on the planet, as I described in Chapter 2, was an impulse that brought us together as a community. Our approach to low impact living was a broad and holistic one that worked across a number of levels and was not simply about techno-fixes: how we chose the fabrics and materials that we built the houses from, the technologies we used to warm them and provide our energy, but also how we made decisions and deliberated on how to change our behaviour as a community to really begin to radically reduce our carbon footprint. As I mentioned in Chapter 2, the approach taken by Lilac is to see low impact living as living lightly in terms of resource use and also our social and economic impact on the planet. How can we find more equal and just ways of relating to others around us (socially, ecologically and eco-nomically), and strengthen more localized and horizontal ways of organizing?

The basics: Lilac's approach to building with natural materials

Right from the beginning, Lilac's approach was driven by a passionate desire to use very low impact and high-performance natural building materials. Straw and wood were our preferred route, as they provided opportunities for elements of community self-build but also because they can be sourced locally and create benefits in terms of local supply chains and purchasing. In the temperate latitudes, we are surrounded by straw and timber. It's amazing that it's not used on a widespread scale. Barbara

Jones, one of the UK's strawbale building pioneers, estimated that 423,000 houses could be built using the 2.37m tonnes of waste straw that is ploughed back into agricultural land annually in the UK alone.[1]

There are so many build options when using natural materials.[2] Our choice of exactly how to build with straw was a difficult one. We spent months researching the pros and cons of different ways of building with wood and straw. Some of us went on a short course about timber frame buildings at the Low Impact Living Initiative (LILI) in London's rural hinterland. We also did a course with Amazonails, the wonderful strawbale outfit that operated in the North of England which pioneered a very community-led approach to building. They taught us the basics of what is called the Nebraska-style, loadbearing, approach to strawbale construction. This is the approach that is more familiar – where strawbales are stacked on top of each other and the bales actually provide the structural strength. A floor plate is placed on top and then compressed down with straps. Lime plaster is then trowelled on to the strawbales, three coats thick. A strawbale building may be built in this way by a relatively inexperienced community led by an experienced instructor. However, what we realized was that our skills and time did not match our enthusiasm. In addition, building our homes entailed much more than just building the actual superstructure of the walls and floors. The joinery, trades fixings, plumbing, plastering, electrics and heating would all have to be done. The Amazonails route offered us the potential of an amazing, involved community-led experience, but we, and the bank, had several unanswered questions around building at such a scale using a loadbearing approach. We got to a point where we still knew we were committed to using straw and timber, but we simply did not see how we would do it in a way that eliminated enough of the risk.

As I outlined in the last chapter, this conundrum was solved when Lilac eventually chose a prefabricated strawbale and engineered timber system called Modcell for the construction of the houses. This system, using Modern Methods of Construction (MMC), offered advantages over traditional strawbale building in terms of structural strength (the wood panel, not the straw, takes the structural load), building insurance, ease and speed of construction. It has a two-and-a-quarter-hour fire certificate, over double the current UK Building Regulations requirement. We found that concerns about mould, infestations and damp are unfounded. The density of straw discourages rodent activity, and the panels are designed to be breathable and prevent the buildup of humidity levels. Modcell is based around individual panels which are built in a temporary 'flying factory' near the construction site where we would take part in their construction. High-precision, cross-laminated timber (called glulam) is assembled into frames and filled with straw, and then finished, by spray, with a lime render. The panels are, literally, as deep as a strawbale, at approximately 480mm. Modcell was more expensive than other traditional construction techniques such as brick and block or timber frame with conventional insulation, but the grant we received from the Department of Energy and Climate Change allowed us to experiment with this method, and to help bring it to market. We saw this as an opportunity to expose straw houses to a larger audience. They wouldn't look like the straw house that the three little pigs built. This is a big perceptual barrier to overcome.

Using straw in any method offers huge advantages for those who want to reduce the carbon emissions from their building materials. It not only delivers low embodied carbon in the construction materials, but also in terms of lifetime energy usage in the home. Natural, plant-based and locally sourced building materials can play a huge role in reducing carbon emissions, given that they sequester carbon through their use. In contrast, conventional materials such as steel and cement have a significant impact on the planet, with the cement industry producing more than 5 per cent of total global CO_2 emissions alone.[3] Using straw in construction is carbon negative, as carbon is stored and then locked up in plant-based construction materials. Barbara Jones documents that one 16kg strawbale alone stores 32kg of CO_2. This compares to an average UK house which produces 50 tonnes of CO_2 during its construction. Modcell claim that a typical 100m² house made using their method sequesters 43 tonnes of CO_2.[4]

Through the grant we received, we were required to meet the UK government's Code for Sustainable Homes (CSH) Level 4 certification, achieving a 44 per cent reduction in 2006 Building Regulation CO_2 (25 per cent on the 2010 Regulations).[5] Again, Barbara Jones is the source of great knowledge here and claims that a typical plastered strawbale wall which is over 450mm thick achieves a U-value of 0.13, more than twice the insulation that Building Regulations in the UK require. Modcell panels at Lilac achieved a U-value of no worse than 0.19 and an airtightness of no worse than 2m3/h/m²@ 50 Pa. For those of you wondering what a U-value is, it's the measurement of the rate of heat loss through a material measured as W/m².K, the lower the number the better.

PASSIVHAUS

Passivhaus is a rigorous, voluntary standard that can create ultra-low energy buildings that require little energy for space heating or cooling. The standard is calculated using the Passivhaus Planning Package (PPP) and involves the following: building designed with an annual heating demand of no more than 15kWh/m² per year; total primary energy consumption not more than

120kWh/m^2 per year; and air leaks of no more than 0.6 times the house volume per hour (n50 " 0.6/hour) at 50Pa (N/m^2). The Passivhaus standard originated from work by researchers Bo Adamson and Wolfgang Feist in Germany and Sweden. In 1996, the Passivhaus Institute was founded to promote and control the standards. There are over 20,000 homes built to passivhaus standards across the world, the majority in Germany and Scandinavia. They may be viewed at http://www.passivhausprojekte.de.

Modcell was based loosely on passivhaus principles. Passivhaus is becoming popular across Europe and the first passivhaus was built in the UK in 2010 in the unlikely place of Denby Dale. A passivhaus requires some considerable adjustments in terms of occupant behaviour. Living in an airtight house requires users to use their ventilation system more and open their windows less. There are die-hard convertees to the strict regulations that surround passivhaus design, but Modcell founder Craig White decided that Modcell would reflect the spirit of passivhaus design without meeting passivhaus standards. On one level this was a pragmatic decision, as the extra uplift in the cost of insulation materials and windows would exclude it from breaking into a broad affordable housing market. Moreover, the Passivhaus Institute lays down strict criteria and certification costs which add further financial burden. The decision also reflected the fact that passivhaus might work better in the more continental climate of central Germany where extremes of hot and cold temperatures are controlled, but in the milder and damp north of England stuck on the Atlantic fringe, householders are more likely to open their windows and want to rely on hot blasts of air from central heating to dry themselves. Thus Modcell is a compromise position – very effective passivhaus-style airtightness levels but not to the exacting standards of passivhaus. A cohousing design approach also presented challenges for passivhaus standards. Extra, and often oversized, windows are added to maximize natural surveillance and neighbourly interactions. These windows can even often be on the northern side of houses so that clusters of horseshoe-shaped homes overlook each other. It's always a compromise and balancing act between what is technically the best and what is socially most desirable.

Our Modcell homes have an annual heating demand of around 30kWh/m^2 per year. While this compares really well against an average space heating demand for existing UK housing stock of 140kWh/m^2 per year, it falls short of the PassivHaus target. However, once a build method achieves these kinds of figures, the performance is very good anyway, and far in excess of what most people will usually experience. This kind of energy performance still equates to a reduction in energy consumption and bills of up to two-thirds for a Modcell house at Lilac compared to existing housing stock in the UK. I used to have gas bills of around £1000 a year in my old, leaky, Victorian red-brick terraced house. Now the cost is about £200. So, beyond these standards, only small further carbon savings are yielded from an extra spend on the building fabric. This is when the law of diminishing returns kicks in. What we realized at Lilac is that to push our ability further to be low impact required an emphasis on the social and community aspects. And this is where our member-led approach came in. We can discuss, debate, learn, share and act together to keep on reducing our dependency on fossil fuels.

Building low impact: dealing with the professionals

The biggest area of work in the development phase was negotiating with the range of professionals we had employed, and then ultimately with the main build contractor. While most of this was done through our project manager Jimm Reed, there also had to be a clear line of communication with us, the client. I helped coordinate this, along with Fran, and then later Joe and Andy. One point of communication was essential, as they needed to clearly know they were dealing with an appointed person who spoke on behalf of the client. In late 2011, when the membership had grown fairly large, we set up a task team called 'professional liaison' to coordinate all the final design work. The work of this team was always busy and often stressful. As I outlined in the last chapter, our task team attended monthly meetings with the project team, and during the build phase we would meet on site to trouble-shoot and make final design decisions. The agendas were endless and challenging. We always had to refer significant decisions back to members and keep an eye on the budget.

We built up a close working relationship with the design coordinator and site manager at Lindum. We also had to coordinate the checking of all the drawings, and the choices among members. The information flow around this group was tremendous and often overwhelming. We held a design choice day where residents came on site to make choices in terms of tiles, kitchen cupboards, carpets and taps. We had to record all this information really clearly across the 20 homes. We created a finishes schedule so that none of the information would be lost (see Figure 4.1). The homes were fairly standardized, so this was an opportunity to add a small amount of personalization. There was a constant inter-play between us, as the client wanting more choice and flexibility, and the contractor wanting to reduce it to keep costs down! What we found was that we were able to encourage residents to limit their desire for choice and further changes in order to keep delays and costs to a minimum. As a cooperative, we were all in this together. One member's decision could have an effect on the rest of us. It actually discouraged people from slipping back into selfish individualism and instead to think about the broader interests of

Plot Number		Kitchen Wall Tiles	Kitchen Flooring	Kitchen Units	Work Tops	Kitchen Unit Handles	Kitchen Sink	Kitchen Taps	U/S Bathroom Flooring (bath and toilet in 2 bed)	D/S Toilet Flooring
2										
2	Brenda Clive	Calypso all three colours random pattern	Prado Jade Vinyl	Scope Walnut	Black Granite	Bow	Double	Thames	Eden Blanc Viny	Eden Blanc
3	Sarah Robin	Calypso Caly 2A	Summer Oak	Scope Ivory	Woodmix Universal	Wooden Knob	Double	Thames	7502 Novilon	Summer Oak Laminate Row
4	Alan Kirsty	Calypso Caly 2A	Traditional Oak Laminate	Scope Ivory	Black Granite	Small Bar	1 and a half	Thames	Novilon 7363 vinyl	Novilion 7363
5A	Maria Avelino	PR648 Goldcrest, Pr630 Kiwi, PR653 Lemon Ice, PR618 Raspberry random layout	Rock Dark Grey vinyl	Scope Ivory	Prime Perlot Granite Crystal	Bow	Double	ABAD20911	8523 novilon 400 cm vinyl	
5B	Liz	Bora cuero – 1 line only horizontally placed. Fill rest of tile area with old tuscan stone	Summer Oak Laminate	Seton Oak	Prima Green Lalique Crystal	Shaker	1 and a half	Thames	Verona Grey Vinyl	
5C	Elinor Jenny	Primatics – Mango, pumpkin, redwood mixed up randomly	Warm Oak Laminate	Scope Ivory	Prima Woodmix Universal	Round Wooden Knob	1 and a half	Thames	Novilan Viva 6118 vinyl	

FIGURE 4.1 An extract from the internal finishes schedule

Source: Lindum Group.

the society. This is a tendency that just wouldn't be as strong with a group of private owner-occupiers. It's a real strength of the mutual model.

Designing Lilac

We co-designed our own homes and the entire neighbourhood. I often forget that. There are not many groups who can say that they put so much time into thinking about, and laying out, the environment they will live in. This member-led design process is central to cohousing, and it is one that we took very seriously. It was a long journey marked by a huge amount of learning and discussion. What we ultimately achieved was not perfect, but it is wonderful. Of course, there are things we would have done better or differently and I will mention these in the pages that follow. But on one level, the process was as important as the final product. It was a way of actually building our community as well as our homes. Designing together meant that we all collectively owned the design process. It wasn't being forced upon us. We were taking back control of our neighbourhood brick by brick, or bale by bale!

We sat down with our architect White Design and together produced a structure for the collective design process. We divided it into four segments, focusing on the whole site, internal layout of the homes, the Common House and the energy strategy. Before we had a session with the architect we held our own meeting to outline and discuss our ideas. We had to be fairly strict, as new members joined with new ideas. We could allow some scope for changes, but as decisions were made, new members had to accept them and join the project on that basis. The following is the full design programme in 2010:

- 31 May: First member-led design meeting: the site (half-day).
- 3 June: Social with architects (evening).
- 4 June: First design meeting with architect: the site (half-day).
- 20 June: Second Lilac member design meeting: internal layouts and Common House (all day).
- 23 June: Second architects' meeting: internal layouts and Common House (half-day).
- 14 July: Third Lilac member design meeting: energy (evening).
- 15 July: Third architects' meeting: energy
- 21 August: Final Lilac design meeting: reflect and finalize (all day and overnight social).

Designing the site

The central idea that guided the site design was cohousing. We saw ourselves as a cohousing community and this involved designing 'in' social interaction and neighbourliness. As I discuss more in Chapter 6, cohousing as a design blueprint usually achieves this through clusters of private homes arranged around shared facilities, usually called a Common House. Cars are pushed to the edges and minimized, creating large car-free landscaped areas. Clearly, there are often concerns about creating cohousing ghettos that are inward looking, so some sensitivity has to be given to external links and how the design permeates out to the surrounding area. During one conversation, Martin, my architect friend, sketched some doodles to reflect these principles (see Figure 4.2). This was a great little schematic of how a horseshoe of homes around a village green created a community feel.

Our site at Wyther Park had pros and cons. It was a large 0.7-hectare L-shaped site that was a former primary school, demolished in 2006 to create a large, flat, empty space. The topography around it sloped from west to east down towards the River Aire around a kilometre away in the valley bottom. The site was built up

FIGURE 4.2 Martin's early sketch of our cohousing vision from 2008

Source: Martin Johnson.

from made ground and so one corner was higher than the surrounding streets. Large Victorian iron railings created a physical barrier between the site and the surrounding inter-war semi-detached housing. We had long conversations about whether to take the railings down, but the local residents actually saw them as part of the area and expressed a preference for them to stay. The north side of the site contained the old school gardens which we intended to keep and return to productive land and a public park.

We were instinctively drawn to the site, as it offered a large southern aspect which we knew would be central to using passive heating from solar gain. Fortunately for us, it also had a huge Victorian sewer through the middle of the site with a 5-metre easement on each side where no building could take place. The volume commercial builders would therefore be less interested in this site, as they could not achieve densities which would yield enough profit. But for us it would be a real feature to have to design and build around this sewer. Difficult and unique sites can actually be an added bonus for community-led groups. Thus, during land searches make sure you dig deep and follow up the odd and quirky sites. These are the ones that will yield some surprising potential.

We had a very early conversation the year before in 2009 about what we saw as the key elements of the project and how we would lay them out on the site. We came up with the following list:

1   Arrange 20 units over two or three large blocks.
2   If two blocks, put together one- and three-bed, and two- and four-bed units.
3   If three blocks, could keep different size of units separate.
4   Arrange blocks to capture south sun.
5   Private gardens to the rear.
6   Communal area to the front.
7   Car parking only at edge of site, not on the site.
8   Discrete play area and food-growing area.

We kept fairly closely to this original list, apart from the fact that in the end we laid our homes out over five blocks. We did some very general layouts of homes. I prepared a very basic and quick sketch, laying out two big blocks angularly in front of the Common House (see Figure 4.3). Roger, another architect friend, also drew a much more beautiful and informative sketch, laying out four blocks in a grid in front of the Common House (see Figure 4.4). We also did a quick tally of how many square metres this totalled, to make sure that what we were proposing was not wildly different from what the local authority would expect in terms of housing densities (see Figure 4.5). What all these sketches did was allow us to develop our thinking which we would have to firm up with the architect.

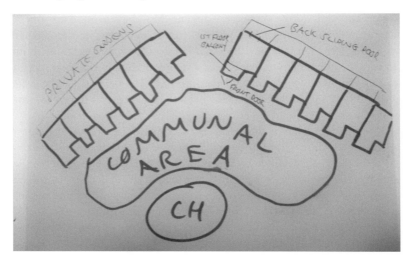

FIGURE 4.3 My very basic initial sketch of the layout of the blocks

Source: Lilac.

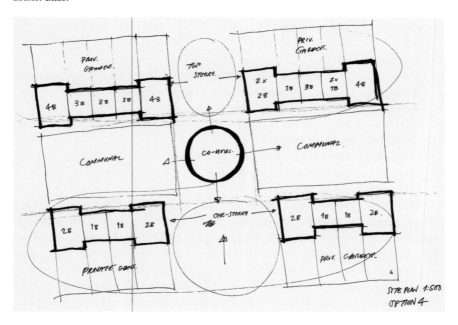

FIGURE 4.4 One of Roger's options showing four blocks laid out in a grid

Source: Roger Stannard.

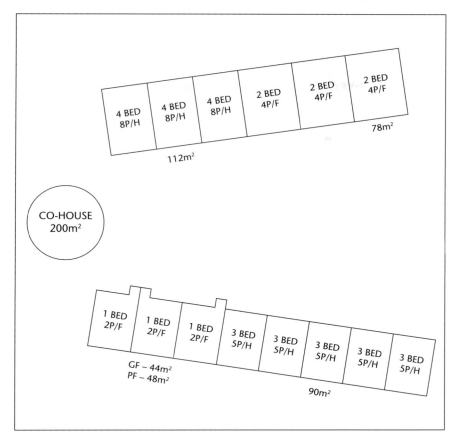

FIGURE 4.5 Our initial ideas on site densities

Source: Lilac.

The membership met for a whole day at the end of May 2010 without the architectural team to try to thrash out our opinion on a range of key aspects for the site. We covered an impressive range of topics:

- Boundaries.
- Cars.
- Interaction with neighbours.
- Aspect/orientation.
- Accessibility.
- Interaction with each other on site.
- Aesthetics.
- Materials.
- Gardens and landscaping.
- Play.
- Common House placement.
- Privacy.
- Housing block layouts.
- Outside gathering spaces.
- Site levels.
- Site safety.

We took the results of this to the architect. In June, we had our first half-day workshop led by White Design. Adriana was helping Craig White at that time. She was from Latin America and had done her Master's thesis on cohousing. She helped us think through the ideas in the first year. Having someone on board who had a natural instinct for cohousing and participatory processes was a real asset. The workshop involved a mixture of discussing our visions for the site at a fairly abstract level with a practical exercise in terms of laying out cardboard blocks on a plan of the site. From this workshop, White Design gave us four options of how to lay out the site. The options varied in terms of how to lay out the blocks, the size of each block and the Common House placement. We eventually went for an option (see Figure 4.6) where the Common House was detached and in the centre, and the homes were arranged in five blocks, two of which were three-storey and contained one- and two-bed flats, and three of which were two-storey houses. This amounted to 20 homes overall, with a total internal floor area of 1518m^2. This gives a total of 43 bedrooms across the site, with an absolute maximum occupancy of 90 people (with a further two guest bedrooms neatly designed into the stairwells of the flats).

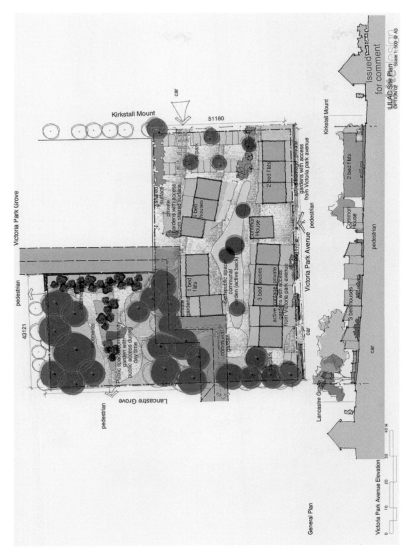

FIGURE 4.6 The basic option we chose with White Design

Source: White Design Associates.

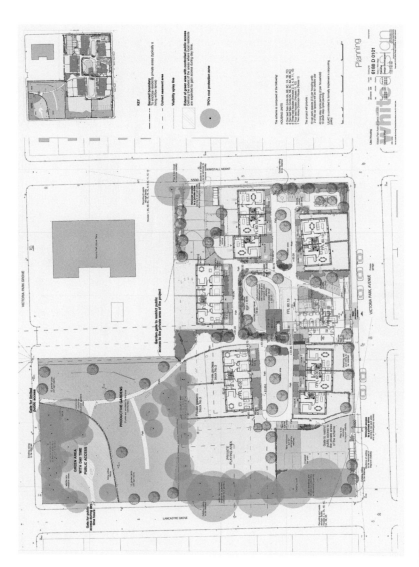

FIGURE 4.7 Final layout of the Lilac development

Source: White Design Associates.

In reality, the 20 dwellings are home to 35 adults and 10 children, or 45 people in total. So there's plenty of room for expansion!

The planners had a number of concerns about the initial layout. They didn't instantly warm to the fact that the private gardens were so small and that so much space was devoted to shared (or to them unregulated) space. There was no adopted highway, no ability for residents to park outside their homes, no natural surveillance of car parks, too few car parking spaces, the homes were not parallel to the surrounding street layout, and they didn't have traditional street frontages but also looked inward towards each other. Clearly, cohousing presents many challenges for the current planning system and its conventions. Some are legitimate, as many of the cohousing principles could lead to inward-facing housing ghettos, a feature good place making needs to avoid. But ultimately, rather than discuss and resolve each aspect individually, our approach was to test our design through the planning process.

Several changes were made to the original option before our planning application could be submitted. This was done to address many of the concerns of the planners, including moving the taller flats to the back of the site to reduce the visual impact of the scheme on the surrounding area, aligning the blocks in line with the surrounding street pattern and placing the larger four-bed homes at the end of the site. The final version of the site plan is shown in Figure 4.7.

The final layout included 25 private allotments at the northwest corner of the site. We designated one for each household, as well as five for those interested from the surrounding streets. We drew names out of a hat to allocate them and almost all of us got an allotment patch in the place we wanted. As Figures 4.9 and 4.10 show, the allotments also include some very basic but really well-designed compost facilities. These are based around seven chambers in which new added compost is gradually turned over and moved towards the other end where it reaches its journey as fully matured compost.

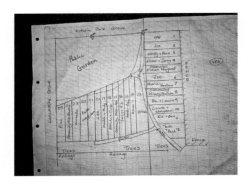

FIGURE 4.8 Allotment allocation

Source: Lilac.

FIGURE 4.9 Our communal composting system

Source: Lilac.

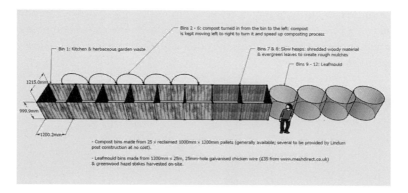

FIGURE 4.10 Schematic drawing of our communal compost system

Source: Lilac.

As part of the site layout process, we spent quite a lot of time talking about the principles for the landscaping of the site with the architect. We undertook a wonderful workshop where we discussed the kinds of things we would like to see in four different zones – with zone zero representing the nearest to our homes and zone four the furthest away (see Figures 4.11 and 4.12). There are some wonderful words associated with home, such as busy, love, me, harmony, refreshing and cheesecake! The things that people associated with the areas furthest away from their homes on site included foxes, compost, fire pits, beehives and chaos.

As you will see from the various plans and photographs of the site throughout this book, the geographical heart of the community is a large pond with decking over it. While this is aesthetically beautiful and brings nature right into the heart of the site, it also functions as a sustainable urban drainage (SUD) system. SUDs are a really crucial piece of climate adaptation infrastructure in cities to reduce the intensity of urban flooding. They attenuate the amount of water run-off from the site during intense rain and storm conditions. The pond collects rainwater from the roofs and other surfaces via a dedicated drainage system. It fills slowly to a certain level and then releases the water to the main city sewerage through what is called

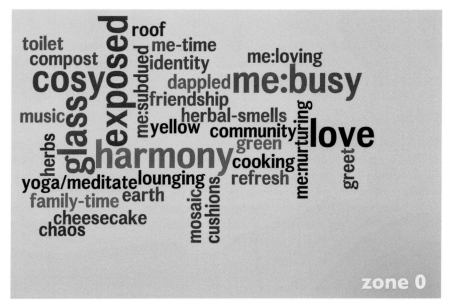

FIGURE 4.11 Word cloud of terms associated with home zone zero (nearest our homes)
Source: White Design Associates.

zone 4

FIGURE 4.12 Word cloud of terms associated with home zone four (furthest away from our homes)

Source: White Design Associates.

a hydro-brake. In a city like Leeds, the old nineteenth-century sewerage system is already at full capacity during heavy rain. We are playing our part to ease conditions as a changing climate brings with it more extreme and varied weather conditions.

Internal layouts

The design of the internal layouts of the homes was again informed by our understanding of cohousing principles – that everyone had a private dwelling but these are normally more compact than a usual home, as shared aspects would be located in the Common House. Our thinking began formally in April 2009 when we held a design day among six members of Lilac, which again Roger helped with. This meeting was held before we formally appointed an architect. We came up with a list of principles that would guide our thinking for the internals. These included the following:

1	South-facing homes – or as near as possible.
2	Houses long and thin (not short and fat) to capture sun as far into houses as possible.

3   Expansive use of ceiling-to-floor glass on south side.

4   Smaller north-facing windows.

5   Open-plan kitchens and living rooms.

6   Beds, bathrooms and stairs at back (north).

7   Living spaces and kitchens at front (south).

8   Private small gardens at back.

9   Twenty units in total.

10   Four house types (six × one-bed, six × two-bed, five × three-bed, three × four-bed).

11   One- and two-bed single-storey flats stacked on top of each other (or as bungalows at front of lower end of site).

12   Use of external staircase for one- and two-bed to minimize space loss.

13   Three- and four-bed houses over two floors.

14   Possible upside-down house for three- and four-beds (i.e. bedrooms on ground floor and living spaces upstairs).

15   No single box bedrooms – all suitable for two people (minimum 10m² but ideally 15m²).

16   Similar benefits for all households (i.e. no units which miss out on essential features).

17   Flexible internal stud walls that can be moved.

18   Single-storey half-width ground floor extension (to front or rear – front might interfere with south-facing solar gain) which creates an alcove garden at ground floor level and first floor balcony.

19   One- and two-beds stacked – so either get the first floor balcony or the ground floor garden.

20   Skylights and use of roof voids to maximize feeling of space.

21   Possible raised-up bedrooms in pitched roof.

22   Doors both front and rear – sliding doors at rear to maximize space.

23   Concentrate routing of services/pipes for easy access.

24   Optional – conservatory glass house at front to maximize heat retention (could be one- or full-storey height).

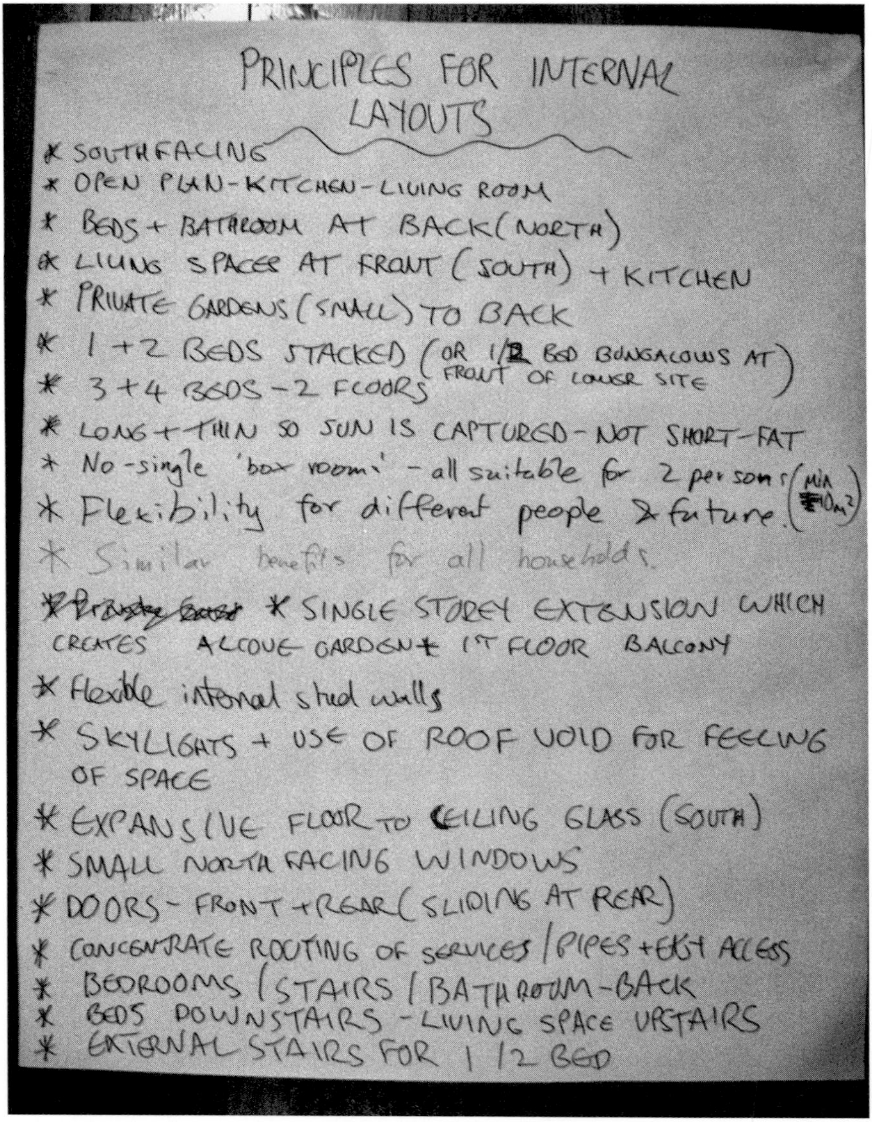

PRINCIPLES FOR INTERNAL LAYOUTS

* SOUTH FACING
* OPEN PLAN - KITCHEN - LIVING ROOM
* BEDS + BATHROOM AT BACK (NORTH)
* LIVING SPACES AT FRONT (SOUTH) + KITCHEN
* PRIVATE GARDENS (SMALL) TO BACK
* 1 + 2 BEDS STACKED (OR 1/2 BED BUNGALOWS AT FRONT OF LOWER SITE)
* 3 + 4 BEDS - 2 FLOORS
* LONG + THIN SO SUN IS CAPTURED - NOT SHORT-FAT
* No-single 'box room' - all suitable for 2 persons (MIN ≥10m²)
* Flexibility for different people & future.
* Similar benefits for all households.
* ~~Privacy~~ * SINGLE STOREY EXTENSION WHICH CREATES ALCOVE GARDEN + 1ST FLOOR BALCONY
* Flexible internal stud walls
* SKYLIGHTS + USE OF ROOF VOID FOR FEELING OF SPACE
* EXPANSIVE FLOOR TO CEILING GLASS (SOUTH)
* SMALL NORTH FACING WINDOWS
* DOORS - FRONT + REAR (SLIDING AT REAR)
* CONCENTRATE ROUTING OF SERVICES / PIPES + EASY ACCESS
* BEDROOMS / STAIRS / BATHROOM - BACK
* BEDS DOWNSTAIRS - LIVING SPACE UPSTAIRS
* EXTERNAL STAIRS FOR 1/2 BED

FIGURE 4.13 We workshopped the internal design criteria

Source: Lilac.

FIGURE 4.14 An early design meeting

Source: Lilac.

We generally stuck to these principles although a few were dropped. The upside-down house with bedrooms downstairs and living rooms upstairs seemed great but just too different. It had been suggested that this is a more energy-efficient design and we had seen it at the Building Research Establishment eco-park north of London. It made sense but we could not find a dataset evidencing the amount of energy saved. In the end we also rejected this option for social reasons, as we wanted houses that had living spaces with direct access to the gardens.

Our first formal meeting on the internal layouts with the architectural team was in June 2010. With the internals there was less scope for broad thinking out of the box, as we had real constraints in terms of cost per square metre and the choice of the Modcell build route. The architect presented us with some initial internal layout drawings and we discussed these (see Figure 4.15). We established a number of preferences at this stage, including the following:

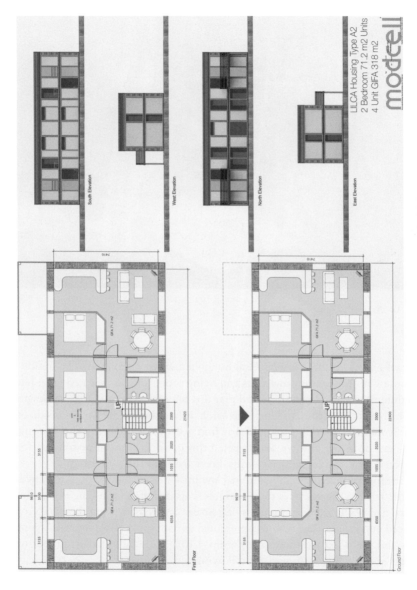

Inside the figure:

LILCA Housing Type A2
2 Bedroom 71.2 m2 Units
4 Unit GIFA 318 m2

modcell

South Elevation

West Elevation

North Elevation

East Elevation

First Floor

Ground Floor

FIGURE 4.15 Early internal designs for one- and two-bed homes

Source: Modcell.

- We wanted a variety of sizes of blocks – two- and three-storey.
- We liked the idea of large open-plan living-kitchen spaces in all homes.
- We liked the idea of roof gardens but saw that there might be limits like making space for solar PV as well as weight issues.
- We thought there might not be much demand for four-bed houses, so limited them to two.

The cohousing design challenge was to ensure that the internal layouts worked so that the houses faced in both directions. They all had to face inward towards the shared area to create a feeling of community, and they also had to face outward to satisfy the planners that they had conventional street frontages to maintain the historic patterning of streets. Therefore, depending on which side of the project a particular block is on, some kitchens face south and some face north, while some living rooms face south and others face north. However, since the living spaces and the balconies on the flats faced towards the interior of the site, their kitchens faced outward. Everything was a balancing act.

The internal layouts went through several revisions. In the end we agreed the following aspects:

- Open-plan living-kitchen spaces.
- Balconies on all flats but not on the houses.
- Good double-sized bedrooms in all homes.
- Three-bed houses to have downstairs toilet but with no shower to make space for a nook area that could be used as a boot room or entrance desk area.
- Four-bed houses to have downstairs shower room for larger families.
- Four-bed houses to have a small recess in ground floor entrance way for shoes/coats.
- Bathrooms to have high-level fanlight to give landing areas natural light.
- Ground floor living areas to have single opening doors on to back gardens.

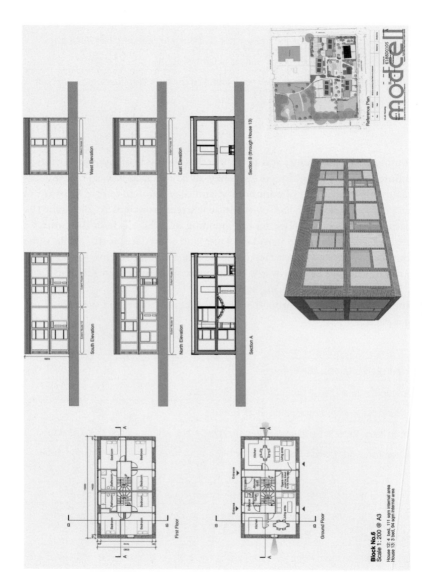

FIGURE 4.16 A typical final home layout

Source: Modcell.

FIGURE 4.17 A typical Lilac living space

Source: Modcell.

The modular, prefabricated Modcell build route gave the homes a very standardized, rectangular feel. The floor-to-ceiling windows, with three in each living space, create superb through-light and cross-ventilation, and the natural materials give the homes a wonderful smell and a deadening sound quality. All of the home types followed the same principles. This standardization really allowed us to achieve cost savings. As I stated earlier, we allowed the residents some level of personalization through individual choice of kitchen units, bathroom and kitchen tiling and flooring. In the end, this did present a number of challenges, as it cost us several thousand pounds more to allow each member to choose largely what they wanted, up to a price limit. Moreover, it added a complexity to the design-and-build process which became a drain on our time and that of the contractor. But it was ultimately worth it. Small elements of individualization really bring each house to life.

THE BALCONIES: AN UNEXPECTED DESIGN CHALLENGE

The beauty of deliberative democracy is that you are never quite sure which issues people are really passionate about, which issues are really important to people, and which issues you are going to have to devote significant time to.

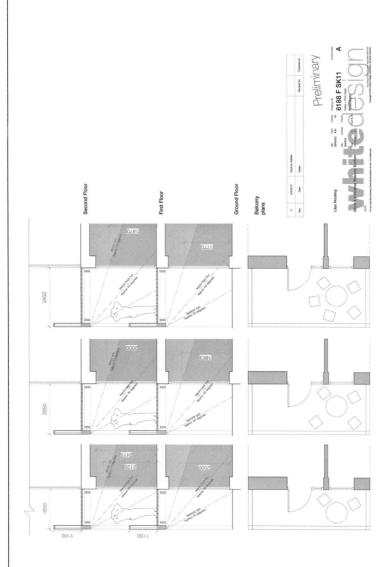

FIGURE 4.18 White Design's balcony drawings

Source: White Design Associates.

The big issue for many of us was the size of the balconies on the flats. Originally we had included them to give the residents in the flats more outdoor sunny space to offset their lack of gardens. Only the ground floor flat has access to the garden at ground level.

The actual width of these balconies became an incredibly stressful choice. Most of it started when the architect placed an indicative depth on the drawings. It was probably around 2.4 metres. At the time I thought it was rather wide but the architect said we should consider it as a miniature garden. Further, shading from the balconies was an important future climate adaptation feature given the potential for overheating in such well-insulated buildings. Happy with the justification for now, although not entirely convinced about the overheating, living in the North of England most of my life, I paid little attention to it in 2009, thinking that this was a detail for a year or so down the line. However, for other people it meant the difference between a sunny or shady living room, or a roomy or narrow balcony space.

As more members joined, conversations about the final depth of the balconies grew. We realized it was something we had to resolve. The residents of the top apartments saw utility in the balconies being as deep as possible to maximize outside sunny space, while some in the middle floor apartments

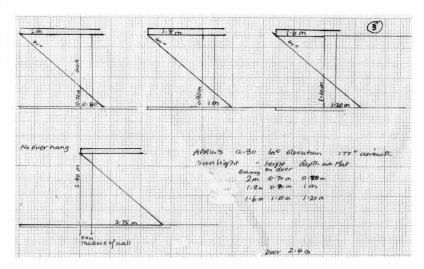

FIGURE 4.19 Erica's line drawings of sun paths

Source: Lilac.

wanted them to be narrower to reduce shading from the balcony overhang. Those on the ground floor were somewhere in the middle, as they had the back garden. The architect drew up some choices of where the sun would fall on different depth balconies of 1.8m, 2m and 2.4m. They showed the sun at midday at the summer and winter solstice. But what about the equinox? Erica, an artist in the middle flat, dug deeper and wanted to know exactly to the centimetre where the sun would fall on any day of the year.

On several evenings people got together and drew out the size of the balconies on the floor and arranged fictitious furniture on them. One became an impromptu gathering between two wheelie bins. Cardboard models were made and torches were shone from angles to replicate the movement of celestial bodies. The original 2.4m seemed too big and was discounted, 1.6m was rejected as too short, and real negotiations started between the 2m and 1.8m options, with the top floor apartment residents realizing how much people in the lower apartments were affected by the shading from above. At a final meeting to decide, pros and cons were listed for the 2m and 1.8m options and finally we decided on the latter. A few people voiced reservations but ultimately they said they could live with 1.8m of wood above them. The top apartment residents were happy that they could seat four people comfortably for potential sunset dinner parties, while the lower flats were happy with the extra 20 centimetres of light fall on the floor. It was only 20 centimetres of timber decking, but it was one of the most discussed and debated part of the whole Lilac neighbourhood.

The Common House

The concept of the Common House is now a well-established central feature of a cohousing community, which creates a geographical heart looking inward towards the community, as well as acting as a permeable interface outward. For all of us at Lilac, the Common House was always regarded as a landmark building in terms of its environmental performance and function as the social hub. It would also help us to save money as a community. It would be the embodiment of the three aspects of Lilac in practice. Designing and conceiving it was a long and twisting process in its own right – as significant as the homes or the site, and for other groups building such an entity it shouldn't be undervalued. Our plans changed, and changed again, due to financial, site and design constraints. We were guided by so many insights and lessons. We visited lots of similar community facilities at other projects, several of us had helped set up and run community facilities, and we had read and been informed by many books.[6] Adriana from White Design had a good idea of what the building should be, and that was invaluable initially.

The initial idea for the Common House was much more ambitious and externally focused, and as such we saw this building as partly publicly funded. We applied for dozens of grants for this building, but none were successful. We had to change strategy as a result, and the cost of the Common House had to be drastically reduced and shared across the members. We asked our quantity surveyor what was the cheapest way of building the Common House. He said it was from traditional masonry and that this would cost about £150,000, including internal fixtures and fittings. This was the figure we ultimately allocated in our budget.

The journey of designing the Common House began in 2009, when we had an initial meeting with Amazonails about whether they wanted to work with us to design and build the Common House using a very participatory approach so that we could all get involved. We had the idea that the Common House could be a loadbearing strawbale construction where we could all get involved, even if the homes were not. That meeting was useful in perhaps reinforcing the substantial time commitment needed and what a huge venture even helping build the Common House would be.

In terms of design, the first thing we did was to have an internal Lilac design meeting dedicated to the Common House in late 2009, where we discussed what kind of building we wanted. It was essential to us that it was built at the same time as the rest of the community so its use was embedded from the outset, it was well-thought-out in terms of integration into the site and routes and flows around it, it offered some opportunities for us to become involved in its build, as well as some for the surrounding community, and it had a gateway function at the entrance to the community.

Reviewing the experience of other projects, we estimated that we needed about $250m^2$ over two floors, with some combination of the following elements:

- Multi-purpose room = $20m^2$.
- Main room = $100m^2$.
- Entryway = $15m^2$.
- Mail and coat area = $15m^2$.
- Office = $10m^2$
- Children's room = $40m^2$.
- Kitchen = $30m^2$.
- Pantry = $5m^2$.

- Laundry = 15m^2.
- Guest rooms = 10–15m^2.
- Toilets = 10–15m^2.
- Common storage = 20m^2.
- Workshop space = 20m^2.

We discussed and ranked the various physical elements and came up with the following elements which were retained as either essential or a high priority for inclusion:

- Welcoming entrance, post and notice-board area.
- Large communal kitchen – dividable with a hatch and shutter.
- Dining area large enough for everyone to eat. This is also multipurpose for other activities (e.g. films and general meetings, exercise (could have folding partition wall)).
- Laundry.
- Guestroom.
- Workshop space and tool storage. Not part of the main structure but could be a cheaper add-on structure that is secure.
- Children's space/play area.
- Shared common storage space – for communally owned stuff only. Not part of the main structure but part of a cheaper add-on structure.
- Outside space/veranda for eating and sitting.
- Nooks and crannies, alcoves, window seats, stair chairs – small areas for chatting quietly.
- Toilets.
- Office space.
- Vegetable, boot sink – in outside space near tool space.

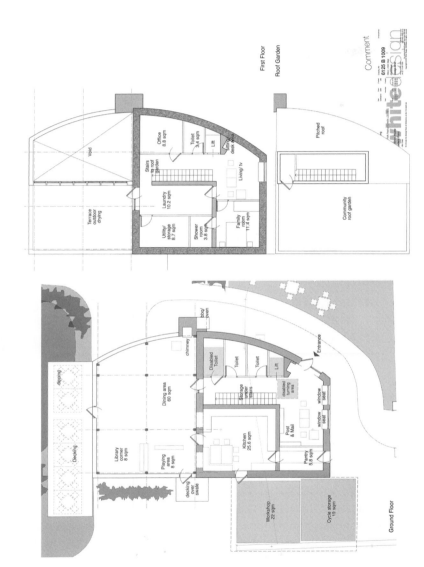

FIGURE 4.20 Adriana's first Common House layout

Source: White Design Associates.

Two other spaces were seen as desirable but fell off the agenda as we faced cost constraints: flexible room (for TV and teen activities), and private office space for members.

We had a meeting on the Common House with White Design in June 2010. At this meeting we reconfirmed our list of priorities based on our initial discussion. Adriana drew an initial design for us which was over 300m². It was a superb building with a curving wall made from hemp or adobe, and a roof garden, with all the features included. But with an estimated cost of double the original budget we couldn't afford it unless we got a grant, and this was looking less likely. We had also become aware that the Modcell route would not fit with this budget, and a cheaper build method had to be sought. What we realized was that the development of the Common House would have to be divided among the residents, with each resident taking on a proportion of extra equity debt to build it. In the long term, however, it's hoped that this initial outlay is outweighed by the subsequent gains in terms of reduced living costs and increased social opportunities.

At a subsequent meeting, we had to redesign the building to meet our estimated budget of £150,000. This essentially meant making really hard choices about which elements were retained. We decided that the essential features we had to preserve in this smaller design were as follows:

- Office, laundry, main dining room, kitchen, lobby/post area, flexible function room, sitting nooks, toilet.

Adriana undertook some quick redesign work to create a new plan of around half the size at 135m². It was designed so that it could be straw, timber or brick. The design was very compact, but still full of features. It included a balcony and window nook to the south side, an overhang to the north over the rear entrance, large opening doors to the rear patio, and a beautiful vaulted ceiling upstairs. There were concerns that there would not be enough seating space in the main dining room for all the adults, never mind the growing number of children. But we couldn't afford anything bigger at this stage. The actual drawing that was submitted and which received planning approval had two future phases approved – the first was a teen room in the attic and the second was a rear extension which would expand the dining area and guest bedrooms towards the decking area. Some real creative thinking led to the creation of a 'lean-to' attached to the Common House, something resembling a shed containing workshop, food store and laundry. This was a brilliant addition and allowed us to add utility without spiralling costs.

Source: Lilac

Source: White Design Associates

Source: Lindum Group

Source: Lindum Group

Source: Lindum Group

Source: Lindum Group

Source: Modcell

Source: Modcell

Source: Modcell

Source: Modcell

Source: Modcell

Source: Modcell

Source: Modcell

Source: Modcell

Source: Modcell

Source: Modcell

Source: Modcell

Source: Modcell

Source: Modcell

Source: Modcell

Source: Andy Lord

Source: Andy Lord

Source: Andy Lord

Source: Andy Lord

Source: Andy Lord

Source: Andy Lord

Source: Andy Lord

Source: Andy Lord

Source: Andy Lord

Source: Andy Lord

Source: Andy Lord

Source: Andy Lord

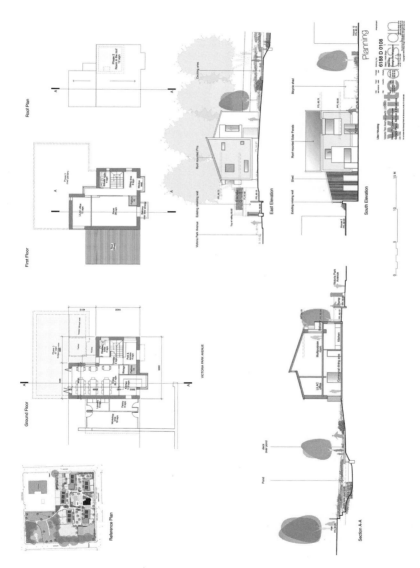

FIGURE 4.21 The final Common House layout

Source: White Design Associates.

By early 2011, we had a design but no clear plan for how the Common House would be built. We were torn between doing it ourselves (through strawbale) and getting someone else to do it. At our April 2011 General Meeting we discussed how to move forward in terms of choosing a preference for how we built it. We drew up a short list of priorities for how it would be done, all of which could be applied to any material we chose. In order of greatest importance they were as follows:

- Capacity matches ability to self-build.
- Extendable – big enough to accommodate everybody.
- Affordable.
- Timing – finished at the same time as the rest of the site.
- Sound evidence base of construction methods.
- Balancing price and utility.
- Acoustics – good environment to talk in.
- Ability to expand, repair and alter later on.
- Looks natural, fits with other buildings.
- Not brick – it's a show-piece of our project.
- Providing training opportunities.
- Round shape nicer than rectangle.

When we sent the tender documents to the shortlist of builders in summer 2011, we still had not decided how we were going to actually build it. In the tender, we stated that we would like to see some options for building the Common House which met our needs. What we realized was that allowing us to help build the Common House would actually add extra costs to the contract, rather than provide a saving. Contractors have to cost for training, risk and supervision, and for working with an external subcontractor who would lead the self-build. This normally outweighs the savings of your labour time, unless you are already an accredited construction worker. It became clearer that we were probably not going to play much of a role in building the Common House, which was a real shame.

The winning contractor Lindum Group came back with a timber frame option which was locally sourced and built. Given that we did not have another option on the table, this seemed perfectly acceptable. The timber frame option allowed us to reduce the amount of steel and concrete, although the actual timber structure was

FIGURE 4.22 View of the Common House from Victoria Park Avenue

Source: Lilac.

FIGURE 4.23 The Common House dining room

Source: Lilac.

FIGURE 4.24 The multifunction room

Source: Lilac.

not visible. We explored various options to make it cheaper still, including members doing the internal fit-out, or even the decoration. In the end, we got the contractor to finish the Common House in its entirety. By this point, it was just so much work running the Society, managing the finances and building the membership that any construction work was simply beyond our capacity. This was a crucial reality check on our organizational capacity.

While not ground-breaking, the actual final product was a beautiful building. It has stunning white rendered walls (more reminiscent of Barcelona than Yorkshire), high vaulted ceilings, surprising and large spacious views over the pond, and interesting nooks. It's also functional and accessible. We spent quite a lot of time finalizing the internal designs of the kitchen and the workshop/laundry space. We got down to the fine detail by drawing out the rooms on graph paper and rearranging all the different elements. Fran spent quite a while thinking about the kitchen layout in a tight space that only measured around 5 by 4 metres (see Figure 4.25). Similarly, Erica spent days drafting, consulting, amending and finalizing the best layout for our shed attached to the common house (see Figure 4.26). It was really important to get all the elements to fit into such a tight space which only measured around 8 by 4 metres.

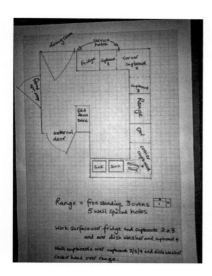

FIGURE 4.25 Fran's drawing of the Common House kitchen

Source: Lilac.

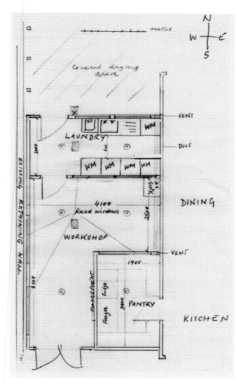

FIGURE 4.26 Erica's drawing of the lean-to

Source: Lilac.

The Common House is a place that is used every day as people pick up post, eat together, meet, collect their mail, check the notice-board, do their laundry, or pop in to get food or tools from the workshop. In the first year, the use of the building was constantly evolving. Getting the Common House into a functioning state was a significant task. The food task team got the shared kitchen and pantry up and running, while a Common House task team took on the interior finishings and drew up a list of items that we needed to buy:

Dining room	
Tables – dining	£1200
Chairs	£1020
Stools	£64
Fireguard	£24
Lightshades	£20
Sideboard	Donated
Curtains/blinds	£200

Multi-purpose room	
Table	£100
Bookshelf/shelves	£100
Toy-box	£75
Curtains/blinds	£60
Projector	£200
Cabinet for media equipment	£50
Bean bags	Free
Child-sized furniture	£40
Children's table	£42
Lightshades	£6
Play mat	£12
Finger guards for door	£8

Office	
Desk	Free
Office chair	Free
Computer, monitor, keyboard, mouse	Free
Printer/scanner/photocopier	£50
Filing cabinet	Free
Lightshade	£3
Desk lamp	Free

Nook

Sofa bed	Free
Lamp	Free
Small bookshelf	Free

Kitchen

Plates, bowls, cups, glasses, cutlery	£420
Set of children's crockery	£10
Oven-to-table dishes	£30
Ladles/serving spoons	£15
Chopping boards	£40
Knives and magnetic strip	£60
Scales	£25
Stock pot	£20
Frying pan	£45
Roasting tin	£45
Set of pans	£40
Colander	£12
Set of kitchen implements	£25
Microwave	£40
Toaster	£40
Thermometer	£15
Mixing bowls	£30
Tea towels	£8
Tupperware/storage	£15
Bread-bin	£25
Blender/mixer	£20
Cafetiere	£16
Step-up stool for children	£10
First aid kit	£19

Pantry

Shelving	Free
Fridge freezer	Free
Storage boxes/tubs	Free
Heavy-duty trolley	£75
Laundry cart	£75

One of the key innovations is that washing machines are provided in the Common House and not in the private dwellings. This presents an interesting perceptual challenge for many of our guests and families when they visit, but it's actually worked out really well. Noisy and dirty machines are taken out of your home, you don't have to buy or maintain a washing machine or the laundry powder that goes with it (see Figure 4.27). Instead, we bulk-buy washing powder and levy an annual charge of £20 per person. Four kilowatts of solar photovoltaic panels on the Common House roof generate free electricity during hours with direct sunlight, so people try to do their laundry during the day. The feed-in-tariff paid on the electricity generated from the solar PV systems in Lilac is pooled and used to cross-subsidize shared utility bills across the site.[7] This is a neat and extremely effective form of monetary cooperation that allows for further cost savings. Several activities that a household would normally pay for (especially energy/food for meals, and water/electricity for washing) have been shifted from private costs and are now effectively subsidized through a common payment.

The workshop is also brimming with high-value, low-use resources such as lawnmowers, power tools and repair equipment which means that individual house-

FIGURE 4.27 The Common House laundry

Source: Lilac.

FIGURE 4.28 The Common House shared tool store and workshop

Source: Lilac.

FIGURE 4.29 The Common House's lobby and post room

Source: Lilac.

holders don't have to buy them or find storage space for them (see Figure 4.28). We also built communal post facilities in the lobby. Airtight houses don't have letterboxes and so the local post person has a key and delivers post to all 20 homes in the lobby (see Figure 4.29). Grabbing your post is an opportunity to say 'hi' to neighbours and check out the notice-board in the lobby. We are also starting to open up the Common House to the local community, hosting activities with a local nursery and socials for local residents. The Common House provides a social focus for the Lilac community on so many levels. Community meals happen at least once a week. We have a meal token system. Tokens cost £3 and buy a substantial meal. The head cook has a spending limit for each meal and is reimbursed from the token money of those signing up. We ask other members to sign up to help clean after the meal as well. Roughly, you have to cook once every six weeks, but in return for this you can receive around a dozen meals. Shared formal duties are fairly minimal. Two that we insisted upon from the beginning are participation in a Common House cleaning rota, as well as a rota to unlock and lock the gate to the public park at dawn and dusk.

The status of Common Houses falls into an interesting legal and financial grey area. They actually function more akin to an extension of the private dwelling of an individual, and so they are not really dwellings in their own right. Therefore, it's not so straightforward that they are businesses which might be eligible for business rates, nor private dwellings which might be eligible for house tax charges. Planning and tax legislation needs to reflect these kinds of hybrid buildings.

Lilac's approach to energy

Our final area of community design–led work related to how to meet our energy and space heating needs. Our approach to energy was one of the areas that could have benefited from much more planning and coordination throughout the design-and-build process. Our overall target was that we had a grant obligation to meet Level 4 of the UK Code for Sustainable Homes (CSH4) (defined as a 25 per cent reduction of the dwelling emission rate over the target emission rate). We were happy with our 'fabric first' approach where we had invested most of our resources in the building insulation fabric of the homes. Basically, the building envelope was incredibly well insulated and achieved very good U-values, as Table 4.1 shows. This would allow us to reduce our energy considerably without significant extra investment. We knew that due to the high level of airtightness and insulation provided by the Modcell system, together with the effective use of daylight and maximization of solar gain, we would achieve low operational energy use. We started out from the estimate that our approach would offer an approximately 70 per cent reduction of primary energy use per unit floor area over the 1990 average for UK building stock.

What we were less sure about was the particular route we would use to heat our homes and our domestic hot water. For a pioneering scheme there are so many options. Initial thinking had thrown up the usual ones around biomass, solar thermal panels, the prospect of district heating, air source pumps and ground pumps. Everyone who had an opinion gave us one, but to get hold of accurate information on costs, usability, efficiency and actual demand needs was proving very difficult. We were also in the middle of a large urban area which is hugely well serviced by

TABLE 4.1 U-values of opaque building elements

Element	U-value $W/(m^2K)$ Lilac	2010 UK Building Regulations
External wall	0.19	0.3
Floor	0.23	0.25
Roof	0.16	0.20
Window	1.3	2.0

Sources: UK Building Regulations (2010) and White Design Associates.

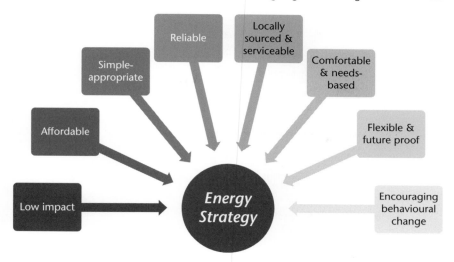

FIGURE 4.30 Energy strategy criteria

Source: Progetic.

existing infrastructure. In this context, it's actually debatable whether going off-grid makes sense in terms of outlay on new infrastructure costs, financial payback times and net carbon emissions reduction.

We held a workshop in July 2010 where we brainstormed a list of principles to guide our approach to on-site energy. These are shown in Figure 4.30.

This was a good start, but it still didn't give us any real choices or decisions. In the autumn of 2010 we enlisted the help of another close friend, Olly. I had built gravity water systems in Mexico with Olly and he had gone on to set up his own energy consultancy firm in Spain called Progetic. We employed Olly to write us a short report that generated a number of energy options which met our principles. Our quantity surveyor had estimated that the total available budget for mechanical services in the project was just over £100,000. This figure included an allowance for renewables as well as the conventional equipment (boiler, radiators, controls, pipework and the new incoming gas supplies). This wasn't enough to cover an ambitious renewables strategy. It was based on what conventional housing projects would deliver. We were fairly limited in what we could achieve.

Olly undertook some detailed modelling on the energy needs of the homes based on various assumptions about the local climate. These included the following:

- Winter design outside temperature: -2.3°C.
- Summer design outside temperature: 26.1°C.
- Design annual precipitation: 0.75mm/day.
- Average annual solar radiation: 2.5kWh/m².day.
- Winter design wind speed: 17.6m/s.
- Average annual relative humidity: 83.5 per cent.
- Average annual heating degree days: 2836.
- Average annual cooling degree days: 737.
- Latitude: 53.81 N.
- Height above sea level: 61m.

Olly stressed that we needed to consider three elements for an integrated approach to energy. These included energy efficiency measures through a rational use of energy-efficient appliances, an emphasis on demand reduction based upon changing resident behaviour, and only then to finally focus on low carbon and renewable energy systems as appropriate. Eight different energy options were generated which met our energy criteria, and several were eliminated due to lack of affordability, failure to meet CSH4, or poor fit to energy needs and the site. In the end, a risk-averse, simple and cost-effective option was chosen, as the excellent performance of the building envelope allowed Lilac to approach CSH4 without significant additional infrastructure and investment. Olly came to Leeds in the winter of 2010 to present his report and make his recommendation. He stated that the most feasible strategy was one that involved the following elements:

- A 29KWp (kilowatt peak) solar pv array across the site.
- Mechanical ventilation with heat recovery (MVHR) in each home.
- High-efficiency gas boilers in each home.
- Solar thermal panels for heating water could be added to the houses if costs permitted.

Olly also presented to us a life-cycle cost analysis for each option. This is important, as it doesn't just reflect the upfront capital costs. Instead, it takes into

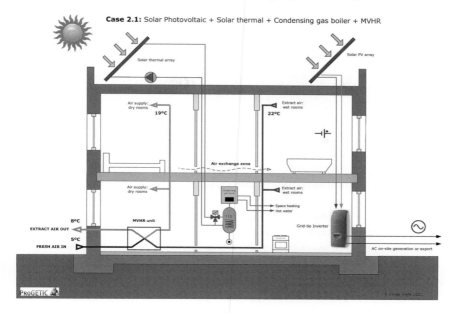

Case 2.1: Solar Photovoltaic + Solar thermal + Condensing gas boiler + MVHR

FIGURE 4.31 Schematic drawing of our energy system

Source: Progetic.

consideration net present value of all capital, maintenance and operating costs, any associated income from tariffs at a set discount, inflation and fuel escalation rate, over a 15-year period. The strategy recommended by Olly had a simple payback time of about 13 years. It was useful to know this, but we were not guided by this payback time because we were paying for everything up front in the total project costs. The feed-in tariff from the solar pv actually just became an extra revenue stream for us to reduce living costs. Our aim was always to balance the need to meet the carbon reduction requirements of CSH4 using the most cost-effective route. We certainly could have exceeded this, but only at a greater cost. To achieve CSH5 or even the top rating of CSH6, we would have had to invest in further measures, including more solar pv, higher performing insulation in the windows, doors, roofs and floors, or switch to a completely different and much more complex and costly strategy such as ground source heating or district biomass. Since we still have gas-powered boilers in the homes, our chosen route does still have a moderate level of carbon emissions from gas. But the overall carbon balance of the energy systems across all our homes is negative due to the greater amount of carbon emissions offset from the electricity generated by the solar pv array and the solar thermal heating units. The following are some further reflections on each of the aspects of our energy system.

Solar photovoltaic (PV) cells

These offered the most cost-effective and highly efficient way to achieve a high rating in the CSH. Offsetting carbon-intensive grid-based electricity with that produced on site scores highly. To get us over our target of CSH4, our contractor designed in 0.75kW of PV in each home. However, it became apparent that a large part of the outlay on the PV system was the inverter and wiring rather than the panels. So we were offered the option of upgrading each home to a 1.25kW peak array for an extra £8000 in total. We accepted this, as it would seriously increase our income from the feed-in tariff. We also installed a 4kW peak array on the Common House. This gave us a total of 29kW peak. I would really recommend maximizing the size of any solar PV system, especially in countries where there is a feed-in tariff. To the dismay of the fledgling solar market, over the past few years the feed-in tariff where the UK government pays for each kilowatt of energy generated from certain micro-renewable sources has been declining. We missed out on the higher tariff of around 35p per kWh (kilowatt hour) generated. We entered the market at a rate of around 15p per kWh. Nevertheless, we estimated that this would yield us an income across the whole community of around £4000, with savings in electricity bills of around £1500. Cleverly, this income is paid directly to the Society and funds utilities (gas, water, electricity) in the shared areas across the site. The 4kW system on the Common House brings extra benefits. All the washing machines are located there and so we encourage residents to set the washing machines for daylight and sunny periods. This means that we are not buying more expensive grid-generated electricity, but using the free electricity generated from the solar PV system. It's a win–win situation if you change your behaviour. You get paid to generate electricity, and you don't have to buy it from the grid if you also use it while you generate.

MVHR units

Mechanical ventilation with heat recovery units are now fairly well-established technologies and are particularly suited for passivhaus-style airtight homes such as ours. They are very good for ventilation and heat recovery, and they reduce humidity and damp, as well as providing a constant supply of fresh air. They are often mistakenly seen as a heat source, but they are actually a heat recovery source. All our homes need to be ventilated anyway, and a MVHR unit offers a route to do this while also recovering heat from activities in the home.

The basics of an MVHR unit are that they have two inlets and two outlets which pass through an exchanger. The home is divided into wet rooms, where the unit intakes from, and dry rooms, where the unit extracts to. Air from the wet rooms (bathrooms, kitchens) is pulled into the unit, with odours and moisture exhausted

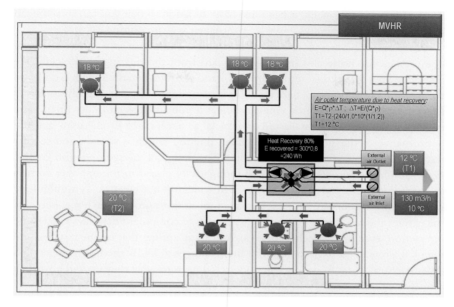

Air outlet temperature due to heat recovery:
$E=Q^*\rho^*\Delta T$; $\Delta T=E/(Q^*\rho)$
$T1=T2-(240/1,0^*10^*(1/1.2))$
$T1=12\ °C$

Heat Recovery 80%
E recovered = 300*0,8
=240 Wh

External air Outlet   12 °C (T1)

External air Inlet   130 m3/h   10 °C

FIGURE 4.32 Schematic of a typical MVHR system

Source: Progetic.

to the outside. The heat is retained and mixes with incoming fresher air and then extracted back into the house through the vents in the dry rooms. The whole system is finely balanced to achieve a set number of air changes in the home. UK building regulations state 0.3l per m². The whole effect is to maintain good-quality air, reduce the buildup of moisture, and odours.

The units we have at Lilac are Sentinel Kinetic made by UK-based Vent Axia. They claim to recover up to 94 per cent of the heat energy that would otherwise be wasted. With a constant fan power of 60 watts at full speed, the MVHR units use a relatively small amount of energy, especially compared to standard electric fan ventilators. Thus this is the most energy-efficient way of providing ventilation and recovering heat. Including an MVHR unit in a house is a clear route to reducing its dwelling emission rate (DER) of CO_2 and thus improving SAP ratings to allow us to reach our goal of CSH4.[8] Sentinel Kinetic units sit above the cooker and also work as an extractor unit. It has a number of features. It has a boost and a purge mode when the fan speed is increased to ventilate the home at a higher rate. It has a summer bypass function that bypasses the heat exchanger, providing free cooling when the outdoor temperature is below the indoor temperature. It also has a built-in humidi-stat, which means that when it detects an increase in relative humidity it will increase the ventilation rate. Finally, it has a low-flow function so that you can turn the fan speed (and hence audibility) down at night when you are drifting off to sleep.

There are still concerns about MVHR units. The motor which drives the fan does emit some noise and this may be heard from the ducting in the ceiling – especially ones that extract into bedrooms – and clearly when the system is on boost the noise is more audible. There is also a constant flow of fresher, slightly cooler air from the ceiling vents which you can detect if you sit or sleep under them. The quality of the unit and installation are crucial to acceptance by the user, and the performance of the system. Well-installed ducting which is straight and regular reduces turbulence and unnecessary noise. The design of the system is also crucial. For example, ceiling vents have to be thoughtfully placed in the opposite corners to room doors to ensure that air flow dead zones are not created. Ten millimetre cutaways under doors are essential to make sure air flows around the home between the extract and the intake vents. It's also a piece of equipment that does need some interaction. Renewable technologies are not static entities that can be installed and then left alone. You have to live with them and get to know them. Many people's dissatisfaction comes from a lack of understanding as to what they do and how they actually work. For us, they are an evolving experiment. We are learning more about how they work and how to use them all the time. But overall, they seem to be contributing positively to the air quality and thermal comfort in our homes.

Gas heating

We never intended to cut our use of fossil fuels completely. Super-efficient gas system boilers in the larger houses and combination boilers in the smaller apartments are used to provide space and water-heating needs. We looked into the possibility of a larger boiler per block but the logistics of the pipe-work were too difficult. The straw-based Modcell houses are actually very good at maintaining a temperature range which does not dip significantly when the houses are continuously occupied. Thus our use of gas central heating has been drastically reduced. Residents have to get used to a delicate balancing act of setting the whole house thermostat along with the thermostatic radiator valves (TRVs) on each radiator. Again these need constant interaction and adjustment.

Solar thermal

This is a tried-and-tested technology with solid performance in terms of meeting a high proportion of domestic hot water demand. It plays a smaller role in reducing CO_2 and helping to meet CSH4 compared to solar PV due to the fact that solar thermal offsets less carbon-intensive gas use rather than more carbon-intensive electricity. While the amount and temperature of hot water is ultimately dependent upon direct sunlight, it is a very good use of the sun's energy. It is a relatively cost-effective and easy-to-maintain technology. In the end we took the opportunity to add solar thermal units to the eight houses at an extra cost. But this extra cost wasn't excessive, as the houses already had system boilers and water tanks, so we just had to pay for the extra pipe-work, controllers and panels.

The solar thermal units work really well, and they can provide some real cost savings through close interaction. Constant observations of the temperature in the water tank are useful to see if a top-up from gas-heated water is needed. The summer of 2013 was a good summer and most of the occupants in the houses found that the panels heated by the sun kept the 300-litre hot water tank with enough hot water for all their needs for almost the entire period from May to October. I was amazed to find that my entire gas bill for the period July to October 2013 was a mere £7! There are still occasional periods in the winter when a clear day will heat the hot water tank to over 40°C. I found that I could have a shower with water at around 30°C, so I only infrequently topped up the hot water tank from the gas boiler. Obviously, for those who like hotter showers at 40°C or above, there will be more reliance on the gas boiler and less reliance on stored heat from the sun. There's also a need to make sure that hot water tanks are occasionally heated to 60°C or above to reduce any risks of the growth of the bacteria legionella.

Multi-fuel stoves

Some members stressed a strong preference for wood burners in their homes. Wood fires in a straw house I hear you scream! However, there were a range of reasons that they were not recommended:

- They represented a significant extra cost. Without being a complete swap for something else, we could not afford them.
- They cannot act as a complete replacement for gas central heating.
- We have a commitment to diversity and equality and accessibility, and expecting members to have to light a fire to have hot water and heating would undermine this.
- There is no feed-in tariff from wood-burning stoves.
- There are logistical issues around delivery and storing wood for 20 households.

However, given the desire for a stove, and a fire 'heart' to gather round, we did install a small 7kW peak wood-burning stove in the Common House. In such a well-insulated building it works well. We chose a steel rather than an iron stove, as it heats up and cools down quicker. This is a better set-up for a busy shared building.

Low impact living: Work in progress

So what's the balance sheet for low impact living at Lilac? We learnt so much and acted so fast over a short period of time, and with such cost constraints, that the outcome was far from perfect. There are a number of lingering issues which it's worth restating here. Actually achieving 0.5 cars per dwelling is still a challenge, as some residents remain locked into workplace car dependency. However, we have almost succeeded here. Second, glitches with the performance and comfort of micro-technologies such as MVHR units remain, and are being slowly addressed. Third, having a much closer relationship with those responsible for the energy strategy, design and implementation is crucial. As I will discuss in the final chapter, having a more integrated approach to mechanical and electrical services in the design phase is essential. This needs to start from the outset.

We are still working towards a full understanding of our home energy systems. We've done a huge amount of on-the-job learning. Very clear and detailed hand-over processes when residents move into their homes is really crucial. We are now exploring a home user energy guide so that members can start to interact with their homes from a more informed perspective. We are also setting up an energy team to share collective knowledge across the project. We are starting to create briefing sheets on the different aspects of our energy system and we regularly use discussion boards and email to share what we have learned. Low impact living, then, is so much more than design and construction. It is a holistic system involving materials, technologies, residents and experts. All these aspects have to come together patiently and coherently.

Notes

1 Jones (2009) is a fantastic starting point for anybody considering building with strawbales.
2 Tom Woolley's (2006) guide to building with natural materials shows the huge range of options ranging across hemp, timber, lime and straw.
3 See Worrel *et al.* (2001).
4 Modcell's website contains a wealth of technical information on the product. See www.modcell.com.
5 The Code for Sustainable Homes (CSH) was introduced in the UK in 2007. It aims to reduce carbon emissions from dwellings and to promote higher standards of sustainable design above the minimum building regulations standards. The Code works by awarding new homes ratings from Level 1 to Level 6, based on their performance against nine

sustainability criteria. Publicly funded homes are required to meet at least CSH3. See Goodchild and Walshaw (2011), Osmani and O'Reilly (2009) and Williams (2012).

6 Several dedicated resources exist in terms of Common House design. See for example, the excellent book by Scotthanson and Scotthanson (2005) which has a chapter on Common House design. Laura Fitch, who works for Kraus-Fitch Architects, Inc. in the USA, provided lots of useful insights on designing Common Houses. See http://www. cohousing.org/cm/article/0504common_house. Grace Kim of Schemata Design has also provided a wealth of information through her Ph.D. thesis (available at http://www. schemataworkshop.com/common-house-design).

7 The feed-in tariff was introduced by the UK government in 2008. It is a payment to households in the UK for every kilowatt they generate from micro-electricity sources. When our systems at Lilac were commissioned, we entered into the tariff at a level of 15.4p per kilowatt hour generated.

8 SAP stands for Standard Assessment Procedure and is the UK government's recommended method for measuring the energy rating of residential dwellings.

5

AFFORDABLE: A GREEN HOUSING REVOLUTION FOR ALL

Lilac's second big challenge is achieving affordability. This is perhaps the most difficult and often overlooked aspect of putting low impact living into practice. But in order that we can all share in, and benefit from, the green revolution it is essential that low impact and community living is an affordable and widely accessible option. This is an urgent task given that the current era is defined by a highly unequal and precarious financial system and speculative and inflationary housing markets. It has become all too easy for green innovations to be exclusive or gated bubbles for more prosperous pioneers. Lilac is deeply aware of that. We may not have fully succeeded but our intention is always to ensure that diversity, equality and justice are at the heart of what we do. Central to our attempts at affordability is an innovative and pioneering form of tenure called Mutual Home Ownership.

In this chapter, I discuss how MHO embeds deep threads of mutualism and togetherness. Practically, I explain how it works, how we modified it and what it means for wider changes in the housing market. But affordability means much more than this. It is also embedded in our cooperative model which strives for economic justice. Moreover, shared patterns of living together and common association offer both measurable and less measurable cost savings, as well as a whole range of well-being effects. These will become increasingly important in the future as sharing resources and informal aspects of the economy begin to replace or support the formal money economy.[1]

Mutual home ownership: the basics

Lilac is based around a new affordability model called a Mutual Home Ownership Society (MHOS). It is an equity-based leaseholder approach to cooperatively owned housing. This model, first proposed by the New Economics Foundation and CDS Co-operatives, lays out the case for intermediate housing that guarantees affordability in perpetuity for its members.[2] The model is a total break from the norm. We were captivated by it as soon as we heard about it. It seemed ideal to meet our commitment to cooperativism and equality. Through hard work, much explaining and constant determination we were able to implement this housing solution that really bucked the status quo. It's not the answer to all housing problems, and it does have its own limitations, not least a dependency on incomes, as well as complexity. But it is, nonetheless, an important part of the complex puzzle that can start to unravel the pervasive and corrosive tendencies towards individualism and commodification in our lives.

So, in brief, what is it? In a MHOS, affordability is defined through the proportion of income spent on housing set at no more than 35 per cent of net household income. It creates an intermediate housing market where rents are above those of social housing but below market price. Professor Steve Wilcox from York University in a 2006 study found that 40 per cent of households fall within the 'broad intermediate housing market' in the UK (see Figure 5.1). This broadly holds true for other high-income countries. The point is that the size of the housing market to meet this demand is inadequate. There's a tenure supply-demand mismatch. The mutual housing market has huge potential to fill this gap, especially given that, as the Commission on Co-operative and Mutual Housing found in its 2009 report, it currently only represents 0.5 per cent of housing in the UK.[3]

Broad intermediate housing market

Not in work	In work but on HB	Not on HB but cannot buy at LD level	Cannot buy at LQ level	Can buy at LQ level

Narrow intermediate housing market

Notes: HB – housing benefit; LD – lowest decile; LQ – lower quantile

FIGURE 5.1 The intermediate housing market

Source: Steve Wilcox.

Lilac is the first MHOS in the UK, and probably the world, and we chose this model to experiment with economic equality in practice. An MHOS is complex and a simplified schematic is presented in Figure 5.2. The MHOS owns the homes and land rather than individual members. The MHOS is owned and managed by its members, namely the residents who live in the homes which it provides. Each member has a lease which gives them the right to occupy a specified house or flat owned by the MHOS. Membership of the MHOS will give members democratic control of their housing. The cost of building the homes owned by the MHOS is financed by a long-term mortgage loan. In our case, this was from ethical bank Triodos. Under the terms of the lease, each member will make monthly payments to the MHOS which will fund the Society's loans and debts, and cover a deduction for service costs.

The cost of buying the land and building the homes owned by the MHOS and financed by the mortgage is divided into equity shares with an initial value of £1. This equity is allocated to households and they are acquired (or paid for) through each member in that household being levied a monthly member charge equivalent to 35 per cent of their net income.

Members pay a deposit equal to 10 per cent of the equity shares they can afford to finance through their monthly payments. In this way, every member, regardless of their income, pays the same proportion, placing the principle of equality at the heart of the model. The number of shares allocated to each household depends on a combination of their income and the cost of their home. (It is important to state throughout that when we refer to 'the cost of a home' we are not just referring to the build cost of the property, but also to a proportion of the cost of the land and the communal facilities that all households access.) The more members earn, the more equity shares they can afford to finance – and the more shares they can afford to be allocated. If the income of a member falls, rather than lose their home, they can sell equity shares if there is a willing buyer, draw on the Society's reserve fund, or convert to a standard rental tenancy. To ensure the sustainability of the project, in Lilac's version of an MHOS, the value of the equity shares allocated to each household cannot differ more than (plus or minus) 10 per cent of the cost of their home. If the households' combined monthly charge (35 per cent of its income) is greater than the amount required to pay the maintenance charge and finance their equity shares allocated to that property, then Lilac's High Earners Policy comes into play. This puts the excess partly towards paying off their debt quicker, and partly towards the Lilac Equity Fund (LEF). I'll explain this in more detail below.

Once all the equity shares have been paid for by a household, they simply pay a nominal 10 per cent of their net income. If a member moves out and sells their shares before they have lived in the MHOS for three years they will only be able to sell the shares at their original value (or a lower one if their value has fallen). For

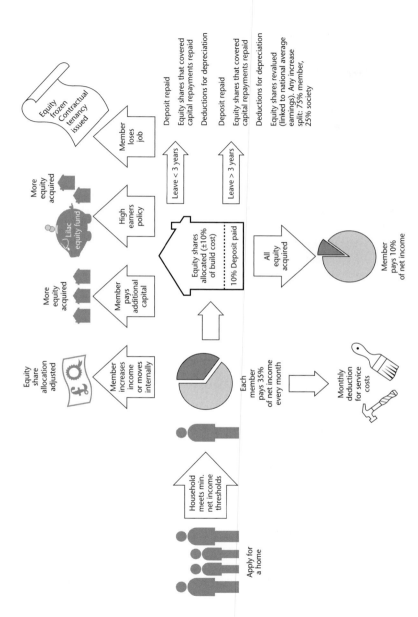

FIGURE 5.2 A simplified version of the Mutual Home Ownership Society model

Source: Lilac.

members who leave after three years, they will receive 75 per cent of the change in value of the equity shares, which is indexed to changes in average national incomes rather than local housing prices. Members can move between properties in the scheme as they become available and as their housing needs change, as long as all the equity shares can be financed by incoming members.

Clearly, Lilac is affordable only within certain parameters. First, a minimum net income for all members in a household is needed to fund the shares allocated to each household. In 2013, these household minimums ranged from just under £15,000 for a one-bed flat to just under £49,000 for a four-bed house. These figures prove to be very affordable, especially when they might be shared between a number of income earners in one house. Table 5.1 shows the net incomes needed for different-sized households to ensure enough income was coming in to service the debt. In the future, Lilac anticipates that as financial reserves are built up a greater range of incomes can be admitted to the MHOS, with less debt needed to be allocated to those on very low incomes. Second, it's not a model that provides housing for the wageless and lowest income groups in society. In the UK you are not able to use state benefits to acquire equity. If a member loses their job, their equity is frozen and they are placed on a contractual tenancy.

Thus, minimum net incomes are needed for the MHOS model to work. Total incomes across the project have to meet an overall minimum in order for all the

TABLE 5.1 Minimum net incomes and deposits needed to live in Lilac (2013 figures)

	Net household income required	
	From	*To*
1–bed	£14,843	£20,315
2–bed	£22,816	£29,870
3–bed	£33,142	£41,365
4–bed	£39,388	£48,497
	Deposit required	
	From	*To*
1–bed	£6,314	£8,873
2–bed	£9,722	£13,020
3–bed	£14,233	£18,078
4–bed	£16,925	£21,184

Source: Lilac.

debt to be serviced. In the case of Lilac, the amount of debt we took on means the net incomes shown in Table 5.1 are needed to service all the debt. Occasional tough decisions are needed when people do not meet the minimum income thresholds. It's a fine balancing act to ensure that all income profiles can service the total debt. Across the project, the households whose incomes mean they take on shares of less than 100 per cent of the cost of a home need to be balanced by those who can take on more than 100 per cent. The mutual model in this respect then is an equalizing device. With time, we hope Lilac will be affordable to those on much lower incomes, especially as project value continues to rise and debt continues to fall. As you will see from Figure 5.3, the equity allocated to homes vary within a range according to whether you take on shares equal to the value of 90 per cent or 110 per cent of the cost of the home, or somewhere in between. In addition, as Table 5.2 shows, the net income needed may be lowered if savings are used to acquire more equity. The affordability of the project also rests on a certain amount of additional capital from members up front. At the beginning, that level was a little over £500,000. Without these contributions from members to acquire equity up front (which have the effect of reducing the overall debt burden of the MHOS), projects would either have to find ways to be drastically cheaper or borrow more money commercially, which brings with it costly interest repayments.

TABLE 5.2 Impact of the initial payment on minimum net household incomes required to live in Lilac

Initial payment	Minimum net income (everyone pays 35% net income to the project)			
	1-bed	2-bed	3-bed	4-bed
£10,000	£13,856	£21,746		
£12,000	£13,435	£21,325		
£14,000	£13,014	£20,904		
£16,000	£12,593	£20,483	£30,928	
£18,000	£12,172	£20,062	£30,507	£36,739
£20,000	£11,751	£19,641	£30,086	£36,318
£25,000	£10,699	£18,589	£29,033	£35,266
£30,000	£9,646	£17,536	£27,981	£34,214
£35,000	£8,594	£16,484	£26,929	£33,161
£40,000	£7,541	£15,431	£25,876	£32,109
£45,000	£6,489	£14,379	£24,824	£31,056
£50,000	£5,436	£13,327	£23,771	£30,004
£55,000	£4,384	£12,274	£22,719	£28,951
£60,000	£3,332	£11,222	£21,666	£27,899
£65,000	£2,279	£10,169	£20,614	£26,847

TABLE 5.2 continued

Initial payment	Minimum net income (everyone pays 35% net income to the project)			
	1-bed	2-bed	3-bed	4-bed
£70,000	£1,227	£9,117	£19,562	£25,794
£75,000	£174	£8,065	£18,509	£24,742
£80,000		£7,012	£17,457	£23,689
£85,000		£5,960	£16,404	£22,637
£90,000		£4,907	£15,352	£21,585
£95,000		£3,855	£14,299	£20,532
£100,000		£2,802	£13,247	£19,480
£105,000		£1,750	£12,195	£18,427
£110,000		£698	£11,142	£17,375
£115,000		-£355	£10,090	£16,322
£120,000			£9,037	£15,270
£125,000			£7,985	£14,218
£130,000			£6,933	£13,165
£135,000			£5,880	£12,113
£140,000			£4,828	£11,060
£145,000			£3,775	£10,008
£150,000			£2,723	£8,955
£155,000			£1,670	£7,903
£160,000			£618	£6,851
£165,000				£5,798
£170,000				£4,746
£175,000				£3,693
£180,000				£2,641
£185,000				£1,589
£190,000				£536
£195,000				-£516

Source: Lilac.

Nevertheless, there are a number of reasons why this model remains affordable: monthly member charges are geared to a constant 35 per cent of net household income to help long-term household planning; members secure a 'foothold' on the housing ladder at lower household incomes and with lower entry deposits; members can buy more shares as their income rises; transaction costs on buying into and leaving are reduced because homes are not bought and sold; and the linkage in the change in the value of equity shares to average earnings rather than local house prices helps reduce risk, dampen increases in value and avoid speculation. This also makes it affordable from one generation of occupants to the next. In sum, the MHOS is a radical departure from conventional routes to home ownership. It promotes resident self-management, decommodifies housing and creates more stable neighbourhoods.

The MHOS model both promotes access to less wealthy groups and discourages wealthier groups who are seeking speculative returns from housing. This is a significant difference to owner-occupied forms of eco- and cohousing. Clearly, there are still limits that need working through, including the lack of sources for accessing development finance, the need for households to meet minimum income thresholds and small deposits, the exposure to risk that comes from the small size of this sector, and dependency on grant funding as well as on additional capital from members.

Making a MHOS work in reality

While the basic principles of a MHOS are relatively understandable, making a new housing tenure type like this work in practice is considerably more complex. We had to make a number of changes and additions to create a viable model. 'What-if' scenarios continued to be generated as we probed deeper into exactly how it would work. Below, I outline some of this detail. The impressive aspect was that none of us was well versed or had experience in housing finance before we started. Much of our thinking was starting from a position as residents who were trying to make a new model work for us, and to ensure that every adjustment we made kept it fair for everyone.

Buying equity

It is now clear that Lilac is not like normal housing. Residents don't rent and they don't buy. Instead they are leaseholders, and their lease allows them to buy equity in the Society. Each member is allocated an amount of equity related to the size of their home (measured in the number of square metres) and we allocate more or less depending on their income. We also allocate equity in proportion to size of gardens and balconies, but we weight it much lower than indoor space. The amount of equity allocated also reflects much more than the house – it includes the cost of the land, grounds, allotment and the Common House.

There are three ways, then, that you can buy or acquire the equity in your home. First, all members acquire 10 per cent through a deposit payment right at the beginning. Second, those with additional capital from, for example, savings or a house sale can acquire some more. There's no obligation to do this, but if they do, they can acquire all their equity more quickly. Once they have acquired all their equity, members pay only 10 per cent of their net income or the level of the current maintenance charge, whichever is greater. Third, as stated above, everyone pays 35 per cent of their monthly net income. The reason it is net and not gross income is that members are allowed to make allowances for statutory deductions (in this case national insurance, tax, higher education loan payments, union dues and pension contributions, the latter which we capped at 10 per cent). Not all of this goes towards acquiring equity. About 4 per cent of it goes towards the home charge which covers maintenance and insurance. And of course, in the early years members' payments are funding bank interest as much as making capital payments. So the amount of equity returned to members who leave in the first decade or so will be lower than those who stay longer.

This figure of 35 per cent may go up if interest rates and the cost of borrowing rise dramatically as they have done in previous eras. A few households have also voluntarily chosen to pay more than 35 per cent of their net income so that they meet the minimum net income threshold. This is testimony to the additional perceived benefits that cohousing brings beyond the most obvious level of payment for your home. The final amount of shares we allocate each member simply reflects a ratio of the total we borrowed against the total yearly debt repayments. There are different payment profiles among members and so households will acquire all their equity at different rates. The profiles below cover most applicants, but some people won't fit into these categories:

- **Low income** – a household with a low income that does not meet the net income threshold to still live in Lilac but have opted to pay more than 35 per cent of income so that they can do so.

- **Low income savers** – a household with low income but with some savings that they have used to acquire equity. This profile allows a household that doesn't meet the net income threshold to still live in Lilac at a level of 35 per cent of net income as they have already paid off some debt so that a lower income is required.

- **Regular income** – a household whose income means they have been allocated between the 90 and 110 per cent range but have not put in any additional capital.

- **High income** – a household whose income means they can be allocated shares which equate to more than 110 per cent of the cost of their home and thus pay into the Lilac Equity Fund (LEF). In this profile, members will acquire all their equity slightly quicker.

- **High income savers** – a household which has put in some additional capital and whose income means they can be allocated shares which equate to more than the repayments on the remaining allocated debt of 110 per cent of the cost of their home and thus pay into the LEF. In this profile, members will acquire all their equity in a much shorter period, partly as they have paid off more debt up front, and partly due to faster repayments.

- **Full payers** – a household which has enough savings to acquire all the allocated equity up front and immediately just pay 10 per cent of their net income, or less if they meet the cap we have set.

The financial situation across the households is actually quite varied. Figure 5.5 shows an illustrative and anonymized snapshot of the equity share allocations among the 20 households. The entire circle represents all the equity shares in Lilac – so that's the entire project costs minus grants and gifts. Each wedge represents one household, and the width varies according to the amount of equity shares allocated to that household. Households such as 's' and 't' are larger houses, while 'g' and 'I' are smaller apartments. What you can see is the uniform 10 per cent deposit, which is shaded darkest at the thin end of the wedge. You can then identify any households which have voluntarily acquired additional equity shares (coloured dark grey). Some have acquired all their equity shares, some have acquired small amounts and others have not acquired any more beyond that which constituted their 10 per cent deposit. Finally, therefore, the amount of remaining debt varies. Some households might acquire the rest of this equity within a few years, while other households might acquire it over, say, a 20-year period.

Figure 5.3 also shows that the amount of equity shares allocated to each household varies between the lower 90 per cent and upper 110 per cent limit of the cost of a home – and this varies according to the size of their income. Thus, for example, 'a' is a household which has been allocated slightly less than 100 per cent of the cost of their home, and which has acquired all their equity shares and therefore only pays 10 per cent of their net income to Lilac. 'B' is a household which has been allocated slightly more than 100 per cent of the cost of their home, and is still paying 35 per cent of their net income every month and has acquired a small amount of additional equity shares. 'D' is similar but has not acquired any additional equity shares.

Figure 5.4 represents the other part of the Society's finances – the household incomes needed to acquire the equity shares. Again, the entire circle shows all the

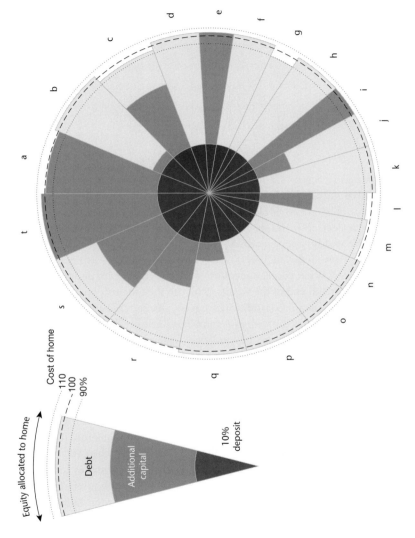

FIGURE 5.3 A snapshot of equity share allocations across the 20 households

Source: Robin Lovelace.

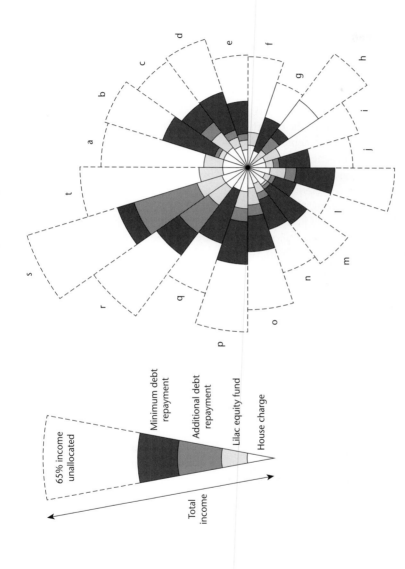

FIGURE 5.4 A snapshot of income profiles across the 20 households, and how payments to Lilac are split across the various components

Source: Robin Lovelace.

incomes across the 20 households – and remember: each net household income has to meet a minimum threshold. This time, the size of the net household income is shown by the length of the wedge – the longer the wedge, the bigger the income. The outermost part of the wedge represented by a dotted line represents household income that is not paid to Lilac. The other shaded components of the inner wedge represent income paid to Lilac. As I explained earlier, monthly household payments to Lilac are set at 35 per cent of net income. For most households on this chart, then, the shaded segments of the wedge together represent 35 per cent of their net household income.

There are four segments here. The innermost segment of the wedge shaded lightest represents the part of the monthly household payment that goes towards the service charge. The second segment represents the part of the monthly payment that goes towards the LEF. The third segment represents the part of the monthly payment that goes towards any additional (or faster) equity payments. Finally, the darkest grey segment represents the part of the monthly payment that goes towards the household's minimum debt repayment. In practice, what you can see from Figure 5.4 is quite a range of household incomes across the Society. This is a positive feature, as it allows scope for reallocation of shares between households if incomes change. You can also see that for those households which have acquired all their equity shares they are only paying the service charge and LEF contribution.[4]

Balancing wealth and equality: what to do with savings and high incomes

We had to modify our model and take pragmatic decisions based on the financial world in which Lilac found itself. One of the aspects of our Western society which Lilac is acutely aware of is the highly uneven distribution of income and savings, which often do not reflect the physical or mental effort and ability exerted at work. Highly perverse and class-based income profiles, family circumstances and opportunities structure our lives. We were keen to address these differences, or at least acknowledge them, rather than ignore them. We wanted to build a community which gave access to a range of households on a variety of incomes. How, is the big issue. So much needed to be talked through, and solutions sought.

The challenge is that the mutual model of home ownership allows for a range of incomes and savings among members, and a sense of fairness has to be instilled in this context. This means different things to different people. Early on, we agreed that wealth can cover both income and savings, and both need to be taken into account in our model. It also might mean inclusiveness for those on lower incomes and not being exploited or squeezed out by those on higher incomes. So there's an upper allocation limit of 110 per cent of the cost of a home and a lower one of 90 per cent. The issue arises that those with very large incomes could actually take on much more than this upper limit.

For this we had to invent what we now call the 'high earners and additional capital investors' policy. This policy pushes the boundaries of housing financing, as it recognizes both income and savings as wealth and uses both to calculate how many equity shares we allocate. The basic idea is to top slice, for the benefit of the society, high earnings or savings, and place them into what we call the Lilac Equity Fund (LEF). This policy applies where 35 per cent of net household income is greater than the house charge and monthly repayments needed to cover the remaining debt (after payment of the deposit and any additional capital) associated with that household.

Payments to the LEF are capped. Our finance team presented very detailed and lengthy information to the wider membership so that we could agree the level of the cap. We discussed a number of different scenarios and finally agreed that the cap would apply to both households paying off debt as well as those who had paid off all the debt – and it would be set as a percentage of the household's allocated shares (in the first instance at 1.5 per cent per year). For example, if a household was allocated £100,000 of equity shares, the maximum annual payment they would pay to the LEF would be £1500. In Lilac the LEF cap ranges from about £1000 up to about £3000. This was a key step, as it aligned this policy to the same principle of proportionality that underpinned the amount of net income payable. Income or savings beyond this level would simply allow a household to acquire their equity shares faster – the equivalent of buying the value of your lease or paying off your mortgage faster. The cap would restrict money actually flowing into the LEF. In this sense, we did not want to overly deter high earners or those with substantial savings, as a combination of modest and lower incomes is essential to the viability of the model. Without a cap, current or future members could easily feel that the LEF was a money pit.

High-earning households pay up to 50 per cent of the excess into the Lilac Equity Fund (LEF) with the other 50 per cent (or more if the cap is reached) used to acquire their equity faster. Where a household has already acquired all of their allocated equity shares and every month are paying 10 per cent of their net income to Lilac (less if they meet the cap), everything that they pay over and above the cost of the maintenance charge is paid into the LEF.

The rationale for the LEF was to put aside some money to help Lilac through any difficult financial periods and with the aspiration that, with time, Lilac would be able to acquire significant equity in itself rather than relying on loans from the bank or other lenders. We wanted those with higher incomes or greater wealth through savings to contribute to the LEF. This was important, as it reinforces the values of fairness and financial equality. We felt that those on higher incomes or with considerable savings should contribute to the sustainability of the project. The LEF actually becomes a tremendously useful rainy-day or crisis fund. The ideas we have generated for its potential use include the following:

- To decrease loans from banks and other lenders in the long term.
- To finance unexpected project costs (such as damages or repairs).
- To finance further building work or extensions.
- To acquire equity shares in the case where, for example, an incoming household was on a lower income than an outgoing member.
- To temporarily meet shortfalls in repayments if a member's income dropped.

We are often asked what stops super-rich households moving in and taking advantage of our model. Technically, there is nothing to prevent this. To start with, in the application process, such rich households may not get on so well with other members and the project's values. A commitment to low impact living may not sit comfortably with a high-income, high-consumption lifestyle. And there is nothing to be gained from moving into Lilac in terms of benefiting from speculative assets. Our experience is that it attracts downsizers and those with surplus capital who are looking to dispose of it to acquire less tangible but extremely difficult-to-acquire assets such as neighbourliness, a greater sense of community and shared resources. The biggest challenge is to make sure that those with more modest incomes can benefit too from these kinds of intangible assets rather than more cash-rich downsizers.

Guaranteeing permanent affordability: homes that appreciate rather than escalate

Our ability to guarantee the affordability of our homes in perpetuity relative to rises in average incomes is perhaps one of the most surprising and challenging aspects of Lilac. The equity shares that a household owns change every year – they appreciate and depreciate. We have linked appreciation to the UK's Index of average weekly earnings (AWE). This is a national gross measure of the increase in wages across all sectors of the economy. It is the only nationally available figure. At the time of writing this was 1.5 per cent. This results in very modest increases in the value of equity locked up in housing, which avoids the buildup of speculative asset bubbles. Given the rocky ride the entire global economy has had at the hands of casino-like housing bubbles, toxic housing debt and irresponsible mortgage lending, we feel that this is an essential contribution to a more sustainable future housing market.

Depreciation is just as challenging a concept. Given that homes in Lilac are not bought or sold, the usual negotiations about what a home is worth and whether any money gets discounted for the state of the property does not apply. Thus the MHOS has to make provisions for depreciating the capital items of a home as they are used by a household. For example, a roof might last 40 years and you might live in the home for 10 years. You have benefited from the use of that roof for 10 out of 40 years of its life. So when you leave, the MHOS deducts from your equity shares 10/40th of the value of a roof. This money is banked until year 40 or thereabouts, when the new roof is bought. The same goes for a list of other capital items such as external windows and doors, kitchen units and bathroom suites. A household may choose to upgrade a capital item at their own expense but they cannot benefit from any extra value from this, unless they can provide evidence, through an independent assessment, that it has increased the value of their home. This would then have to be approved and agreed by the Society. Essentially, upgrades are for the household's own use-value rather being able to realize this in cash terms through an increase in the value of their equity.

Thus, in terms of goods in the marketplace homes in Lilac are rather more like cars than houses. Their value goes up year on year in relation to what consumers can afford but not excessively so, and their value depreciates annually and linearly due to wear and tear by the owner. It really does get people thinking differently about their housing. This is the challenge of our age.

What happens when households come and go?

Coming and going is not straightforward. Members are acquiring a 20-year lease, so it's similar to buying a home in terms of commitment. The reason it is capped at 20 years is to avoid a legal situation called 'leaseholder enfranchisement' where, after a period of 21 years, a leaseholder is entitled to acquire the freehold title of their house. This would effectively demutualize parts of the MHOS. In return for the lease, the member takes on the responsibility to pay for a certain amount of equity allocated to their house. Leaving a MHOS entails cancelling your membership and then reassigning your equity to whoever comes in to take over your home. The main point, just like a conventional mortgage, is that if you cannot realize the value of your property from an incoming occupant then it's likely you won't move. You essentially have to wait until a new occupant comes along. A house may have acquired all or only some of their equity. A final statement will tell them the value of this, taking into consideration appreciation and depreciation. As mentioned, the real innovation behind the MHOS is how it dampens equity value by pegging it to wages rather than house prices, thus avoiding homes in Lilac becoming an asset bubble that people can speculate on. Members may only obtain any increase in the value of the equity if they have lived in their homes for three years or more – again another mechanism to reduce high turnover and instability in the community. Even then, the value of the increase is shared, with the household getting 75 per cent of it and the Society retaining 25 per cent.

As with any lending arrangement, in the early years more of your repayments go towards paying bank interest. Thus the longer the member lives in the mutual home ownership project, the greater proportion of money will go towards buying their equity rather than paying bank charges. Understandably, people have suggested to us that this kind of model sets itself apart from the normal housing market and may lock members out of returning back into it. This may be partly the case, but unless efforts are made to tackle housing speculation, greater problems of locking out a whole generation from accessing decent housing will continue. The hope is that there will be a steady growth of this kind of project throughout the country and beyond through which members can move. It creates a kind of parallel mutual housing market which can combat speculation on a much wider level. We made a picture to represent what people take with them in different scenarios (see Figure 5.5).

On leaving, equity acquired by the household is repaid. This amount of money taken out of the Society has to be replaced either through the incoming member, by allocating shares internally to other members who can afford them, surplus from the equity fund, or remortgaging from the bank given that the entire project will increase in value year on year. Clearly, this latter option is the least desirable given that it's the most expensive route, and is only really possible in future years. In a real

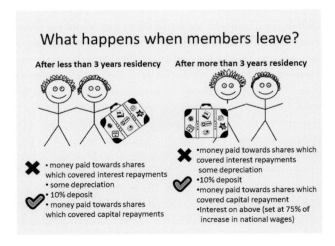

FIGURE 5.5
What happens when you leave Lilac?

Source: Lilac.

emergency, if all the other routes were exhausted, various other third sector lenders can be accessed to plug shortfalls, albeit at slightly higher interest rates.

Managing complex finances at the grassroots

We reached a certain point where Tash, in her role as treasurer, would explain complex algorithms and mathematical assumptions through spreadsheets and PowerPoints. She managed and monitored the project finances from our cramped home office using several computer spreadsheets. The whole operation had to shift away from being reliant on Tash and run from our home. What we needed was a professional and reliable solution to how we handled complexity through a user-friendly interface that could enhance common understanding across a diverse membership. We couldn't go any further without a dedicated financial manager which we didn't have and couldn't afford. We asked around to see what software packages were out there that could help us. There weren't any. We really were breaking new ground. But we had a capacity issue.

As luck would have it, Tash's brother was a software designer who specialized in making interfaces that were human-friendly, as his company put it. What we needed was to distil all the complexities of the MHOS model, and the complex formulas that calculated how they are allocated, appreciated and depreciated in a way that each member could interact with. We needed to be able to manage and check that everything was working, monitor the cash flow of the Society, and provide members with a transparent way of checking their finances.

It was in this context that Dwell was born. Dwell is now an amazing piece of user-friendly software that we had to conceive and get someone to design and build. In the end, the Society chose Tash's brother's company Maldaba, to do this. They had the perfect combination of high-level mathematical thinking combined with a passion for creating interfaces, so other people don't have to be good at maths! We spent several workshops chatting to Maldaba about how Dwell would work so that they could go and build it (see Figure 5.6). Dwell holds all the information on leases and payment histories, and is our online tool for tracking maintenance requests, of which there were many in the early days! Dwell includes the following:

- Unit management.
- Document repository for paperless filing.
- Maintenance module for handling routine, cyclical and end-of-life/planned maintenance.

MALDABA
SOFTWARE DEVELOPMENT FOR HUMANS

- Administrators will be able to declare members as self-employed, and can choose to draw an average salary over the last 1/2/3 years of income information.
- Users can link Income/Expense information to files in the Document Store.
- The 12-month date-period for Income/Expenses will be set by the member.
- Some items will carry rules (such as Pensions, which will be capped how much can be considered an expense.)
- The system will calculate a member's 10% deposit based on income information stored.

Dwellings

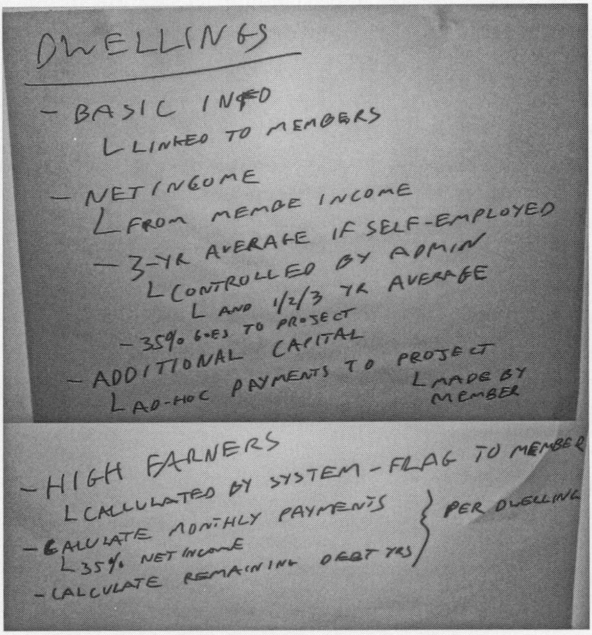

- Dwellings' basic info will consist of the following (as agreed in the proposal):
  - Address
  - Size

Olive House 32 Holmes Road London NW5 3AB
07866 462 710 admin@maldaba.co.uk www.maldaba.co.uk
Maldaba Limited Registered in England No. 5187518 VAT Registration No. GB 9402303 66

Ref: MDB/13/061/Phase1_Workshop Page 3 of 5

FIGURE 5.6 Designing Dwell

Source: Maldaba.

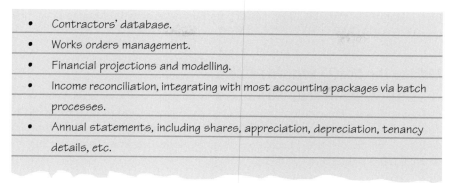

- Contractors' database.
- Works orders management.
- Financial projections and modelling.
- Income reconciliation, integrating with most accounting packages via batch processes.
- Annual statements, including shares, appreciation, depreciation, tenancy details, etc.

Dwell is a wonderful concept, although the name was a difficult choice. We wanted something that didn't sound too techie or managerial, but which felt homely. Dwell in many ways is like a close friend that helps you interact with the Society. I've come across many groups who have confidently told me that they have all the in-house financial expertise they need. That has given me a wry smile as I imagine their workload increasing to breaking point as they try to manage this as a bedroom operation. However, as with all grassroots initiatives people have to come to their

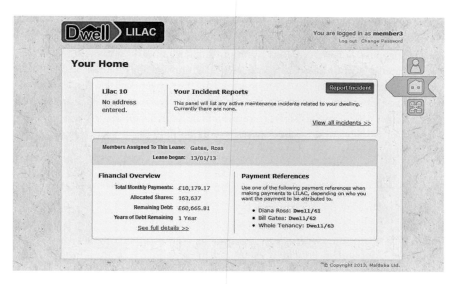

FIGURE 5.7 A ficticious member's home page on the Dwell website

Source: Maldaba.

own conclusions. Dwell is a key part of community capacity building to enact low impact living.

Making the MHOS work legally

Given the complexity of the MHOS there is quite a significant legal framework that underpins it. This was crucial to protect the interests and mutual status of the Society. As with all areas of Lilac, legally there was a huge amount to think through and create for the first time. Each aspect is quite pioneering in its own right and it's worth having a quick look at them.

The Rules

Unlike private limited companies, the governing documents of cooperative societies are called Rules. Ours date from 2009 when we incorporated as a legal entity. It sets out our objectives, our powers, and our roles and responsibilities. As I discussed in Chapter 3, Lilac is a bona fide member cooperative registered as an Industrial and Provident Society (IPS). There are upsides and downsides to this kind of legal structure. The downside is that the public will regard a bona fide member cooperative as more narrowly focused on the interests of a small group (unlike a cooperative for the benefit of the community which has a broader focus on the interests of a much wider public). But we took the decision to be a bona fide member cooperative because we really wanted to prioritize member-led self-governance and self-management within a smaller cohousing context. We could have created a Community Land Trust (CLT) acting as a broader community inter-est framework in which the MHOS would sit. However, we felt that this would create a complex two-tier structure of governance which was not necessary. In the longer term, a CLT is probably a useful vehicle which could own and govern a number of smaller cohousing cooperatives. The following is an extract from our Rules which sets out our objectives.

The objectives of the Society shall be:

[a] The provision, construction, conversion, improvement or management on the Cooperative Principles as set out in Appendix 1 to these rules [the 'Cooperative Principles'] of housing exclusively for occupation by members of the Society under the terms of a lease granted to them by the Society or under

---

the terms of a tenancy of property owned or managed by the Society solely or jointly with another member or members which shall, if it is a lease granted to them by the Society:

- include rights to purchase equity shares in the portfolio of residential properties owned by the Society;
- exclude all rights for a member to purchase the individual dwelling s/he occupies;
- exclude any right to dispose of or assign the lease to any person other than to a person who is a member or prospective member of the Society in accordance with the terms of the lease and with the prior written consent of the Society;
- include the right of the member to assign his or her equity shares in the Society when they assign their lease in accordance with its terms or at such other times with the consent of the Society as the equity share scheme in the lease permits for a value determined by the formula for valuing equity shares set out in the lease;
- require the member to assign the lease to the Society or, at the Society's direction, to a member or prospective member of the Society on ceasing to be a member.

The rules are a hefty and important document and over the years we have tried to distil its essence so that it is widely understood by the members. Early on, I did this visual summary of it so that we could explain really simply to people how the Society functioned as a legal entity at a very broad-brush level (see Figure 5.8). One of the interesting things this shows is the different levels of quorum. For example, at our general meetings we need one-third of the membership to be present and for our board we need half of board members to be present. To make structural changes high levels of agreement are needed. For example, to change a rule it requires the agreement of two-thirds of people at a meeting, and to dissolve the Society would require, namely the agreement of three-quarters of its members. However, as I explain in the next chapter, we use consensus decision making in all our meetings. Thus we would only ever vote if agreement could not be reached at three consecutive meetings using consensus. Up until now this has never been the case. And because consensus works so well it's not likely that we will ever have to fall back on voting.

The rules set out that we are a particular kind of cooperative, a Mutual Home Ownership Society, that issues equity shares to its members. In the rules, it is explained in the following way:

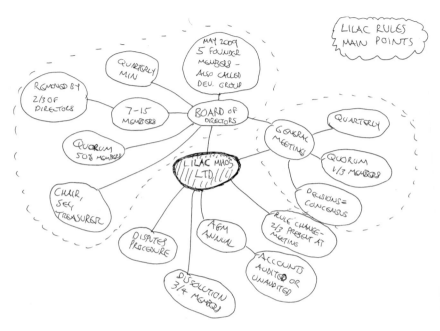

FIGURE 5.8 My sketch of how Lilac functions as a legal entity

Source: Lilac.

> The Society shall be entitled to enable members to hold an equitable interest in the value of the housing assets owned by the Society through owning and financing equity shares issued by the Society. The total value of the equity shares issued by the Society shall not exceed the initial value of the housing assets owned by the Society on the date on which the housing owned by the Society first became available for occupation by members.

Options agreement

The rules were only a starting point in the legal framework which runs Lilac. As we developed our membership base we realized that we needed a mechanism which committed members to the project. After all, people could say they wanted to live in Lilac and then simply walk away later on. This binding commitment was achieved through a document called an Options Agreement which all members had to sign before their homes were ready to be occupied. It basically gives residents an option on their home. It's also more endearingly known as a 'put and call agreement'. What this refers to is that when the member is 'called' on to take up the lease, the Society has an obligation to 'put' it to them. This is refreshingly simple compared to the legal speak we had to interpret over the years.

The Options Agreement is signed by each member when they pay their deposit.

Every household pays a deposit equal to 10 per cent of their allocated equity shares. We stipulated that members had to pay 5 per cent of this before we bought the land, or the whole 10 per cent if they joined after we bought it. These deposits gave us our war chest and locked in the members to the scheme so that we knew we had a viable project. The bank, for example, would not sign off our loan until we could prove we had reached 75 per cent commitment to occupancy before the build even started. We achieved this and we were full well before the project was complete. This shows the real demand for this kind of low impact living arrangement. The Options Agreement had an end date. If that date was reached, the members would have their deposits repaid and the project would presumably be wound up. Thankfully this was never reached!

The lease

The lease is the key document that underpins the relationship between the member and the Society. It sets out how the MHOS works and the obligations on behalf of the member and the Society. Responsibilities are shared in the lease. We were very clear who was responsible for what. The full list of shared maintenance responsibilities is given in Table 5.3.

The lease and the rules sit together as two halves of an integrated whole. Having two documents is an oddity of the arcane nature of English cooperative law. At the time of writing, moves were afoot to bring the UK into line with many other countries and create a unified cooperative legal framework so a separate rule and lease document would not be necessary. In order to maintain the mutual status of the Society, the lease requires the member to remain a member of the MHOS until they assign their lease and equity shares to an incoming member. Any notice of termination of membership of the MHOS actually constitutes a breach of the lease, allowing the Society to terminate the member's occupancy and assign the lease and equity shares to a new member.

We spent a whole year drafting and checking one particular part of the lease – Schedule 6 – which explains the workings of the MHOS. This was the first time it was done and it had to be explained in some detail. Tash and I would pull our hair out as we had to patiently explain it to each other and then get our solicitor to draft it into legal speak. Things would get lost in interpretation so we had to redraft it again! It had to be exactly right, which was rather terrifying. It was like sitting an exam without much guidance, or even anyone who would mark it. But you still

TABLE 5.3 Maintenance: who is responsible for what in the lease?

Society's responsibilities:

1 Lilac is responsible for maintenance and repair of all exterior walls and roof.
2 Lilac is responsible for all cabling and plumbing, pipes, sewers, drains, mains ducts, conduits, gutters, wires, cables, channels, flues inside and outside of the house.
3 Lilac is responsible for external decoration of the buildings.
4 Lilac is responsible for equipment for gas, hot water, space heating, electricity (light fittings, etc.), basins, baths, sewerage and sanitation in homes.
5 Only the society can apply for planning permission.

Member's responsibilities:

1 Member is responsible, and hence pays, for repairs due to negligence or intentional damage.
2 Member is responsible for keeping unblocked pipes, sewers, drains, ducts, conduits, gutters and watercourses inside or only serving the property. Member would pay for any unblocking or obstructions so that services are in working order and the lavatories properly cleaned.
3 Member must keep windows and doors serviceable and replace light bulbs, fuses and broken glass.
4 Member may decorate at their own cost in accordance with our home modification agreement.
5 Members must keep their gardens cultivated and well maintained (in line with front gardens agreement).
6 Member must keep windows cleaned and grounds tidy.
7 Repairs done by the member do not impair or reduce the environmental performance of the building.
8 Member must return the property in 'as good condition as when they arrive' evidenced by photographs. Member must pay for any repairs that need doing. This may be done by member or it is taken out of ES on leaving if not done so.
9 Member must use the recycling and rubbish facilities provided by the Society.
10 Member cannot put up aerials or signs.
11 Member cannot apply for planning permission.
12 Member cannot make any new connections to pipes or cabling without the Society's permission.

Source: Lilac.

had to get an A+. Even Schedule 6 runs to four pages. The following is a small extract to give you a flavour of the kind of text we had to write.

SCHEDULE 6 EQUITY SHARE SCHEME

1   The Monthly Charge shall be 35 per cent of Net Disposable Household Income (as defined in the Appendix) (or such other percentage as shall be determined by the Society in general meeting acting reasonably). The Monthly Charge of the Member must be sufficient to service 90 to 110 per cent of the Society's loan repayments relating to the Member's portfolio, such sum to be reviewed from time to time by the Society acting reasonably.

2   If a Member's Net Disposable Household Income rises the Society can require the Member to be allocated such further Equity Shares in the Society which the Member is deemed by the Society (acting reasonably) to be able to afford. The Member is obliged to accept such further Equity Shares and to finance them, provided that the Member's Adjusted Monthly Charge is equal to or less than the Net Disposable Household Income limit in Clause 1 above.

3   If an incoming Member cannot afford to be allocated all of the outgoing Member's Equity Shares, the Society can require an existing Member to be allocated the remaining Equity Shares of the outgoing Member pursuant to Clause 2.

4   While the value of the Equity Shares of the Member shall increase from the date the Member occupies the Property, on vacating the Property the Member shall only be entitled to any increase in value if the Member has lived in the Property for more than 3 years. The increase in value shall be the same amount as the equivalent increase in the Index of Average Weekly Earnings (or any successor index thereto).

5   The Society will establish the Lilac Equity Fund to accept contributions from Members who meet the criteria set out in the Society's High Earners and Additional Capital agreement from time to time or those who have acquired the full amount of their Equity Shares deemed necessary by the Society acting reasonably (as defined in Clause 7 below), such shares to reflect the amount required to finance the Development Costs apportioned to the Property together with any capital improvement or repair costs. The Lilac Equity Fund will be utilized for the benefit of Members in accordance

with the agreement agreed by the Society in general meeting from time to time.

6   At the Base Valuation Date each Equity Share shall have a value of £1.

7   The total number of Equity Shares issued by the Society to Members shall comprise:

7.1   the total Development Costs;

7.2   the additional Equity Shares issued by the Society acting reasonably to fund capital improvements or repairs to the Development;

7.3   additional Equity Shares issued by the Society acting reasonably to reflect the value of improvements approved by the Society and carried out by the Member to the Property (or carried out by the Society), such value to be assessed by an independent valuer appointed by the Society (acting as an expert and whose decision shall be final and binding).

DIY conveyancing

One of the ways in which we really kept costs down was to do as much legal work as possible ourselves. Our solicitor, Ian Moran, was incredibly helpful. Right from the beginning he was always available for a meeting to explain the finer details of what we were trying to achieve in legal terms. There are so many tasks to be done in terms of preparing leases, submitting documents to the UK Land Registry, and paying Stamp Duty Land Tax (SDLT) to the UK government's Treasury Department. What we were actually doing in legal terms was selling 20 homes. Normally this would all be arranged by solicitors and the buyer would simply turn up at a solicitor's office at a prearranged time to sign several forms and all would be done and dusted – for a fee of course. Much of this we realized we could do ourselves but it took an incredibly long time. Many evenings were spent preparing detailed mail merges and letter templates, filling out forms, collecting information and getting signatures from dozens of members. It saved us thousands of pounds but took hundreds of hours!

There was a long learning process and many phone calls to agencies to make sure we were doing the right thing. We had to have many conversations with the government's tax office to try to explain and clarify to them exactly who and what we were. This took rather a long time because what we were doing was brand new in terms of housing tenure. They couldn't quite understand what we were and how to charge us in terms of taxation. Similarly, we had to figure out how to deposit a house lease to the Land Registry. This was amazingly complex and involved getting together quite a few documents which included: the lease itself, an application form, a form signed by a solicitor confirming the identity of the leaseholder, a similar one for the Society, a confirmation letter from the bank and a confirmation letter from the local authority. There is an impressive and complex amount of legal work that sits silently behind the pleasures of community life. I urge groups to go into this fully prepared.

The wider affordability benefits of mutualism

One of the things about Lilac as a member-led cooperative is that first and foremost we are a financial cooperative. In monetary terms, we stand and fall together as a community. This also means we have many safeguards built in to support our members in times of financial hardship. Here is what Lilac typically can do before it would have to take the drastic measure of terminating a member's lease:

- Residents might have mortgage protection insurance to cover payments.
- Change to a rental contract and get housing benefit if eligible (shares frozen).
- Lilac Equity Fund could be used to fill temporary payment gap.
- Resident uses savings to pay off equity shares, so lower net income is sufficient.
- Other members with higher incomes take on some of the shares.
- Residents move to a smaller property.
- In the final instance, residents are given notice to leave Lilac.

These safeguards have incredibly positive well-being effects. Knowing that you will be fully involved in decisions affecting your housing situation, as well as the security provided by being part of a cooperative that is legally bound to look after your interests, is incredibly beneficial. Mutual forms of tenure and more communal living arrangements, then, offer a whole host of opportunities that can also make living more affordable. Some of these are measurable, some less so.

One of the main forms is the extra financial security offered by the mutual tenure type, especially with outgoings on housing set at 35 per cent of net income. This may have to go up if interest rates rise but in general it should stay at that level. This figure may seem a little higher or lower depending on previous experience.

But the main benefit is that it provides continuity for the duration that the member is acquiring equity. As is clear now, the monthly member charge also includes so much more than the home. It includes access to the Common House, shared landscaped areas, allotments, as well as a range of social relations between members. Member-controlled housing offers further real benefits in terms of the well-being and happiness of residents. The extra financial security is something for which people in Lilac state they are happy to pay extra for that piece of mind that they are involved in managing their own housing. All residents would be equal participants in figuring out solutions if things went wrong.

Beyond actual financial outgoings on housing, there are a range of other financial benefits that the cohousing and cooperative model offers, all of which can further extend affordability. The following are a few of them that we observe on a daily basis. I've made some rough estimates of cost savings against various items, and taken together these could offer substantial weekly savings to a household's outgoings.

- Intra-community lending becomes quite widespread in a cohousing context on an informal or formal level. For example, somebody could make a batch of jam or cook some pizza and share the surplus with their neighbours. These kinds of gifts could save a household around £5 per week.

- Tools are shared in the workshop which means that people don't have to buy a whole range of garden and DIY items such as lawnmowers, rakes, spades, power tools and ladders. These could save a household around £100 a year.

- Shared storage areas such as workshops and on-site laundry facilities means that extra storage space and washing appliances can be reduced within individual homes. This reduces the number of square metres needed for each home and reduces the build cost. For example, it may be possible to reduce the size of a home by 5m^2, reducing the debt allocated to that house by about £6000.

- Services may also be provided and offered within the community. One of the most obvious is childcare on an informal or formal basis, and this can save a household a considerable amount of money on a weekly basis. A household sourcing a full day's childcare from within the community could save around £40 per week.

- Communal meals are also one of the most visible ways in which a community can save money. Bulk buying and bulk cooking for group sizes of over 20 can offer direct savings per meal. For example, shared meals in Lilac are cooked and served for each member during twice-weekly community meals for £3 per person. Children under 5 eat for free. Eating shared meals could reduce a household's outgoings by £10 a week, especially since less energy is used compared to cooking privately.

- Since we only have ten parking spaces for 20 homes we had to commit to a certain amount of car sharing and pooling. From day one, we actually achieved this target with several households sharing cars. This brought immediate gains because the cost of running a car was equally shared between various neighbours. A few people actually sold their cars in order to share a vehicle. We also chose a location with very good connections to cycling and bus networks which meant getting around the city while also being less dependent on a car was more likely. Car borrowing is also widespread, which is really useful for household members who only want very occasional access to a car but don't want, or cannot afford, to buy one. Sharing a car can save over £1000 per year, as costs for tax, maintenance, insurance and servicing are all shared. Car pooling can save even more as the actual capital costs of vehicles are divided.

- Shared learning goes on in such a dense network of people around a whole host of issues such as gardening, home cooking or even child rearing. Rather than access courses for a fee, there's a huge amount of skill sharing occurring which is offered free by neighbours. There's also a range of occasions when popping to a neighbour's house can find an answer to a DIY, electrical or computer problem. Such activities could mean, for example, a household saving money because they do not have to buy in the services of external contractors.

- Shared laundry facilities can also yield real savings. As well as not having to buy and maintain washing machines, washing detergent is bought in bulk at lower prices. Electricity and water is also paid for communally. All this could add up to savings for a household of £200 per year.

In summary, Lilac represents a fairly complex and multifaceted approach to trying to embed patterns of low impact living which show a commitment to economic and social, not just environmental, justice. We mainly try to do this through our clever and pioneering Mutual Home Ownership Society model. But it is also about a context where shared and more cooperative living can bring direct cost savings to daily life. These need to be constantly explored and new areas found to reduce the overall environmental and economic footprint of a neighbourhood.

Notes

1 See Schor (2010).
2 The report *Common Ground* by the New Economics Foundation and others back in 2003 reviewed the different types of mutual and equity housing products on the market and first proposed the Mutual Home Ownership Society model. See http://www.cds.coop/about-us/publications/common-ground-for-mutual-home-ownership. See also Woodin *et al.* (2010).
3 See Commission on Co-operative and Mutual Housing (2009).
4 Figures 5.3 and 5.4 are for illustrative purposes only. To preserve the confidentiality of member finances, it is not appropriate to present absolute figures.

6

COMMUNITY: COOPERATING COLLECTIVELY

As much as constructing walls, Lilac builds community. It's odd to think of it in that way. But the social fabric, rather than just the physical fabric, is actually central to Lilac. What's the point of creating beautiful places without a community that is going to nurture and thrive in that place? Community building is often overlooked. It's the less visible aspect behind all the day-to-day busy-ness of construction, policy and planning issues. This chapter explores Lilac's efforts to build and maintain a strong community. Rather than seeing buildings and people separately, then, we need to think in terms of co-dependency. A low impact project is a set of complex inter-actions between social, cultural, emotional, technical, legal and ecological systems. Together, they form a holistic, interdependent whole.

Overall, our approach is defined by the idea of cohousing and in this chapter I'll explain what this means to us and how we put it into practice, and why we want to organize our lives collectively. It will look at our evolving approach to how we make effective decisions together, how we deal with problems and try to overcome them, and how we use community agreements to do this. It will also explain how we operate as a membership society and how we recruit members, as well as how we reach out to the local community.

Cohousing: building a life together

Lilac has always thought of itself as a cohousing community or project. This has been really useful. It is an internationally recognized movement, and one that is growing in the UK. It functions on a number of levels. At its most basic, it is a design methodology for how planners, architects and community groups can co-design homes, putting interaction and neighbourliness at the centre. More profoundly, it is a way of living that challenges the increasing fragmentation and individualization of modern life. And it is also part of longer attempts to make cities more people-centred.[1]

Cohousing is an established method of building community-led housing, typically with a range of around ten and up to 40 dwellings. Below that there is not enough critical mass, and above that a feeling of community becomes diluted and fragmented. The exact size of the cohousing movement is difficult to discern due to variations in definition and the frequent turnover of projects. But to get a scale of the sector internationally: there are hundreds in Denmark which is commonly understood as the birthplace of the cohousing movement, around 300 in the Netherlands and over 100 in North America. According to the UK Cohousing Network, in 2013 there were 16 cohousing communities in the UK, with 45 in development. Smaller numbers also exist in Australia, New Zealand, Germany, France and other Scandinavian countries. The evolution of cohousing has taken different paths in different places. The early Scandinavian examples, especially in Denmark from the 1960s, were very much based on highly egalitarian values, and grew to a considerable proportion of national housing stock.[2] North American cohousing communities flourished during the 1990s and were part of a distinctive new 'urbanist approach' to downtown renewal which responded to the excesses of American urban blight, sprawl and the dominance of cars by introducing more people-centred and fine-grained approaches to urban design. However, some are relatively gated and costly developments, which to some extent has done little to alleviate the problems facing inner-city USA.

It's too early to discern any particular trend within UK cohousing. Some share a history with more radical and counter-cultural intentional communities while others have merely replicated the Anglo-Saxon preoccupation for owner-occupied tenures. More interestingly, and a route where Lilac fits in, is that there is a productive overlap being forged between cohousing and the growth of community-owned and mutual housing that is affordable in perpetuity. There is a natural affinity between cohousing and cooperative housing, as many cohousing groups seek to manage their own affairs, and place community values over profit. So it's important to stress that cohousing is not a tenure type. But a priority is that as cohousing continues to grow, it also promotes affordable tenure types that remain so in perpetuity.

Cohousing focuses on the idea of designing housing to promote more interaction between residents using a mixture of individual dwellings around shared spaces, often based on certain kinds of 'intentional' values that help shape group behaviour and ethos. These values may vary from explicit ones, to more implied and less visible ones. It's worth stating that we don't formally see ourselves as an intentional community which overtly foregrounds values be they spiritual or ecological. Nevertheless, Lilac's name and values are directive enough to attract residents with a strong commitment to social and environmental justice in the first instance.

WHAT IS AN INTENTIONAL COMMUNITY?

The definition of an intentional community normally relates to a situation where groups of mostly unrelated people live together dedicated by intent to a specific common value or goal. There can be many types and intent can relate to lifestyle, values, goals, political or spiritual outlook or size. In intentional communities individuals have largely chosen to live together for some common purpose. Attempts are made to build a community together which in some way is more fulfilling than mainstream society around them, and usually involves going beyond accepted norms and traditions.[3]

There are a number of benefits that cohousing schemes proclaim.[4] First, the design process is normally led by the residents and so it more clearly responds to their needs and circumstances. This is one place in the city where a greater sense of democratic participation and ownership prevails over how the built environment develops. One of the most notable features of cohousing design is the absence of on-site vehicle access. It's literally a breath of fresh air and is probably the one single planning aspect that could be changed easily to transform neighbourhoods across cities. In cohousing, gone are adopted highways that cut through and scar neighbourhoods, active parking frontages (what's the obsession with a view of your car?) and bewilderingly high parking ratios (many suburban new-builds stipulate over two parking spaces per dwelling). In cohousing, car reduction is combined with car separation and car-free home zones to increase safety, interaction as well as reducing carbon emissions related to car use. In come pocket car parks located on the edge of sites which are heavily landscaped, formal car pools and informal car sharing. This leaves swathes of central land devoted to community amenities and nature. Thus, in terms of design, residents are in control and have an intimate connection with how the site is designed and evolves around them.

Second, there is a clear commitment that the overall design master plan and site layout will actively increase community interaction and natural surveillance. This is achieved in various ways such as through the alignment and grouping of homes, locating shared facilities that are used daily at the geographical centre, and creating overlooked, frequently used vantage points such as kitchen windows which face inward. Third, the close proximity of housing and the shared facilities also promote natural opportunities to increase safety and informal support for those who may need it (older residents, those less physically able or mobile). For these reasons, cohousing options are often very popular among over-55 age groups and single-occupancy households in their later years. There is nothing like the prospect of retirement to get you thinking about what kind of environment you are going to grow old in. Clearly, cohousing is not sheltered housing for the elderly, but senior cohousing is an increasingly popular idea as the post-50s generation look towards later life and seek less isolated and more fulfilling patterns of interaction. However, inter-generationality is also key. A rich diversity of ages and generations is essential to create lively and supportive communities. Cohousing projects that become retirement ghettos simply do not offer the same kinds of well-being outcomes that more inter-generational communities will.

In this sense, fourth, cohousing offers the benefit of private self-contained homes with shared co-located facilities. Complete immersion in communal living can, for many, become overwhelming after a while. Cohousing gives residents an opportunity to close the front door away from the rigours and demands of living in a community. Fifth, cohousing offers opportunities to reduce living costs through pooling resources. As discussed in the last chapter, this may happen formally through on-site laundry, tool and food stores, swap shops or swap boards, and informally through a host of sharing with, and lending to, neighbours. This democratic and interactive nature of cohousing creates opportunities through which low carbon behaviour changes can be pushed forward. Cohousers can adopt a range of community policies, agreements and sharing arrangements to tweak and modify behaviour in a way that would never really happen in a regular street. Sharing also leads to direct carbon savings, although these need to be still actively quantified. Think, for example, about a communal meal with one oven being used rather than 20 separate ones, or five shared washing machines rather than 20 occasionally used private ones.

Building our membership the cooperative way

What underpins Lilac as a community is that we are a membership-based cooperative society. Thus, from the outset, residents own and run their own neighbourhood. This creates a fundamentally different starting point compared to those who just loosely associate or co-locate. As a legally registered cooperative society, all members and those wanting to join have to subscribe to the International Cooperative Principles.

Lilac's membership policy has evolved over the years. The founders became the first members. We didn't formally launch our membership until late 2010, 18

INTERNATIONAL COOPERATIVE PRINCIPLES

Cooperatives around the world generally operate according to the same core principles and values, adopted by the International Co-operative Alliance in 1995. Cooperatives trace the roots of these principles to the first modern cooperative founded in Rochdale, England in 1844. The seven principles are as follows:

1   Voluntary and Open Membership. Cooperatives are voluntary organizations, open to all people able to use its services and willing to accept the responsibilities of membership, without gender, social, racial, political or religious discrimination.
2   Democratic Member Control. Cooperatives are democratic organizations controlled by their members – those who buy the goods or use the services of the cooperative – who actively participate in setting policies and making decisions.
3   Members' Economic Participation. Members contribute equally to, and democratically control, the capital of the cooperative. This benefits members in proportion to the business they conduct with the cooperative rather than the capital invested.
4   Autonomy and Independence. Cooperatives are autonomous, self-help organizations controlled by their members. If the coop enters into agreements with other organizations or raises capital from external sources, it is done so based on terms that ensure democratic control by the members and maintains the cooperative's autonomy.
5   Education, Training and Information. Cooperatives provide education and training for members, elected representatives, managers and employees so that they can contribute effectively to the development of their cooperative. Members also inform the general public about the nature and benefits of cooperatives.
6   Cooperation among Cooperatives. Cooperatives serve their members most effectively and strengthen the cooperative movement by working together through local, national, regional and international structures.
7   Concern for Community. While focusing on member needs, cooperatives work for the sustainable development of communities through policies and programmes accepted by the members.[5]

FIGURE 6.1 Monitoring our membership with post-its

Source: Lilac.

months after the Society was founded. Launching the membership offer was a leap of faith. We had no idea whether people would join the project. We were clear that we wouldn't launch our membership until enough work had been done on the core aspects of the project. Our concern was that new members would distract from the ability to have a clear direction that was not up for negotiation in the early days. But it only took around two years to recruit all the members we needed to fill the scheme. The development group closely monitored numbers of applicants and actual members, as this was the ultimate test of our success. We had a battered piece of flipchart paper and some post-it notes which we used to update avidly at every meeting (see Figure 6.1). By late 2012 all the homes in Lilac were allocated. We initially ended up with a fairly diverse range of 33 adults and nine children. In terms of age range, there are adults in almost every age decade, with a noticeable subgroup over the age of 55. Our oldest member is nearly 80! Teenagers are noticeably absent, something which will come with time given that most of the children are below 10 years of age. In terms of occupation type, the majority of people in Lilac work in the voluntary, public and charitable sectors, with a noticeable amount of people working in health and education. There are also a few people who are retired.

During the development period, we made huge efforts to advertise our membership as far and as wide as possible. We placed adverts on the outside of the site, we delivered thousands of leaflets, we posted ads in the local paper, we wrote commentaries in newspapers and magazines, we ran public events, made table mats for local cafés, and we even did a big mail out to the local authority's housing waiting list (see Figures 6.2, 6.3 and 6.4). Some of these were more successful than others. The most successful seems to have been word-of-mouth and actually meeting prospective Lilac members in person at the events we ran.

Our first membership policy was fairly lengthy. We wrote a document outlining the process for applying to Lilac before it was built, and this ran to 24 pages. The following is an extract from it.

FIGURE 6.2 A banner at the site advertises the last two homes available

Source: Lilac.

FIGURE 6.3 A Lilac publicity evening, with the Lord Mayor of Leeds in attendance

Source: Lilac.

FIGURE 6.4 A table mat advert made for the local café

Source: Lilac.

HOW TO APPLY FOR MEMBERSHIP IN LILAC

There are a number of stages an applicant has to go through to apply to become a member of Lilac Mutual Home Ownership Society. Remember you can undertake many of these stages at the same time and you can move through the stages as quickly as you like.

1   Become a friend. The first stage is becoming a friend of the project. This costs £5 per year and involves completing a friendship form which may be posted or emailed to us. An example Friendship form is attached. New friends of Lilac are invited to join our announcement email list.

2   Buddy system. If you express interest in considering full membership of the Society, then we allocate you a buddy. This is a current member who is a first point of contact for questions you may have and allows you the opportunity to find out more.

3   Attend socials. We hold regular socials so that people interested in living in Lilac can meet other members and informally find out more about the project. These are advertised on our website, on the general email list and through our Membership Officer. It is a prerequisite of our application process to have attended at least one social event.

4   Inductions. We hold monthly inductions for those who are seriously considering applying for membership. These are normally mid-month in Leeds city centre and last for three to four hours. We cover in detail all the information you need to know to make a decision about whether you wish to apply.

5   Prospective member status. At or after the induction you can inform our Membership Officer that you want to be considered as a prospective member – this is someone who has attended an induction and as a result of this is actively interested in joining and wants to find out more. We ask for a time commitment of one hour per week to help make the project happen. Prospective members can attend our regular general member meetings as observers only.

6   Applying to become a full member. Each month we have a wave of membership. If you have attended at least one social event and an induction session and decide you want to apply, you will need to send us an application form by the beginning of the month. Your application form will then be circulated to every adult member of Lilac for consideration. Applicants

have to be approved by every adult member. We set up 'meet the applicant' events where you can meet all the members. It is essential that applicants have met current members and that they have met you.

7   Acceptance as a full member. At the end of the month we will inform you if you have been accepted. You will receive an acceptance letter informing you that you have been accepted by all current full members. This letter will inform you of the current cost of your 10 per cent deposit. Acceptance is subject to a number of criteria that Lilac requires. Within two weeks of you receiving your acceptance letter, we need the following:

- A credit check. We ask you to undertake this with Experian and give us a full copy of the resulting report, including credit rating.
- Financial information and proof of earnings. We require a copy of your most recent P60, wage slip, tax returns (if appropriate), a statement of any debts, information regarding any statuary loan repayments (e.g. student loans), and proof of savings if you intend to use these to put into Lilac. If you have recently changed jobs or expect to change jobs in the near future you will also need to provide relevant information regarding this, such as expected income. If you are self-employed you will need to provide the last three years of your accounts and tax returns so that we can calculate your average income.
- If you intend to put in more than a 10 per cent deposit you will need to let us know how much this will be and provide evidence of the source (e.g. proof of savings or house valuation). If you intend to sell your house to provide funds we require a time frame for when you will put your house on the market. We would expect your house to be on the market a suitable amount of time before (this could be 6–12 months).

8   Full member status. Once we have the above information we will ask for three commitments for you to become a full member:

- Financial commitment. Within two weeks of receiving your acceptance letter, pay an initial 5 per cent deposit in the form of loan stock. We will advise you of the exact amount after receiving your financial information and the approximate time you would be expected to pay your deposit. This deposit reflects your household income and the build cost of your chosen home, and will be as accurate as we can make it before the project is finally built. For those who apply after 1 April 2011, it is likely that we will require the full 10 per cent deposit on acceptance. Only on final completion of the project will we know final build costs, and at this stage your deposit may also be slightly adjusted (up or down).

- Time commitment. A minimum of an average of two hours per week to the development and maintenance of the project *or* four hours per week if you want to join the development group/management board. We also ask all members to keep up to date with meeting minutes, attend quarterly general meetings and the AGM, and attend some of our social events to meet potential members.
- Legal commitment. Sign our 'put and call agreement'. This is a pre-lease agreement which creates an obligation between Lilac and its members that they will sign a lease when called upon to do so.

Those who have wanted to live in Lilac have largely been self-selecting. We have not had to rely overly on recruitment as our strong identity and values spoke widely for us. Beyond subscribing to the rules and principles of the cooperative, we asked all applicants to read and agree with our core vision statement and ethical policy. The ethical policy is used to guide who we will work with as an organization. When we first recruited members, we stated that prospective members must also meet a number of criteria which were used to guide decisions on allocations. There was no weighting or ranking inferred. We left this to a matter of judgement for each situation. The original criteria were as follows:

1 Responding to needs based on issues of (dis)ability, mobility and medical issues.
2 Diversity: Lilac strives to build a diverse community in accordance with our values and hence there are certain people/groups we may particularly want to ensure are part of Lilac to increase our diversity.
3 Add to the rich spread of ages.
4 Skills that may plug or relieve a gap in essential skills required for Lilac's functioning.
5 Length of time in waiting pool.
6 Ability to meet the minimum income/savings required to finance the level of equity shares and to ensure that the sum total of the net incomes across the project is sufficient to meet all debt repayments.

7 Suitability of house size requested. The maximum house size in bedrooms that can be allocated to a household would normally equal the number of residents in that household plus one: for example, three people can have a four-bed house, but one person cannot have a three-bed house. This is general guidance and each case will be considered on its own merits.

8 Subscribing to the core values and ethical policy of Lilac.

9 Being approved by all other members, including get-on-ability.

10 Previous contributions to Lilac in terms of work and helping out.

However, what we found was that having such heavily defined criteria did not serve us well. With hindsight they were far too prescriptive. Issues emerged when we tried to apply those criteria towards the end of the development phase. What transpired was a whole host of subjective opinions and interpretations from existing members as to how much each applicant met certain criteria or not. How diverse is one over the other? How get-on-able are they? Soon after, we moved away these criteria and introduced a much more clearly defined housing allocation process where applicants were ranked only chronologically in terms of when they applied. This was a huge learning point for us. We tried to engineer a complex set of criteria that would select perfect applicants who reflected social diversity, but also that we would all get along with. We were seeking the impossible. At the end of the day, we were trying to seek perfection in an imperfect world. A more realistic route to living together is to accept people as they are and develop robust processes through which people can explore and discuss their differences, and also protect the core interests of the Society. This doesn't mean cohousing can be left to become an elitist ghetto. For Lilac, our commitment to cooperativism and economic equality through the MHOS is enough to ensure that fundamentally we are an open and progressive community.

The regular socials became central events. They allowed members of Lilac to socialize as well as opportunities to meet applicants so that they could find out about the project and whether it was suitable for them. We ran a number of events ranging from monthly pub nights, to country walks or 'bring-a-dish' events. We also held informative events where we showed films or held discussion evenings to discuss wider issues associated with the project. The formal inductions became tremendously important. We insisted that anyone considering applying attended these inductions so that they at least understood the basics. We found that there was so much to explain about Lilac that these events lasted four hours! Inductees would come out with their heads spinning, either fully geared up to the prospect or overwhelmed by the complexity of what was on offer.

Reaching out

Building a strong community did not stop at our membership. We found such a demand among emerging groups and policy makers for what we were doing. A year before we moved in we held a day-long workshop called 'Learning from Lilac'. Ninety people attended, all of whom seemed hugely inspired by the combination of pioneering elements our project represented. The day we moved in we also hosted a visit by the then UK housing minister, Mark Prisk, who was joined by TV celebrity Kevin McCloud, known for his showcasing of eccentric and inspiring ecobuilders in his *Grand Designs* TV show.

A big chunk of what Lilac does is about inspiration and research. We see ourselves as a learning community, not just in terms of member education, but in terms of providing examples for others to learn from. We set up a task team called 'Learning, research and replicability' which now organizes regular site tours so that we could respond to the interests and learning needs of outside groups, and find ways to build momentum to grow cohousing and cooperative housing solutions. The first was held in November 2013 and attracted over 60 people. We created a briefing sheet for each of the three aspects of Lilac to try to convey the basic information (see Figure 6.5).

We also became very good at press work. Over the years we had a range of excellent press commentary, some of which focused on the potential controversies around building with straw. However, much of it was extremely positive, as the examples below show. Alan, one of our founder members, who had worked in campaigns and communications, worked out a promotional strategy for us around the following themes:

- **Online communication:** Lilac website, email lists, websites, facebook, youtube.
- **Face-to-face communication:** launch event in local area, celebration of each new wave of members, external conferences, socials for friends and members, buddy system, resident/tenant meetings, meet local groups, presence at local festivals and community days, door-to-door leafleting, crib sheet.
- **Printed communication:** leaflet/flyer, posters, acceptance letter to new members, Lilac handbook/information package for new members, newsletters, business cards.

LILAC

BRIEFING SHEET

Affordability

Lilac is an innovative and pioneering cohousing project completed in March 2013 in Bramley, Leeds in the UK. It features 20 homes and a shared common house built from straw bales and timber. Lilac is a member-led not-for-profit co-operative and aims to share It's learning with others. This series of briefing notes outlines the various aspects of the Lilac model and its key features. They can be downloaded from the website.

- Lilac is the UK's first Mutual Home Ownership Society which delivers 100% permanently affordable housing

- It is an intermediate housing product (homes are not owned or rented)

- The MHOS owns houses (and land) and issues leases to members

- All members pay a deposit equivalent to 10% of the build cost of their home.

- Every member pays 35% of their net income to Society

- Members can buy additional equity

- Once all equity is acquired members just pay 10% of their net income

- Minimum net household incomes are needed for each size of home

- Members are allocated equity shares in the Society dependent on their income and home size

- Each household must take on equity of the value of their home's build cost (+/- 10%)

- Moving on: leavers get the money they pay towards their equity share

- if resident for more than 3 years members get a share of increase or decrease in value of equity shares (linked to national earnings NOT housing market)

'Our use of the MHOS model can help to tackle the housing crisis, and give people and real say over how their homes are managed'

Lilac: the UK's first affordable, low impact cohousing neighbourhood

www.lilac.coop   info@lilac.coop   twitter@lilacleeds

Lilac Mutual Home Ownership Society Ltd. Registered as a Co-operative Society No 30689R

FIGURE 6.5 Briefing sheet which we used at our open days

Source: Lilac.

- **Media communication:** local newspaper, magazine, TV and radio covering key points in our process, national newspapers, magazines, advertising (some paid, some not).
- **On-site communication:** a site sign, show home, Lilac training events, site confirmation announcement.

ECO-FRIENDLY: The Lilac scheme aims to be both ultra-green and affordable to less-well-off families

It's the straw age in village of the affordable future

BY LAURA BOWYER

AN ECO-VILLAGE planned for Leeds could be the first of its kind in the country.

The low impact living affordable community (Lilac) proposed for the old Wyther Park Primary School in Bramley would be unique because of three key elements – low environmental impact, affordable housing and community focus.

The project will be ultra-sustainable, made from straw and timber and part-built by its residents, with hardly any artificial heating.

It would be the first of its kind to be affordable to low-income families. A salary of £16,000 would enable someone

to buy into the shared ownership scheme.

The scheme's final designs, by architect White Design Associates, will be on view at Leeds Central Library on Monday evening.

Treasurer and co-founder Tash Gordon said: "Our aim is that this will be the first of many similar schemes in Leeds.

"It will put Leeds on the map

as one of the UK's first cities to have a genuinely community-led approach to affordable and super-green beautiful houses for ordinary people – which will offer really low bills, a safe car free home zone and shared facilities in a common house.

"This is going to transform the way we build our houses in Leeds."

The project is planned for completion in 2012 and there

are 10 homes left for members to sign up to at the launch on Monday.

Residents have to be members of Lilac and are approved by other members. They will pay around 35 per cent of their monthly income towards their equity share.

The group intends to submit designs to Leeds City Council for planning permission soon.

Membership officer for the project, Kirsty Hughes, added: "Lilac really is one of the first of its kind in the UK. Our houses are affordable to those on modest incomes, they are built to really high ecological standards from natural materials like straw and timber, and there will be a really strong sense of community."

laura.bowyer@ypn.co.uk

YORKSHIRE EVENING POST 19/11/10 P28

FIGURE 6.6 Press coverage in the *Yorkshire Evening Post*

Source: *Yorkshire Evening Post*, 19 November 2010, p. 28.

Making real democracy

Our evolving organizational form

Lilac's organizational structure is an evolving entity. It has grown organically as the project has expanded is scale and complexity, and has changed in response to discussions about how best to evolve as an organization. Right at the beginning of the project in 2008 when we set up the Society as a legal entity, a fairly centralized 'Development Group' was formed by the co-founders. This worked well in the early years when foundational decisions needed to be made by a small group to take the idea forward. This group would meet every two weeks and each member of the group would be responsible for different areas: finance, land/legal and membership were the main ones. Over three years we mainly met at mine and Tash's house. Bi-weekly meetings would often last three hours and energy levels were tested to their limits. Both Tash and Kirsty gave birth to children during this period. Many meetings were shaped and interrupted by breastfeeding, listening to waking babies on child monitors or late starts due to problems getting the children to sleep. These were highly productive and stressful times.

This small group, which fluctuated between five and eight members, led much of the negotiations on the financing and legal basis of the project. But without the constant support of the other members it would not have been possible. There were highs and lows, but somehow we managed to synchronize them so that we were never all despondent together! But as the Society grew and new members joined, the workload and expectations for this small group also grew and we had to move away from a small and focused group. We reached a point in 2011 when the development group simply struggled to manage the workload. It was time to change it.

In 2011, we held our first community away-day, which has been repeated annually ever since. These were really key events that brought us all together in ways that we weren't prepared for. They allowed us to grow and mature, to learn to listen to one another and to tackle central issues. The 2011 event was held over two days at a wonderful woodland retreat outside the Yorkshire valley town of Hebden Bridge. We employed a professional external facilitator from the Institute of Cultural Affairs (ICA) based in Manchester who was an expert in strategic planning for groups using consensus decision making as a formal tool. He worked with us over two days using a process that the ICA call Participatory Strategic Planning to map out our overall vision as an organization, our strategic direction, an assessment of the obstacles to achieving these, as well as action planning for implementation.

OUR VISION AS A COMMUNITY

During our away-day in November 2011, we defined our overall vision of what we wanted to see in two years' time as a result of our action. The eight aims we settled on are set out below and it's wonderful to reflect that we largely still meet them all.

- Offering inspiring solutions for sustainable living.
- Creating a beautiful, productive, stimulating space.
- Supportive, kind, respectful community.
- Good relations with the wider community.
- Sharing workloads happily and equitably.
- A functional and sustainable MHOS.
- A fun place to live.
- Agreements and processes which enable.

During this away weekend we thought a lot about what would block us from meeting our vision and how we could overcome these obstacles. The following is a summary of the discussion.

Blocks to achieving our vision:	What will allow us to overcome these blocks?
Communication	Residential annual retreat
Managing expectations	Workshops on key issues
Taking on, letting go of roles	Role play for conflict resolution
Isolation, engagement, participation	Every member runs at least one skill share workshop
Financial insecurity	
Personal conflict	Regular Lilac shared meals from now on
Illness, life changes	
Chaos, unpredictable events	Personal reflection time at the start of meetings
Power imbalances	Set time limits on one person/group doing a particular group
Too much work, not enough fun	

Blocks to achieving our vision:	What will allow us to overcome these blocks?
Seeing people for what they do, not for who they are	Workshop for skills and knowledge sharing
Processes/vision not owned by everyone	Consistent practices and processes across teams
Bogged down in day-to-day matters – not strategic and reflective	Move from single-person roles to working groups
	Annual strategy meeting
	Monthly discussion forum

What came out of this event was a restructuring of our organizational form to create more equally distributed working practices which moved away from the development group. We adopted a decision-making structure based on three levels of decisions, which was adapted from the Tacoma Cohousing project in the USA. We made this into a decision-making grid (see Table 6.1).

We divided up the work into eight self-directed and participatory task teams to undertake routine decisions based on a pre-agreed remit. These included the following:

- Membership
- Landscape
- Finance
- Maintenance

- Publicity
- Process
- Community outreach
- Learning/Research/Replicability

The process team is responsible for maintaining effective decision making across the Society and helps with meeting planning and agendas. The task teams meet as frequently as is necessary, but usually around once per month. The boundaries of these task teams necessarily need to be fluid, as work, tasks and priorities change during the project. Participation in any task team has a limit of about three years and then members move on.

We now hold general meetings every three months. These are responsible for strategic decisions and direction where proposals, sent in advance, are discussed, amended and ratified. The general meetings are very ordered events. We have a facilitator and a set agenda which only deals with items sent in advance. We use

TABLE 6.1 Classification of decisions within Lilac

	Routine	Significant	Major	Emergency
		(A decision only needs to meet one criterion in this column to be significant rather than routine)	(A decision only needs to meet one criterion in this column to be major rather than significant)	
How much money is involved?	Spending that is already budgeted for	Spending that is already budgeted for if the decision is being made by a task team, or unbudgeted expenditure under £100 if the decision is being made by the Board	Unbudgeted expenditure over £100	
What impact does it have on a community agreement/how important is it?	There are no changes to community agreements	There are minor changes to community agreements	Changes the nature of the project, or The decision is ambiguous in relation to Lilac's values or ethical policy	Need to be made quickly to avoid significant delay or cost to the project
Which members and teams need to be involved?	The decision clearly falls within the remit of one task team, and can be made by this task team	The decision is made by the task team/the Board; however, there is a clearly defined process for all members to input their comments, questions and concerns If the decision falls within the remit of more than one task team, it is also a 'significant' decision	The decision is made at a General Meeting by consensus	The decision must be made at an emergency Special General Meeting
What if a member objects?	If a team member raises objections to the decision and the team cannot resolve those objections the decision must be treated as significant'	If a Lilac member raises objections to the decision, and the team cannot resolve those objections, the decision must be treated as 'major'. Any objection must be made within two weeks	In a situation where consensus of members could not be agreed, the decision must be deferred to a further meeting. This can happen for a maximum of three meetings. If after three meetings	

TABLE 6.1 continued

	Routine	Significant	Major	Emergency
			meetings consensus is not achieved, the decision must be made through a majority vote (see Rule 37)	
How does it get communicated and decided?	Achieve consensus within the team, and Posting the decision in the minutes	The decision can be implemented by task teams or the Board, and do not need to be made at a General Meeting. However, task teams and the Board must communicate clearly with the membership by:	By consensus at a General Meeting. If consensus is not reached, a second meeting on the topic will beheld. If consensus is not reached at the secondmeeting, a third meeting will be held. If at the third meeting, consensus is still not reached, the decision will be made by a vote in line with Rule 37	
	Before implementing the decision, the team must resolve any questions or concerns raised by any individual team member	Announcing to all members that the decision is under discussion Establishing a clearly defined process for collecting and responding to comments, questions and concerns (individual members must have adequate time to comment, a specified time must be stated, and a response mechanism defined) Documenting comments, questions and concerns, and addressing them in the minutes or other communications.		
		Task teams/the Board must then:		
		Achieve consensus within their team, and		
		Post the decision in the minutes		

Source: Lilac.

TABLE 6.2 Template for proposals to a General Meeting

Proposal title:

Proposer's name:

Date:

Summary:

Level of decision:

Background:

Justification/goals:

Recommended action:

Three pros:

Three cons:

Alternatives:

Source: Used with permission of Diana Leafe Christian, from her forthcoming book on governance and interpersonal dynamics in intentional communities and member-led organizations. Adopted from Bea Brigg's book, *Introduction to Consensus*. DianaLeafeChristian.org.

templates for proposals and minutes of meetings, and this has really given us consistency and clarity (see Table 6.2).[6]

We continued with a smaller board of members partly to comply with our legal obligations but also to give us a body that has an overview function for the legal and financial running of the MHOS within the remit set by members. One of the challenges for the Society is to continually ensure workloads remain at a sustainable level. We have a treasurer team of two people who have an overview of the Society's finances and report to the Board. They sit within, and are supported by, the wider finance team. We also have a nominated secretary and a shadow secretary who works with them.

In 2012 we met again for our annual away-day. It was a unique moment as the project was nearing completion. There was excitement and frustration in equal amounts. There had been a few tense, but ultimately useful, discussions especially as we started to explore the detail of several areas of community life and community agreements. The overall feeling underpinning this away-day was to uncover these tensions and find ways for us to begin to trust each other, and respect and tolerate each other's differences so that we could live together. Our process group organized some activities which really allowed issues to be explored in some detail.

The process task team had been canvassing opinion on any potential blocks we might face in terms of reaching agreement on issues. We used a tool called 'bricks and light bulbs' to explore these obstacles. During the day we built a large brick wall from them. We added to them and discussed them. In small groups we looked for solutions, or light bulbs, that could address these blocks. We distilled them down to a small shortlist of issues we felt were still crucial to address. In order of importance, these were as follows:

- Workload: work not shared fairly, equally or sustainably.
- Rules: concern of having too much control over people's lives.
- Values: not understanding the deep values/politics that different people hold.
- Trust: not trusting each other.
- Taking care of each other: feeling excluded and needing to talk about hard subjects.
- Values: Achieving a balance between different people's ideas of the vision.

COME DINE WITH ME

One format which we found extremely successful was a workshop called 'Come dine with me'. The workshop, drawing on the title of a popular TV programme, used an established fishbowl method for group communication. Participants are seated round a table with the aim of discussing an issue. They are free to leave the table, and other participants are free to join. In our version there were three food courses, or conversations, each with a title. We chose the 'Come dine with me' title to explore issues of communal food, a topic where members had different preferences, ethical views and dietary requirements. We needed to find a method which would simply allow people to be heard and explore areas of commonality. One conversational round explored issues of meat/vegetarianism/veganism which allowed us to recognize that while individuals had their own food politics, a pragmatic approach was required which allowed residents to share meat or dairy in the community's public spaces. Another round explored views on what kinds of food local residents from outside Lilac could bring into the Common House.

In June 2013, just after we moved in, we had a workshop with inspirational cohousing writer and activist Diana Leafe Christian. This was a formative event for us. Diana's work over the years has been crucial for groups to develop self-awareness and how to build capacity and deal with problems. What she focused on with us were the blocks that groups face in terms of flourishing as a community. For Diana, three aspects are crucial for a healthy, thriving cohousing community to emerge: community glue, good process and communication skills, and effective project management. All three aspects have to be co-present, and if they are they offer the preconditions for good community governance (see Figure 6.8).[7]

We also explored the idea of 'good enough' decisions. A problem for projects is when they strive to find perfect solutions. Instead, democratic decision making is much more processual and messy. Good practices come from experience and a decent amount of trial and error. Therefore, decisions should be sought which are good enough; that is to say, they are clear, and safe enough to try. They can be monitored, revised and improved. We have found this really useful and it has relieved the pressure away from having to get it right from the outset.

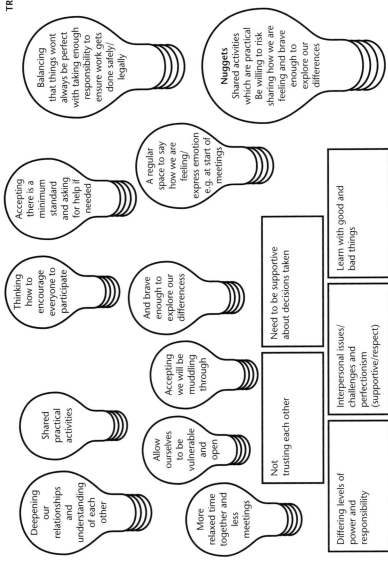

FIGURE 6.7 Brick and light bulb exercise on trust

Source: Lilac.

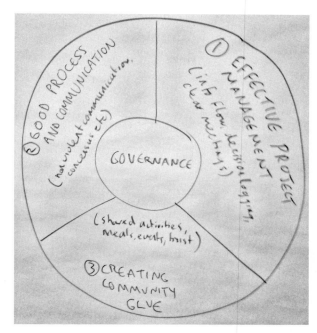

FIGURE 6.8 Three aspects of a healthy, thriving community

Source: Used with permission of Diana Leafe Christian, from her forthcoming book on governance and interpersonal dynamics in intentional communities and member-led organizations. DianaLeafeChristian.org.

In the autumn of 2013 after we moved, we shifted the emphasis of the board. No longer was it concerned with the development of the project which had pre-occupied us for four long years. Instead, we based it around a 'hub-and-spoke' model. Each task team nominated a spokesperson for one year who acted as a 'spoke'. These spokes together formed what we refer to as the hub. The treasurer and secretary teams also sit in on this. We focused quite a lot on member education to make sure members of the board felt all right with their role and responsibilities that came with it.[8] We thought long and hard about our remit and came up with an initial threefold structure that covered healthy governance, strategic vision and planning, and financial/legal overview (see Figure 6.9).

Direct democracy in practice: using consensus decision making

For cohousing to work well, it requires deliberative and direct forms of democracy which brings residents together to formulate and implement aspects of community life, resolve conflicts and mediate opinions.[9] For Lilac, the formal cooperative structure is the democratic heart of the project. Very simply, every member has an equal voice. One member, one vote. There is no chairperson with a casting vote, no central committee with a power of veto.

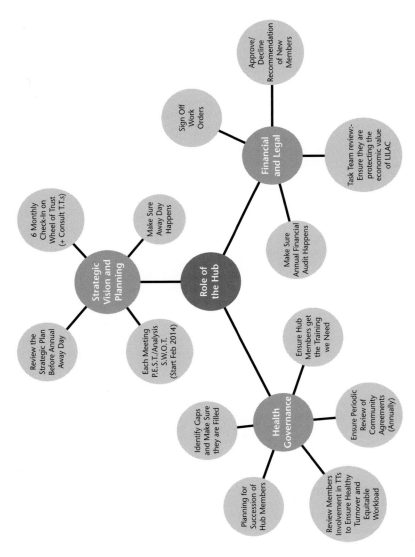

FIGURE 6.9 The role and remit of the hub

Source: Lilac.

But beyond this, we also opted to use formal consensus decision making rather than simple majority voting. As we put it in our vision statement, we work in a horizontal way through working groups which are accountable to the wider group, with all decisions reached by consensus. We use consensus decision making because we value the participation of every member of Lilac. So what is consensus decision making? It is simply a way of making decisions where there is a commitment to find outcomes that are acceptable to all. Instead of using majority voting, for example, where the majority of those present at any given meeting could show their hands to favour a particular outcome, consensus works quite differently. It's a longer and more creative process which takes account of everyone's needs. Consensus is about finding common ground with decisions reached in a dialogue between equals. It's a formal recognition of the equal rights of others, not in the sense that they have the same amount of voting powers as everyone else, but that everyone is equally committed to finding outcomes that are the best for a group. In good consensus decision making, no one is left in a minority with a decision taken against their will. This kind of approach to decision making requires a really well-thought-through and clear process.

In consensus, a number of deliberative steps are taken to ensure that decisions are not rushed, there is much discussion on topics, and that outcomes may be owned by everyone. Of central importance is a commitment to work towards the best interests of the group, rather than just using decision making to fulfil individual needs or opinions. It's a really challenging process for those (including me!) who normally like to be heard over others and usually feel certain that they are right. What consensus tries to do is unleash the creative genius of decision making in a group context, rather than falling back on established ways of doing things, or expert opinion. In the last resort, individuals do have a power of veto in the form of a block on a final proposal. But what this often largely represents is a lack of thorough discussion on the topic or misunderstanding. Those well versed in the use of consensus decision making would see the use of a blocking veto as a breakdown in good communication.

When genuine opposing views do emerge, creative solutions can be found to deal with their concerns. A whole range of tools and techniques exist which may be used to help groups explore difficult or controversial topics so that they can reach outcomes which everyone can live with. Thus consensus is a very powerful process for building communities and empowering individuals. Since all members can agree to the final decision, or at least agree not to block it and to try it, outcomes are usually much more robust and durable.

Historically, consensus has worked in all types of settings: small voluntary groups, local communities, businesses, even whole nations and territories such as the Muscogee Nation. Many housing cooperatives and social enterprises also use consensus successfully such as Radical Routes, a network of housing and workers' cooperatives in the UK which use consensus decision making. At Lilac, we broadly use the decision-making process adopted by Radical Roots, the network of independent cooperatives. This involves distributing proposals two weeks in advance of a general meeting, and anyone wishing to modify or discuss a proposal has to discuss his or her concerns with the proposer beforehand and reach an outcome prior to the general meeting.[10] Consensus decision making has also been used within the peace, environmental, anti-globalization and social justice movements as well as being the mainstay of the Quaker religious movement. It's popular in these settings, as such groups believe that the methods for achieving change need to match their goals and visions of a free, non-violent, egalitarian society. At large demonstrations around the world, many mass gatherings, actions and events involving several thousand people have been planned and carried out using consensus to reach decisions.

Clearly, consensus decision making is not the solution to all problems, and depends heavily on full commitment by those participating and the use of good processes and well-trained facilitators. Consensus is a different approach to decision making, so it is essential that people are clear about its underlying ideas. It is only a tool, and only as good as the commitment of the group using it. A number of sticking points may emerge, many of which stem from lack of experience in consensus rather than being inherent to the process. It takes time to unlearn ingrained patterns of behaviour based around more hierarchical decision making. Seeds for Change, a group specializing in consensus training in the UK, provide some of the best insights and training on the use of consensus, and the following are a few of the common problems they highlight:[11]

- As in any discussion those with more experience of the process can manipulate the outcome.
- There can be a bias towards the status quo: even if most members are ready for a change, existing policies remain in place if no decision is reached.
- Sometimes it can take a long time to look at ideas until all objections are resolved – leading to frustration and weaker commitment to the group.
- The right to veto can be a lethal tool in the hands of those used to more than their fair share of power and attention. It can magnify their voices, and be used to guard against changes that may affect their power base and influence.

- Those who do more work or know more about an issue will have more power in a group whether they like it or not. This is a two-way process – people can only dominate a group if others let them.
- Where people are not united by a common aim they will find it difficult to come to the deep understanding and respect necessary for consensus.

Getting consensus decision making right is so important that we have asked all our members to undertake training. Allowing misunderstandings or differences of opinion to fester invisibly between members and between decision-making meetings can be incredibly counter-productive for the daily life of any community. As discussed earlier, we also use a clear template for making proposals and bringing them to a general meeting. We have also begun regular discussion evenings where any items that may form the basis of a proposal in the future are discussed in a relaxing non-decision-making environment. This is a useful way to share views and to explore issues that may be the source of potential disagreements and conflicts. It's a great way to start to find common ground in a non-pressured and more sociable environment.

There are lots of great tools and activities that groups can use to help them with their consensus decision making.[12] These include the following:

- Conversational go-rounds or paired listening.
- Ideas storming.
- Straw polls, temperature checks, opinion lines.
- Lists of pros and cons, plus-minus-interesting.

Lilac uses a fairly structured approach to developing and agreeing proposals, through a number of stages.[13] A proposal is discussed with pros and cons elaborated upon. Concerns are raised and then the proposal is amended until it is in a form that people are happy with. Participants are then asked if there are any major objections (blocks) or minor objections (normally called stand-asides), and then those assembled are asked to actively acknowledge if consensus has been reached. Some groups do this with hand signals which can add an extra layer of fun as well as efficiency to consensus meetings. Figure 6.10 sets out this sequencing.

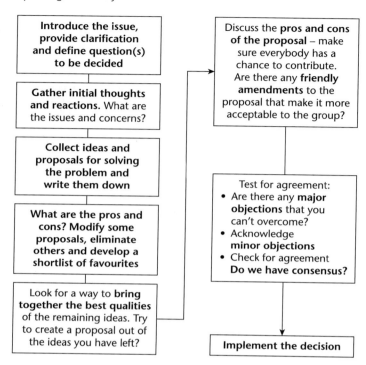

FIGURE 6.10 Consensus model flow diagram

Source: Seeds for Change.

We have also built in the safety-valve that if, after three meetings, we have not come to an acceptable outcome, we can use our simple majority voting protocols. We have also been exploring a further modification of consensus decision making called the N-Street method, eponymously named after the pioneering Californian cohousing community. This method is based on the approach that if a resident blocks a proposal then that person has to take on the responsibility of creating a process with others to find a solution. There can be up to six meetings over three months to do this. If the decision cannot be reached after this, then it is reached using a 75 per cent supermajority vote.[14]

LILAC Community Agreement [template v.1]

Why?

Here you would write a short statement explaining any background or important context. Please do not just state YOUR views – these have to be the views of the Society. This is not a space to express your own strongly held beliefs. Any assumptions/assertions have to be reasonable, backed up and defensible in public.

Aim

Try and summarise the aim of the policy in one clear sentence. Eg: 'The aim of Lilac's chewing gum policy is to reduce and ultimately eliminate the amount of chewing gum dropped in the communal areas'. An aim has to be SMART (specific, measurable, achievable, relevant, timely).

Definitions

Here you need to spell out any technical or specialist terms eg:

kWh = kilowatt hour

Aspects

Here you need to lay out the different aspects of the policy. Please be clear about the difference of intention: must means required to, should means recommended, and preferred is more optional. So please try and phrase things as follows:

Lilac members are required to.... (must - strongest)

It is recommended that....(should - middle)

It is preferred that....(weakest)

1. Lilac members are required to not use washing machines in their own homes
2. It is recommended that Lilac members do not leave their doors open at night
3. It is preferred that Lilac members use the communal areas for drying clothes
4. etc etc

Responsibility

Here you need to state who is responsible for what
Please only use 'member' 'society' etc. Do not use general terms such as 'we' 'you' 'community'. Clear responsibility has to be stated.

Exceptions

Please note any exceptions, for example, guide dogs, those with disabilities etc.

Revisions

In line with Lilac's decision making arrangements, if necessary policies can be reviewed annually if necessary.

Lilac Community Agreement. Topic XXX. Number XXXX

FIGURE 6.11 Lilac community agreement template

Source: Lilac.

Community agreements

The Society has collaboratively produced a number of community agreements using a standard template which outline expectations and limits on different aspects of community life (see Figure 6.11). Members are free to propose a community agreement and to put it forward as a proposal for discussion, amendment and then ratification. These cover areas such as pets, communal cooking, use of the Common House, front gardens, equal opportunities, vulnerable adults, the use of white goods, housing allocation and diversity. Some have foregrounded areas of disagreement and have still not been fully worked through. In the early days, there was a desire to try to create an agreement for many areas of life at Lilac. There was a tendency emerging to use the community agreements to overprescribe and micromanage life in the neighbourhood. But what we realized as we started to live together was that some of the best ways of reaching agreement was to simply share space and to openly discuss issues and differences. We are still finding a balance between legislating for what we see as really important areas, and allowing more flexibility in other areas to find the best solution.

NAMING OUR STREET

Such a pioneering project required a new name. Over a number of weeks we put ideas forward and researched the different meanings of street names. So, what kind of place is it? Lilac is an enclosed site, surrounded by the old Victorian school fence. It lent itself to something intimate – a mews, court, yard or grove. We also came across garth, an old Norse name for a cloistered courtyard. But what would work for a name? Its eco credentials also made 'garden' sound suitable. A few distinct themes emerged. It was an old school, so 'Old School Garden' was an early favourite. It also seemed an appropriate way to mark the significance of the history of the site. Others preferred something more forward looking that embraced our future impact. A derivative of Green and Hope and the fact that we had a view over the valley led to the name 'Greenhope View'. In the end, both were rejected by some members, the former for resonating too closely with members who had an earlier passion for 'Old Skool' hip hop and cringed at the prospect of saying their address, while some others felt that 'Greenhope' went too far in terms of sounding too ecological and would only increase the commune stereotypes associated with our site.

We are very good at knowing what we didn't want. Anything royalist was out (Victoria Gardens), as was anything legalistic (Old School Court). Ultimately, our concept and Society name worked as a useful compromise, and with the ending 'grove' we became 'Lilac Grove'. There are in fact one or two lilac trees on site that were spared by the bulldozers, and while we will never have a grove of them, the link back to our founding idea has given us a clear sense of place. In those early days of intense decision making, the naming of the site was incredibly important. We had a clear idea of what we could and couldn't live with. But a street name is just a street name. How many odd-sounding places do we know, whose historic origins have become obscured by the passing of time?

Refining the art of conversation the non-violent way

One of the things that we have committed to as a Society is the use of non-violent communication (NVC) techniques. There is a long tradition of NVC and we have spent some time training ourselves in workshops so we can better use them in our daily lives. NVC was developed by Marshall Rosenberg in the 1960s. Rosenberg is an inspirational American psychologist and founder of the Centre for Nonviolent Communication. It also functions as an effective conflict resolution process. In summary, NVC focuses on three aspects of how we communicate: self-empathy (which is about tuning into one's own experience), empathy (which focuses on listening to others drawing on a compassionate approach), and self-expression (which attempts to allow individuals to express themselves authentically to inspire compassion in others).

NVC is a hopeful approach that assumes all of us have the capacity for compassion. It helps people identify established patterns of thinking and speaking that lead to communicative violence. NVC proposes that if people can identify their needs, and those of others, less conflictual ways of community can be achieved.[15] We are exploring NVC in practice through an occasional study group. What we are finding is that it takes a huge amount of effort to adopt a whole new way of communicating. NVC really does provide a challenge to the ways in which many of us have grown up communicating with each other.

The art of community building

Building a community of members has been probably the most challenging, but also most rewarding, aspect of the Lilac project. Reflecting back on the past six years, the most important, and sometimes undervalued, work of community building has been around good communication and decision making. This created the vital bedrock for everything else we wanted to do – design our neighbourhood, get through the planning process, negotiate money and land, and construct our homes. And community building is simply an art with very few shortcuts available. It is open to interpretation. It takes time, patience, trust and listening. And this is not a work of art that is static. It's a collage which is added to every day through diverse interactions. And the moments of joy and happiness, as well as frustration and sadness, give this collage its rich texture.

Notes

1 See Gehl (2010) and Jacobs (1961).
2 Cohousing in Denmark dates back to the early 1960s and the work of a number of pioneering individuals. For example, the Danish architect Jan Gudmand-Hoyer worked with several groups to set up communities and wrote an influential and provocative article entitled 'The missing link between utopia and the dated one-family house' which led to a surge of interest in cohousing. In 1967, Bodil Graae wrote a similarly influential and provocative article entitled 'Children should have one hundred parents' which led to a huge interest in multi-generational communities. Denmark has benefited from formal state legislative support for cohousing, government-backed loans as well as professional bodies backing cohousing projects. Cohousing as a concept now permeates into much of the way that housing is delivered in Denmark. See Marcus (2000) and Bamford (2005).
3 See Sargisson (2007, 2009).
4 There is a huge and established literature on cohousing. A small sample includes: Jarvis (2011), Durrett and McCamant (2011), Field (2004), Bunker *et al.* (2011), Williams (2005), Sargisson (2012), Meltzer (2005), McCamant and Durrett (1994), Scotthanson and Scotthanson (2005) and Fosket and Mamo (2009).
5 See http://ica.coop/en/what-co-op/co-operative-identity-values-principles.
6 We borrowed many of these ideas from Diana Leafe Christian. Her work and further resources may be found at http://www.dianaleafechristian.org.
7 See Christian (2003). Her website also has some excellent resources on how groups can use the Sociocracy method to extend their practices of good community governance. See www.dianaleafechristian.org.
8 There are several excellent guides. See corporative UK's Simply Governance resource (http://www.uk.coop/simplygovernance), and the International Cooperative Alliance's Good Governance Charter for Housing Cooperatives at http://www.icahousing.coop/attachments/Good%20Governance%20Charter_6%20web.pdf.
9 There are some excellent resources out there for groups to improve their democratic processes, including starhawk (2011).
10 See http://www.radicalroutes.org.uk/publicdownloads/introrra5.pdf.

11 These pointers are from a chapter they wrote called 'Doing It without leaders' in a book I co-edited: *DIY: a Handbook of Changing our World.*

12 The Institute for Cultural Affairs (ICA), for example, has developed numerous resources for participatory processes. See http://www.ica-uk.org.uk/participation-resources. Resources I have also developed with the Trapese popular education collective are available at http://trapese.clearerchannel.org/resources.php.

13 This method for generating proposals is from Seeds for Change. See http://www.seedsforchange.org.uk/consensus.pdf.

14 More information on this particular way of using consensus may be found at http://www.cohousing.org/node/1592.

15 For a good introduction to NVC look at The Centre For Nonviolent Communication website at http://www.cnvc.org/ and Rosenberg (2003, 2005).

7

LEARNING FROM LILAC

There are many lessons that may be drawn from a project like Lilac that is so different and broad ranging. What I do in this chapter is reflect on some of the lessons that will, hopefully, be useful to a range of people reading *Low Impact Living*. I cluster these into the following: emerging community groups attempting to take their own project forward; those in the construction and the development sector who will be helping groups build projects; practitioners such as architects, quantity surveyors and engineers who will be working with these groups; and representatives in local and national governments who will be using policy and funding streams to enable similar projects. These lessons and recommendations are necessarily broad, as I am aware that I do not want to make this too UK focused. Enabling frameworks, policy mechanisms and funding streams are notoriously changeable and heavily context dependent, and we should be cautious about building strategic advice around them.

Individually, the lessons Lilac offers are not necessarily original, as many have been part of long-established and successful attempts to set up community-led, mutual, cohousing or eco-village projects. However, the originality comes from their combined effects which together point to a transformatory step-change in the art of place making – based on a combination of low impact living, economic equality and community self-management. These start to significantly challenge the business-as-usual model of city development and the intense and corrosive individualism that has become the hallmark of urban life over the past 30 years. Retrofitting a stronger sense of community and togetherness back into cities is an urgent task.[1] This is a real game changer. But it isn't a one-size-fits-all approach. Instead, everyone involved in making these projects happen needs to adopt a particular attitude and approach – one that does not dogmatically stick to the crude profit bottom line, or ways of acting inherited from the past. This is really challenging for the commercial housing construction sector. But it is essential for the delivery of community-led projects. What is needed is constant dialogue, flexibility and, most of all, time, to reach common understandings, build trust and avoid confusion.

Before I explore what may be learned from Lilac, it's worth reflecting on what life has been like over the first year. The time-scale of one year is almost too short to assess the success of a project. Groups who actually manage to bring their project to completion need to recognize that the first year will be a very particular kind of experience – one that is full of frustration and joy in equal amounts. The first year of living somewhere should really be seen as a natural extension of the development phase. It is marked by settling in, establishing procedures, debugging systems and snagging defects. Not only will individuals be under quite a lot of pressure in terms of moving in and setting up their own home, the whole community will be finding its feet. Almost every interaction will be novel and full of possibilities and challenges. In the early days of a project, making time to still have fun, as well as listening and finding out the needs of others around you, is essential. It is likely to be over longer periods – five or even ten years – that a project and its residents will really start to flourish.

Our arrival on site coincided with spring 2013. The first six weeks were taken up with all the residents moving in, as well as the contractors moving off site. As spring became summer, the community's energy turned towards the shared aspects of the site – landscaping the natural areas and the Common House. The landscape task team designated 'area coordinators' for the various landscaped areas around the site and we all busily beautified, gardened and planted. We also set up a Common House task team to help furnish it and set up all the basic equipment we needed, and prepare the guest bedrooms for visitors that are located in the stairwells of the apartment blocks. By the time autumn and winter arrived, there were still many areas left untouched, and plans unstarted. It's important not to feel overwhelmed by the amount of tasks that need to be done in the life of a community. Unlike a conventional housing development, cooperative and community-led housing projects have the advantage of allowing things to develop gradually with time, in a way which is organic and also reflects the capacity of the residents. So, rather than thinking about everything being completed in the first year, it's useful to lay out all the tasks a community wants to achieve over the first 12 months, two years and five years. We are building up quite an interesting set of potential ideas and plans for future years, including a children's play area (featuring a high zip wire, tree-house and free play area), wildflower meadow, pizza oven, pergola and seating area, and of course a hot tub and sauna! Many of these will come to fruition; others may take a back seat and take much longer to emerge. But the important point is that tasks are treated with joy and an exercise in community building.

We had our share of frustrations in the first year. There were occasional misunderstandings. There was fatigue over too many emails and the sheer amount of work we had to do to make sure our legal and financial procedures were in place and good enough to run a multi-million-pound entity. But we always made sure that we created plenty of time for fun and shared activities in the first year. We ate together at least twice a week in the Common House, and there were several shared celebrations for birthdays, the passing of the seasons and during holiday periods. It's difficult to assess overall the first year of life in Lilac. It has been really different for different people. My overwhelming impression is rather like being on a rollercoaster – full of surprises and unpredictability mixed with joy. In a way, I am glad that the first year of living in Lilac is now over and that the community can really emerge and define itself. The first year is a small step on a much longer journey. But it is one that we are taking together. I think the following African proverb really sums up the kind of journey we are on: 'If you want to go fast, go alone. If you want to go far, go together.'

So what helped Lilac succeed?

Before I look at the lessons that Lilac offers, I want to pull out what I see as underpinning Lilac's success. There are a few things that really catalysed us into action. Some were very context dependent, others offer more generalizable points.

First, the pioneering and inclusive vision gave us political purchase and social clout. People recognized that we were up to something big, and for the right reasons. We were pioneers with a social zeal for progressive change. We were doing the things that needed to be done and thinking the things that needed to be thought. As a cooperative society, we could also wear our badge of social equality and cooperation proudly. It creates a warm, inclusive feel. To outsiders you are not dealing with self-interested or profit-motivated people. Rather, we affirm long historical traditions. This was really useful when in front of funders, planners and local authority officers who are used to profit-hungry developers trying to dodge or minimize social obligations.

Second, there seemed to be few alternatives or short cuts to six years of hard work. Time and again we encountered a perseverance test. We had to simply maintain morale and keep going when we encountered hiccups, barriers and potential disasters. I've documented a fair few in this book. But rather than trying to anticipate them, groups simply need to be prepared for the unexpected as they arise and hold on to their longer term vision. This also means having a strong group and a mix of personalities who can weather constant setbacks. The overall message is that it is

difficult, as it actually just takes so long to think through such a pioneering methodology for developing an affordable and low impact cohousing neighbourhood.
There are now some short cuts and time savings, many of which may be yielded
from the contents of this book as well as other sources. However, the bottom line
is that these projects will take the time they need if they are to emerge sustainably,
in a social and ecological sense.

Third, a core initial group with a clear vision and sense of direction is paramount.
In the early days, groups are tremendously in flux. Participants come and go, and
there is a rapid accumulation and turnover of ideas. From a single point, ideas
expand and the project becomes more broadly conceived. At a given point, direction and commonality needs to be extracted from this huge amount of information
in what is called the 'groan zone' to focus the project back down. This whole
process through divergence to convergence can take a while, possibly up to one
year. But groups need to be aware where they are at in this journey and not to get
stuck or demoralized. This way of looking at group thinking is called 'the diamond
of participatory decision making'.[2] It's a useful way to think about how to focus in
the early days. For us, part of this was having a small group which gathered information and then set the basic parameters of the project (size, location, materials) as well
as developing a business plan before this was taken out to recruit a wider base.
Similarly, bringing in professionals at the right time was vital. Every group gets to
a stage beyond which they need further advice. Too early, and the idea generation
process can get stifled; too late, and the group could wither through fatigue.

Fourth, the support we received from statutory agencies (in our case Leeds City
Council and the UK government's Homes and Communities Agency) was crucial
to Lilac. Local and national agencies are still the major players in terms of policy
and finance. They are the enablers. We secured land at an affordable market value
with logistical support through an exclusivity agreement. We also benefited from a
substantial grant which allowed us to get through planning and experiment with
modular and prefabricated strawbale construction. In this age of austerity, these kinds
of grants seem more distant, but arguments need to be made about where public
funds are allocated. There is public money. It is just poorly distributed. We were
also fortunate to have a very supportive bank lender. There is a real lack of willing-
ness to lend to projects like ours among the mainstream banks, and this needs urgent
attention.

Finally, key to our success were our members. With such a broad and large
project, there was work to do on so many fronts that this could only be tackled by
a well-organized, sizeable group of people. Our members became advocates for the
idea, reinforcing our vision and sharing it with others. This kind of group advocacy
immediately sets Lilac apart from the highly individualistic responses inherent in
many solutions to climate change. Our membership-based approach also allowed

us to discuss issues, and ultimately this led to more robust decisions that people owned, rather than feeling that they were imposed from above.

A more critical look at Lilac

Lilac is a living model. It's not a utopia. It's full of imperfections, complexities and difficulties, and many of the assumed benefits will only be fully tested as the years pass. It's worth dwelling on some of the areas for further work.

The MHOS model, for example, is complex and only now is being fully tested. Its complexity could be a barrier to its wider take-up. It has so many twists and turns, and relies on so many complex formula and algorithms that it's difficult to understand at an everyday level. However, very few of us suppose that we fully understand a mortgage or loan agreement when we agree to borrow money from a bank. What is needed are trusted software tools and intermediaries which can help spread and implement the model. Further, while the MHOS model is a useful rebalancing devise that can offer housing to those facing barriers, it cannot do everything. It must not, for example. replace social housing and a core commitment from the welfare state to fund public housing at an affordable sub-market level. The mutual sector needs to grow, but not at the expense of public housing. It is better that it's seen as a replacement for private sector rented and owner-occupied housing that is at the core of house price inflation and speculation. The challenge remains to create a more generalized model of affordable, mutual housing that can be implemented in lower income, urban communities. By growing the size of mutually owned cohousing, we can keep pushing the boundaries of affordability. And any project committed to social justice has also got to keep an eye on exclusions and discriminations that may emerge unintentionally in terms of class, ethnicity and gender.

Second, more work needs to be done to create a sustainable delivery model which avoids burnout and over-concentration on founding members. This is not unique to cohousing projects. Most pioneering projects rely on the energy and vision of those 'burning souls' who establish projects. It will always be a small group of people who are prepared to break the norm and defy the status quo. This is a challenge personally for those involved, but also in terms of the health and impact of the wider community. Like many grassroots projects, Lilac relied on a small group of founders, who worked extremely hard for an intense period of time. It also created work and knowledge hierarchies which take time to unravel. The sheer size of the perseverance test is also overwhelming. Relying on spare time and skill sets as non-professionals, groups have to draw on all their reserves as well as determination and passion.

Third, there is the constant challenge of replicability. Socio-technical studies view projects like Lilac emerging in micro-level, niche, protected spaces. These spaces represent a window of opportunity to change dominant socio-technical regimes.[3] But there are concerns about the extent to which these niche innovations can diffuse their ideas into wider society. Projects are often so context dependent, and Lilac was fortunate to benefit from government grants. However, the logic is that these grants are used to get a project to market, and fund the substantial extra costs which riskier pioneering reference projects represent. So what can be done to break out of the niche? I'll point towards some of these below, but they include capacity-building and enabling intermediate institutions, as well as limiting the market dominance of certain kinds of more commercial providers who tend to inhibit creativity and grassroots innovation.

So what can be learned from Lilac?

For community groups

There are so many areas a group has to attend to that advice is far-reaching and diverse. Below are some pointers, grouped around the main lessons as I see them.

Time and timing

In most areas of life, timing is everything. Knowing when to wait is as key as knowing when to act.[4] There has to be a recognition of where a group is at in the development process. Different stages require radically different skill sets, resources and time commitments. Further, there has to be a realistic assessment of group capacity, time and the actual length of the development journey. In our case it was six years. This can be trimmed, but never at the expense of good group formation. Bringing in various professionals is also crucial. As the Lilac example shows, after three years we could go no further without a project manager, and then we quickly acquired a full suite of other professionals. Being professional led too early or too late will either lead to an erosion of autonomy, or over-commitment, confusion and possible collapse.

Dealing with risk

The ability to manage risks is a very important feature. I mean this at a very personal and intuitive level. Groups will encounter decisions which represent significant risks. But let's differentiate between reckless and competent risk taking. Risk in any situation has to be assessed. It's not just about abandoning caution and seeking adventure. Groups will benefit from having competent risk takers who are familiar with dealing with, and assessing, risk in other spheres of their lives. There will be

TABLE 7.1 Lilac's risk register, January 2009

Category	Risk/ consequences	Level of risk	Control/ Action	Responsibility	Target date(s)	Progress
Financial Physical Operational Personal Strategic, or Reputation	5 Catastrophic 4 Major 3 Moderate 2 Minor 1 Insignificant	5 Almost certain 4 Likely 3 Possible 2 Unlikely 1 Rare	Avoidance (eliminate) Reduction (mitigate) Transfer (outsource or insure) Retention (accept and budget)			

Source: Lilac.

moments when huge choices have to be made in terms of costs, procurement routes or contractors. Getting the right advice is also crucial here. But this also entails getting advice from the right experts who want to inform rather than influence. The difference is crucial for group independence. On one level, groups have to be left to make their own mistakes, but also guided so that those mistakes do dot lead to collapse. We adopted a risk strategy fairly early on. This allowed us to identify all the risks we could see ahead, but importantly plan how we would reduce or mitigate them. Funders will want to see some kind of risk matrix as part of your business planning. Our risk register (see Table 7.1) allowed us to classify each type of risk in terms of intensity from insignificant to catastrophic, and likelihood from rare to almost certain. It also allowed us to determine how we were going to mitigate against that risk and plan for it.

Embracing personalities

Any healthy, functioning group will contain a variety of personality types. It is important to combine introverts and extroverts, doers and thinkers, leaders and followers, collaborators and lone workers, listeners and speakers, and those of a more agitational as well as a conciliatory nature. They will play different roles at different times. The extroverts and doers will be very good in the early stages, and at the broad-brush activities. The introvert thinkers will be essential for listening and providing community glue, and for quietly contemplating solutions to difficult problems.[5] What is also needed is people who act in the here-and-now, as well as horizon scanners, those who are always pondering the long term. It would be perfect, wouldn't it, if we could all encapsulate these tendencies within ourselves, being constantly responsive to the needs and moods of contexts and others around us? But alas, most of us are largely programmed to act and respond in ways that have always worked for us. It is this recognition of differences that can help a group, and be revelatory in terms of getting an overview of how good internal group communication can flourish. Groups may want to formally assess what kinds of personality types they have amongst them to help them identify gaps or areas of over-dominance.[6]

Communication

Effective internal communication is essential. A balance between email and face-to-face meetings, as well as formal and informal exchanges, has to be struck. Protocols and templates really help, as outlined in Chapter 6. Being able to communicate clearly and assertively with professionals and practitioners is also essential. We did this through a single point of contact which had a mandate from the membership and worked under the remit of the board. This contact gave the external world of contractors confidence that they had a clear line of communication with the whole community, and relieved concerns that they would not be flooded by multiple, or contradictory, correspondence and views. What groups have to realize is that the complex and personable levels of communication they may want with professional teams can add up to significant risks and potential extra costs for them. Anything that means more work or time simply adds further costs. So groups have to be disciplined and restrained when engaging with the external world, and have more scope to be deliberative and thoughtful in their internal affairs.

For the development industry

The development sector is diverse, incorporating large-volume builders, small bespoke outfits and self-builders. In some contexts like the USA, developers have emerged from within the cohousing community to provide services to emerging projects.[7] Overall, the larger scale mainstream development sector lacks certain skills and competencies to be able to develop long-term working relationships with the cohousing and cooperative community. There are a number of reasons for this. The first relates to differences in the profit bottom line. No matter how supportive of particular projects, most developers will not be able to show the kinds of cost flexibility that small-scale projects need. Second, more sensitivity to the potential of time delays is needed. Developers want to get on and off site as quickly as possible to minimize costs. Put simply, the longer a building site is operational, the costlier the project to everyone. Fast time-scales can be imposed on pioneering projects which do not allow for problem solving and thinking time on issues that arise as the project is being built. More off-site predevelopment work is often needed. Third is lack of experience and exposure to the nature of large and complex membership and community-led projects. Most developers are used to negotiating with single, experienced representatives who are delivering repeat work or easy-to-understand development templates. It is *terra incognita* when a developer has to slow down and understand the requirements of a diverse group. Moreover, the democratic and deliberative nature of groups means that decisions can be changed, which may cause problems during the development process.

Developers should take seriously the need to get to know individual groups, as well as the idea of cohousing. When this is only done tokenistically it can lead to frustration and delays. Secondees from community organizations can be helpful for developers. They can act as interpreters between often diverse languages. A central part of this understanding is recognizing that developers are not just dealing with housing managers or client representatives. They are also dealing with a client group who are future residents and self-commissioners of their neighbourhood and home. In this context, the personal and the professional are deeply entwined. Developer-residents are likely to scrutinize details very closely. Reactions to poor design decisions, misunderstandings and delays can provoke extremely strong and emotionally charged reactions. These are not the kinds of daily interactions that developers are used to. But their recognition is crucial for a workable relation to emerge. A sustained level of interaction is needed to constantly explain and mutually agree on design aspects and choices as they develop through a build stage. This requires staff within development firms who have the time and inclination to build up a close relationship with members of community groups who may have higher than average levels of expectations about how the development process may turn out.

What is needed is clear and detailed information for groups to be able to make decisions. We were presented with several decisions to make in a short time-scale. Sometimes, we lacked the knowledge and experience to understand the full nature or impact of the choices we were making. These cropped up in areas like depth of balconies, placement of radiators and windows, layout of electrical equipment or choice of internal materials. One area that needs further attention is the relationship with subcontractors. Usually a contractor is chosen, as a community group will feel they are aligned with their values, and that they have shown that they understand the group. However, subcontractors are often a different story. They are not usually chosen by the community. Rather, they are brought into the process by the contractor, often on cost grounds. Subcontractors may not be primarily motivated by the nature of the project, its aims and aspirations, wanting instead to deliver the job on cost. At the coal-face on site, the actual workers will want to get the job done as quickly as possible. Of course, this doesn't mean that they are not interested in innovation or breaking the mould. It's just that there are so many practical limits in the working day that constrain meaningful engagement.

Community-led groups need to be aware that different types of development contracts can create different experiences during the development phase. We used a JCT (Joint Contracts Tribunal) Design and Build Contract. This is a familiar contractual route in the UK and is designed for construction projects where the contractor carries out both the design and the construction work. It gives the client group cost certainty which is often the main priority. But it places the contractor in the driving seat, with all other professionals novated, or transferred, under their control. This can reduce the role of the architect, and as a result, a commitment to the design intention and coherence of the project becomes more challenging. Other types of contract however, where the architect takes the leading role, may expose the client to less cost certainty. So it's a fine balancing act. Partnership contracts are a productive route where parties work together to find solutions, everyone shares the risks and also any variations in cost. For example, JCT has created a 'Constructing Excellence' contractual route for when 'participants wish to engender collaborative and integrated working practices'.[8] The wider point is that mechanisms for more collaborative relations need to be established to deliver pioneering and non-traditional projects. A dedicated delivery vehicle owned and managed by the community-led housing sector would be useful in this context.

The finance and land sector also needs to recognize the unique situation of community self-builders and custom-builders. It's fair to say that emerging cohousing groups will have little development finance behind them in the early years. They will rely on a mixture of seedcorn grants or internal loans from members, family and friends. Lenders, landowners and developers need to make allowances for this. Financial balance sheets will be precarious and a number of mechanisms may be used. Landowners could offer exclusive agreements for groups to negotiate on land while they attend to arranging loans, planning and surveys. These crucial few months can allow small community-led outfits to get ahead of larger developers who have huge cash reserves and are prepared to take a bet on acquiring vacant land. The practice of land banking is really problematic for community groups. Large developers will literally buy sites and bank them in their stocks for long periods of time to artificially inflate values or distort market conditions in their favour. Legislation is needed to regulate and reduce this kind of activity. Split or deferred payments for land can also be really useful. For example, we benefited from paying for our land in two instalments, with the second payment required six months after practical completion of the project. Developers can also help small groups with their development cash flow by grouping together and delaying payments or forward scheduling invoices. This basically offers small entities access to lines of credit from developers who can afford it.

For practitioners

Not all practitioners have detailed experience of working with community groups. Architects, quantity surveyors and engineers are accustomed to working with a dedicated team of professionals who are competent with specialized knowledge. Therefore, in a similar way to development contractors, many practitioners can further develop their understandings of how large, diverse community groups and membership-led organizations work.

Professional practitioners may be centrally involved in the conception and design of cohousing projects from the outset. Co-production is a real necessity, and taking it seriously and doing it well is vital. To collaboratively design projects is a powerful way to bond. However, it takes particular skills and dedication to co-produce a project. Roger Hart's work with children which led to his idea of the 'Ladder of Participation' is a useful tool to demonstrate the way that, without good ground-work and trust, many relationships can be based on mere informing and consulting, rather than empowering and engaging.[9]

Appropriate facilitation skills are central here, as is devising a set of activities which are substantive rather than tokenistic. Practitioners need to be aware of the dangers of an approach based on the extraction of ideas over interaction. Information may be taken at a crude level and reinterpreted in a way which loses their meaning and strips them of their values. Designating a consistent representative within each external practitioner entity is really needed to build up trust, continuity and coherent information flow. Practitioners should also be prepared to be given quite a detailed project brief which guides the project throughout. This brief needs to be reviewed periodically to assess whether the project is experiencing any 'mission creep' away from initial intentions. This briefing process is something that Lilac did not do enough of. Having a clear design statement early on is invaluable. This involves being able to record and retrieve decisions quickly and accurately.

For local and national agencies

The holistic challenges that pioneering projects represent entail a considerable rethinking of the way urban space is used, planned and integrated. Cohousing presents so many challenges to the planning system and the way that city space is allocated – reducing car ownership, reducing size devoted to individual dwelling space and increasing that devoted to spared facilities, the creation of central, car-free, landscaped shared spaces, integrating productive growing space, maximizing resident interaction, designing convivial spaces, using new ownership and tenure mechanisms for land and housing, and providing activities that integrate new projects with existing communities. The limitation of current policy and planning frameworks to achieve these kinds of aims cannot be underestimated. Fragmentation of the understanding of the challenges within statutory agencies is still the norm, as is risk aversion and a best-value approach to the management of public assets. City officials are fully able to be innovative – and they need to be encouraged to do so more, as well as draw on workable examples from elsewhere which show how things can be done differently.

At the heart of a cohousing revolution are enabling institutions that are well resourced and can respond to the needs of innovative groups. Pioneering projects are inherently a challenge to slower moving government structures, be they at the local or national level. For good reasons, government bureaucracies are not easily swayed or shifted. However, the kinds of step changes needed to tackle and address the range of challenges outlined in this book are going to push the daily life, and values, of governments to new limits.

Local authorities need to see community groups as equal partners and fellow custodians in the delivery of policy and well-being outcomes at the neighbourhood level. Problems such as climate mitigation and adaptation, energy descent, economic equality, the stewardship of public assets and social cohesion are too large, unwieldy and complex to be solved by the state alone. More distributed forms of networked power, where the state acts as an enabler, can mobilize local communities to the challenges they face. This is a historic challenge for the state – to let go, to trust and to enable. At the heart of the ecological, affordable housing revolution are some far-reaching institutional changes. An enabling role is an equal and collaborative role which allows ideas, ingenuity and innovation to flourish. We can actually see many fragments of this. Local authorities have long embraced the sustainability agenda through Local Agenda 21 frameworks. More recently, many have developed climate change strategies with challenging carbon reduction targets. Progressive networks of cities and their leaders such as C40 Cities, the Covenant of Mayors and ICLEI-Local Governments for Sustainability are demonstrating what can be done.

Of course, in an age dominated by global financial capital there is only so much the local or the national state can do. States are situated within a wider context of corporate interests and lobbying which is eroding the democratic mandate between the state and its citizens. Increasingly, they are also being squeezed by centralized power above them at supra-state level. One of the tasks, then, is to reclaim the state.[10] What this means is to reclaim the historic redistributive and social justice functions of the modern state as they continue to be slowly eroded.

Broader lessons

There are a number of other broader lessons that projects like Lilac offers. First, projects which go beyond the status quo have to recognize the interconnected and complex nature of the challenges they face. Making sure our efforts to embed forms of low impact living also meet the 'triple bottom line' of economy, ecology and equality is essential.[11] To deliver these measures requires working simultaneously across a range of institutional and governance frameworks and scales, as well as behavioural, cultural, legal, financial, planning, ecological, community, design and governance issues. The ability to achieve this is extremely difficult. It makes the task at hand complex, and challenges conventional wisdom in terms of the functioning of housing markets, landownership, building fabric choices and community self-governance. All this is only reinforced by the silos and specialisms that most professions, especially central government departments and large-volume housing builders, operate within. Part of the response is to set up novel partnership-based delivery mechanisms to deal with the interconnected and holistic nature of the challenge, as well as tensions and conflicts that inevitably arise from engaging with vested interests, slow-moving bureaucracies and even hostile elements of the status quo. Seeking out friendly allies here is really crucial. Projects need to acknowledge and use, rather than overlook, the political tensions and conflicts they generate as a result of working towards various, and often competing, futures for cities and their neighbourhoods.

Second, as I stressed earlier, low impact living can also drift into forms of place making that are parochial, inward-looking and exclusive. The rise of gated residential communities across the globe has been quite astonishing over the past two decades. These communities are driven by fear and a desire to socially segregate from what are perceived to be less desirable, or dangerous, groups. They are increasingly leading to a labyrinthine patchwork of defendable urban enclaves and quarters, with streets and entrances literally gated and closed to restrict and prohibit entry. This deeply erodes interaction and a sense of community in cities.[12] It is a tendency that eco-minded and community-led housing projects must avoid at all costs.

Third, the agenda that projects like Lilac represent means something quite profound for how we understand localities. A very different ethics of place is needed that is ecologically robust, economically viable and socially equitable. It needs to recognize and build upon the myriad links and networks upon which pioneering projects depend. Every day, a cast of thousands of people and projects that stretches the planet is brought into play. Recognizing these 'distant others' and how we impact and depend upon them for our daily lives is essential for building more inclusive and open places in which to live.[13] In our efforts to create the kinds of projects outlined in this book, we must always be mindful of reducing our negative impacts upon others.

These kinds of experiments also entail a radical rethinking of what is commonly understood as a city. How settlement forms and neighbourhood patterns will emerge in future scenarios that are both more localized and egalitarian, as well as able to limit dangerous levels of GHGs and the use of fossil fuels, and adapt to a changing climate, are all considerable questions. It is likely that what we have comfortably come to recognize as places during the age of hyper-industrialization and oil dependency will be radically transformed. Part of this may be through necessity as price signals, resources and governments change. But more and more, groups will actively change the rules and intervene in the ever unfolding story of what urban places could be like in the future.[14] Actual outcomes are less certain. Some of these could be transformatory and people-centred. Others could be more sinister and repressive.

Fourth, pioneering projects have a triple personality – engaging at an everyday level with the way the world is, struggling against convention, and also aiming for a different future.[15] Projects act within the constraints of existing planning, financial and regulatory frameworks, and cultural and behaviour norms. At the same time they agitate, seeking to intervene in the structural origins of problems, rather than responding passively to external shocks and changes, as well as developing new ways of urban living that challenge growth-based neoliberal policies. They represent inspirational laboratories, acting as educators, overcoming inaction and confusion, providing compelling examples and innovative experiments in future adaptations that can tackle climate change and energy scarcity.

Finally, constant vigilance and intermediate milestones are needed to assess what is being achieved and in what directions pioneering projects are taking society. There are some really important junction points ahead. Projects could become a roadmap for rebooting and deepening the highly unequal capitalist money economy, further embedding market relations, commodifying land and resources and social divisions between the haves and the have-nots. I've already highlighted the dangers of cohousing, as it contains tendencies towards a more egalitarian model based on co-ownership and maximizing access, as well as a more privatized model based upon individual homes for sale at open market prices. Eco-developments, villages and cohousing schemes are a more familiar part of the landscape in prosperous suburbs, semi-rural towns, liberal college towns or more progressive small cities. They need to spread to more unlikely locations for their benefits to be widely shared – such as struggling inner cities or declining industrial towns. A commitment to affordability, accessibility and economic equality needs to be at the heart of roadmaps for future low impact living. And, of course, the important question remains: 'how would we know if we have been successful?' Project building is as much about the journey and how we get there, as our destination. The values that underpin our work, the styles and tools we use to organize, the kinds of relations we build along the way, and the lessons we share are all part of the low impact living revolution.

Priorities for the future

I constantly meet other groups who want to draw on what we have done, want to put their dreams into reality. But many don't achieve this. One of the conundrums is that we are dealing with a model with huge potential demand but a low 'conversion rate' into reality. There seem to be many potential blocks, challenges and barriers along the way for a real growth of low impact living projects. What can be done?

First, more capacity is needed. There needs to be support and education, especially for groups who want to adopt a cooperative, mutual model. Specific skills are required in terms of how groups can manage their own organizations and finances as well as use more direct forms of decision making. Chapter 6 pointed out several resources here. Similarly, local authorities and agencies can unleash potential and build capacity in groups through training about how policy and planning works. Local policy champions can be very useful, whose role it is to signpost, open doors, make introductions, translate and explain. At some point, local agencies need to ring-fence resources and land for a small amount of risk taking and experimentation. This can generate reference projects that others can follow and that policy makers can learn from.

Second, there are a whole set of issues related to project financing. As we've seen, projects like Lilac have cash flow issues in the early days, especially to get them over the first few hurdles like planning agreements, land purchases, architects' drawings and engineers' reports. Seedcorn funding from national or regional agencies can really help here. For example, as a result of what we did at Lilac, the UK government launched a multi-million-pound fund to get more community-led housing projects off the ground. Start-up capital from commercial lenders is also another route, and there are lots of social entrepreneurs and venture capitalists out there who are willing to lend money. However, interest rates can be prohibitively high. What the mutual and cooperative sector need specifically are its own sources of start-up capital and seedcorn funding. At the moment, further funding is also required to fill the gap in 'loan–value' ratios. Put simply, most projects can only borrow around 70 per cent of the value of project costs. Most conventional developers fill this gap through either large cash reserves built up from development profit, or in the case of social housing, from government grants. Finance solutions need to be found for the cooperative and community-led sectors to plug this gap.

Inter-project lending will also be really crucial. As projects develop and start to build up their own capital, they can lend this to other new start-ups. In addition, progressive developers could hold back a certain percentage of profits and use these to seed further projects. This could be built into cash flow models. Once innovative new financial models have been tried and tested by pioneering projects, the hope is that more high street lenders will get involved in supporting them.

Third, reforms of land markets are really crucial. The practice of land banking needs to be regulated, and reduced, to allow a level playing field of access for smaller community groups. Finding suitable land is one of the real obstacles for emerging groups. Putting derelict land and that 'banked' by large speculative developers back onto the market is essential to get local land markets operating again in the interests of those who live there. Further, the cooperative and community land trust sectors could use their resources to acquire and allocate land to suitable emerging projects. Local authorities could designate strategic housing land as experimental sites for pioneering projects. Local authorities could also transfer land assets to the mutual and community-owned sectors, and recognize them as partners in the public stewardship of land.

Finally, innovative delivery mechanisms need to be developed. As I pointed out in the last chapter, in other countries cohousers have created their own community-led development vehicles to deliver a larger number of cohousing units. In Scandinavia, large cooperative development vehicles also deliver homes in their thousands. For example, HSB, the Swedish Cooperative Housing Association, encompasses 3903 cooperative local housing companies comprising 317,000 homes.[16] This should be a priority in all contexts because it has a number of benefits. First, it allows profits to be reinvested into the sector and to seed other projects. Second, it allows the benefits of volume building where the unit cost of each house is dramatically reduced the more you build. Third, it allows standard templates to be used which can further reduce costs. Fourth, bulk purchasing arrangements and longer term subcontracting relationships with other not-for-profit entities can further reduce costs. This can help localize supply chains, reduce the building industry's carbon footprint, and reinforce local jobs and skills. Larger networks of member-led housing can also tackle issues such as carbon reduction and fossil fuel dependency at a broader scale. Finally, there are a whole range of less tangible benefits associated with the increased accountability that goes with a greater say in how neighbourhoods are built. This is particularly the case with development companies which are partly, or wholly, community owned.

So this concludes the story of Lilac, for now. Whether you are thinking, researching, designing, building, or living somewhere, I hope this field-guide for ecological, affordable, community building has been of some help. It does feel as if we are at the beginning of an exciting period when there could be a substantial new round of growth of low impact living projects. I urge you to be part of it in whatever way, and make your own dreams a reality. And I hope it is now clear that, for me, a low impact living revolution is not one worth having, unless it is deeply embedded in economic and social justice, as well as a desire to reconnect the strong bonds of togetherness and association that have been eroded over recent decades.

A final comment. Pass on, borrow, adapt, reuse, or recycle the ideas in this book. You can even make a carbon copy of Lilac (although if you do I imagine you'll be in touch for some advice!). But don't profit from these ideas. Don't lock them behind corporate firewalls or expensive patents. Creating a rich commons of ideas and practice is the best route to respond productively to these challenging times. What we have tried to do through Lilac should also not be fragmented. The only low impact living revolution worth backing is one that is widely accessible and reteaches us the deep practices of how to build community. Clarify and strongly state your dreams, visions, values and motives. Hold onto them. They will guide you well in the darkest days. Don't let them be derailed by the dead hand of the status quo, bureaucratic structures, or the enticements of a fast buck. With a good team, an open heart and a desire to communicate, clear aims, strong values, a lot of perseverance, help from anyone that you care to ask, and of course, some luck, you are likely to succeed. Go for it.

Notes

1 See Hemming (2011), Sennett (2012).
2 See Kaner *et al.* (1998).
3 See Geels (2005).
4 See Partnoy (2012).
5 See Cain (2013).
6 There are lots of personality tests that may be used. A useful starting point includes the Myers-Briggs-type indicator (MBTI). See http://www.myersbriggs.org/.
7 See e.g. http://www.cohousingpartners.com and http://www.cohousingco.com.
8 See http://www.jctltd.co.uk/category/partnering-contracts.
9 See Hart (1992).
10 See Wainwright (2003), Monbiot (2001).
11 See Pavel (2009).
12 See Minton (2012).
13 See Massey (2004).
14 See Chatterton (2010), Vanderbilt (2010).
15 The work of John Holloway (2010) has been useful in stressing that all anti-paradigmatic projects are both in, against and beyond capitalism.
16 See http://www.hsb.se/hem.

REFERENCES

Agyeman, J. (2005) *Sustainable communities and the challenge of environmental justice*, New York: New York University Press.

Anderson, K., Bows, A. and Mander, S. (2008) 'From long-term targets to cumulative emission pathways: Reframing UK climate policy', *Energy Policy*, 36(10): 3714–22.

Anderson, W. (2006) *Diary of an eco-builder*, Totnes: Green Books.

—— (2009) *Homes for a changing climate: Adapting our homes and communities to cope with the climate of the 21st century*, Totnes: Green Books.

Angus, I. (ed.) (2009) *The global fight for climate justice*, London: Resistance Books.

Atkinson, A. (2007) '"Sustainable development" and energy futures', *City: Analysis of Urban Trends, Culture, Theory, Policy, Action*, 11(2): 201–13.

Bamford, G. (2005) 'Cohousing for older people: Housing innovation in the Netherlands and Denmark', *Australasian Journal of Ageing*, 24(1): 44–6.

Barber, B. (1984) *Strong democracy: Participatory politics for a new age*, Berkeley: University of California Press.

Bauman, Z. (2001) *Community: Seeking security in an insecure world*, London: Polity Press.

Bicknell, J., Dodman, D. and Satterthwaite, D. (eds) (2009) *Adapting cities to climate change: Understanding and addressing the development challenges*, London: Earthscan.

Bond, P. (2010) 'Climate justice politics across space and scale', *Human Geography*, 3(2): 49–62.

Bulkeley, H. (2005) 'Reconfiguring environmental governance: Towards a politics of scales and networks', *Political Geography*, 24(8): 875–902.

Bulkeley, H. and Schroeder, H. (2008) *Governing climate change post-2012: The role of global cities – London*, Tyndall Centre Briefing Note 34, Oxford: The Tyndall Centre for Climate Change Research.

Bulkeley, H., Castan-Broto, V., Hodson, M. and Marvin, S. (2010) *Cities and low carbon transitions*, London: Routledge.

Bunker, S., Coates, C., Field, M. and How, J. (eds) (2011) *Cohousing in Britain today*, London: Diggers and Dreamers Publications.

Cain, S. (2013) *Quiet: The power of introverts in a world that can't stop talking*, London: Penguin.

Calthorpe, P. (2013) *Urbanism in the age of climate change*, New York: Island Press.

Chamberlin, S. (2009) *The transition timeline*, Totnes: Green Books.

Chatterton, P. (2002) 'Be realistic: Demand the impossible. Moving towards "strong" sustainable development in an old industrial region?', *Regional Studies*, 35(5): 552–61.

—— (2010) 'The urban impossible: A eulogy for the unfinished city', *City*, 14(3): 234–44.

Christian, D.L. (2003) *Creating a life together: Practical tools to grow ecovillages and intentional communities*, Gabriola Island: New Society Publishers.

Commission on Co-operative and Mutual Housing (2009) *Bringing democracy home*, London: CCMH.

Condon, P. (2010) *Seven rules for sustainable communities: Design strategies for the post-carbon world*, New York: Island Press.

Cook, M. (2011) *The zero-carbon house*, London: Crowood Press.

Co-operatives UK (2012) *The UK co-operative economy 2012: Alternatives to austerity*, Manchester: Co-operatives UK.

Dawson, J. (2006) *Ecovillages: New frontiers for sustainability*, Schumacher Briefings, Totnes: Green Books.

De Angelis, M. (2007) *The beginning of history: Value struggles of global capital*, London: Pluto Press.

Department for Communities and Local Government (2010) *Summary of changes to the code for sustainable homes technical guidance – 2010*, London: DCLG Publications.

Department for Energy and Climate Change (2010) *Energy consumption in the UK*, London: DECC.

Desai, P. (2009) *One planet communities: A real life guide to sustainable living*, London: Wiley.

Dobson, A. (2003) *Citizenship and the environment*, Oxford: Oxford University Press.

Dorling, D. (2011) *Injustice and why social inequalities persist*, London: Polity Press.

Douthwaite, R. (1999) *The growth illusion: How economic growth has enriched the few, impoverished the many and endangered the planet*, Gabriola Island: New Society Publishers.

Durrett, C. and McCamant, K. (2011) *Creating cohousing: Building sustainable communities*, Gabriola Island: New Society Publishers.

Egan, D. and Marlow, O. (2013) *Codesigning space*, London: Artifice Books.

Evans, J. (2011) 'Resilience, ecology and adaptation in the experimental city', *Transactions of the Institute of British Geographers*, 36(2): 223–37.

Fairlie, S. (2009) *Low impact development: Planning and people in a sustainable countryside*, London: Jon Carpenter.

Featherstone, D.J. (2008) *Resistance, space and political identities: The making of counter-global networks*, Oxford: Wiley-Blackwell.

Field, M. (2004) *Thinking about cohousing: The creation of intentional neighbourhoods*, London: Diggers and Dreamers Publications.

—— (2011) *Housing co-operatives and other 'mutual' housing bodies*, Warwick: Consult.

Fosket, J. and Mamo, L. (2009) *Living green: Communities that sustain*, Gabriola Island: New Society Publishers.

Galeano, E. (2001) *Upside down: A primer for the looking-glass world*, London: Picador.

Geels, F.W. (2005) *Technological transitions and system innovations: A coevolutionary and socio-technical analysis*, Cheltenham: Edward Elgar.

Gehl, J. (2010) *Cities for people*, New York: Island Press.

Global Humanitarian Forum (2009) *Human impact report: Climate change. An anatomy of a silent crisis*, Geneva: Global Humanitarian Forum.

Goodchild, B. and Walshaw, A. (2011) Towards zero carbon homes in England? From inception to partial implementation, *Housing Studies*, 26: 6.

Hall, P. (2013) *Good cities, better lives: How Europe discovered the lost art of urbanism*, London: Routledge.

Hamdi, N. (2004) *Small change: About the art of practice and limits of planning in cities*, London: Earthscan.

—— (2010) *The place makers guide to building community*, London: Earthscan.

Hansen, J., Sato, M., Kharecha, P., Beerling, D., Berner, R., Masson-Delmotte, V., Pagani, M., Raymo, M., Royer, D.L. and Zachos, J.C. (2008) Target atmospheric CO2: Where should humanity aim?', *Open Atmospheric Scientific Journal*, 2: 217–31.

Hardt, M. and Negri, A. (2009) *Commonwealth*, Cambridge, MA: Harvard University Press.

Hart, R. (1992) *Children's participation: From tokenism to citizenship*. UNICEF Innocenti Essays, No. 4, Florence: UNICEF ICDC.

Hawken, P. (2007) *Blessed unrest: How the largest movement in the world came into being*, New York: Viking Press.

Heinberg, R. (2004) Powerdown: *Options and actions for a post-carbon world*, Gabriola Island: New Society Publishers.

—— (2005) *The party's over: Oil, war and the fate of industrial societies*, Gabriola Island: New Society Publishers.

Heinberg, R. and Lerch, D. (2010) *The post carbon reader*, Gabriola Island: New Society Publishers.

Heiskanen, E., Johnson, M., Robinson, S., Vadovics, E. and Saatamoinen, M. (2010) 'Low-carbon communities as a context for individual behaviour change', *Energy Policy*, 38(12): 7586–95.

Hemming, H. (2011) *Together: How small groups achieve big things*, London: John Murray.

Hodson, M. and Marvin, S. (2009), '"Urban ecological security": A new urban paradigm?', *International Journal of Urban and Regional Research*, 33(1): 193–215.

—— (2010) 'Urbanism in the anthropocene', *City*, 14(3): 299–313.

—— (2011) 'Can cities shape socio-technical transitions and how would we know if they were?', in Bulkeley, H., Castan-Broto, V., Hodson, M. and Marvin, S. *Cities and low carbon transitions*, London: Routledge.

Holloway, J. (2010) *Crack capitalism*, London: Pluto Press.

Homer-Dixon, T. (2006) *The upside of down: Catastrophe, creativity and the renewal of civilisation*, London: Souvenir Press.

Hopkins, R. (2008) *The transition handbook*, Totnes: Green Books.

—— (2013) *The power of just doing stuff: How local action can change the world*, Cambridge: Green Books.

Intergovernmental Panel on Climate Change (IPCC) (2007) *Fourth assessment report of the IPCC: Climate change 2007, synthesis report*, Geneva: IPCC.

—— (2012) *Managing the risks of extreme events and disasters to advance climate change adaptation: Special report of the intergovernmental panel on climate change*, Cambridge: Cambridge University Press.

—— (2013) *Fifth assessment report of the IPCC: Climate change 2013, synthesis report*, Geneva: IPCC.

Jackson, H. and Svensson, K. (2002) *Ecovillage living: Restoring the Earth and her people*, Totnes: Green Books.

Jackson, T. (2009) *Prosperity without growth: Economics for a finite planet*, London: Earthscan.

Jacobs, J. (1961) *The death and life of great American cities*, New York: Random House.

Jarvis, H. (2011) 'Saving space, sharing time: Integrated infrastructures of daily life in cohousing', *Environment and Planning A*, 43(3): 560–77.

Johnston, S., Parzen, J. and Nicholas, S. (2013) *The guide to greening cities*, New York: Island Press.

Joll, J. (1979) *The anarchists*, London: Methuen.

Jonas, A.E.G., Gibbs, D. and While, A. (2011) 'The New Urban Politics as a politics of carbon control', *Urban Studies*, 48(12): 2537–44.

Jones, B. (2009) *Building with straw bales: A practical guide for the UK and Ireland*, Totnes: Green Books.

Kahler, M. (ed.) (2009) *Networked politics: Agency, power, and governance*, Cornell, NY: Cornell University Press.

Kaner, S., Lenny, L., Toldi, C., Fisk, S. and Berger, D. (1998) *Facilitator's guide to participatory decision-making* (2nd edn), San Francisco, CA: Jossey-Bass.

Kellogg, S. (2008) *Toolbox for sustainable city living*, San Francisco, CA: South End Press.

Kennedy, C.A., Cuddihy, J., and Engel Yan, J. (2007) 'The changing metabolism of cities', *Journal of Industrial Ecology*, 11(2): 43–59.

Kropotkin, P. (1972) *Mutual aid: A factor of evolution*, London: Freedom.

—— (1987) *Fields, factories and workshops tomorrow*, London: Freedom.

Kunstler, J. (2006) *The long emergency: Surviving the converging catastrophes of the twenty-first century*, London: Atlantic.

Lerch, D. (2007) *Post carbon cities: Planning for energy and climate uncertainty*, Santa Rosa: Post Carbon Institute.

Linebaugh, P. (2008) *The Magna Carta manifesto: Liberties and commons for all*, London: Verso.

Littler, J. (2009) *Radical consumption: Shopping for change in contemporary culture*, Maidenhead: Open University Press.

Lynas, M. (2007) *Six degrees: Our future on a hotter planet*, London: Fourth Estate.

Manzi, T. (ed.) (2010) *Social sustainability in urban areas: Communities, connectivity and the urban fabric*, London: Earthscan.

Marcus, C. (2000) 'Site planning, building design and a sense of community: An analysis of six cohousing schemes in Denmark, Sweden, and the Netherlands', *Journal of Architectural and Planning Research*, 17(2): 146–63.

Marshall, P. (1992) *Demanding the impossible: A history of anarchism*, London: Harper Collins.

Martinez-Alier, G. (2009) 'Socially sustainable economic de-growth', *Development and Change*, 40(6): 1099–119.

Mason, P. (2012) *Why it's kicking off everywhere: The new global revolutions*, London: Verso.

Massey, D. (2004) 'Geographies of responsibility', *Geografiska Annaler: Series B, Human Geography*, 86(1): 5–18.

McCamant, K. and Durrett, C. (1994) *Cohousing: A contemporary approach to housing ourselves*, 2nd edn, Berkeley, CA: Ten Speed Press.

Meinshausen, M., Meinshausen, N., Hare, W., Raper, S.C.B., Frieler, K. and Knutti, R. (2009) 'Greenhouse-gas emission targets for limiting global warming to 2 degrees C', *Nature*, 458(7242): 1158–62.

Meltzer, G. (2005) *Sustainable community: Learning from the cohousing model*, Victoria, BC: Trafford.

Mertes, T. (2004) *A movement of movements: A reader*, London: Verso.

Middlemiss, L. and Parrish, B.D. (2010) 'Building capacity for low-carbon communities: The role of grassroots initiatives', *Energy Policy*, 38(12): 7559–66.

Minton, A. (2012) *Ground control: Fear and happiness in the twenty-first-century city*, London: Penguin.

Monbiot, G. (2001) *Captive state: The corporate takeover of Britain*, London: Pan Books.

Mulugetta, Y., Jackson, T. and van der Horst, D. (2010) 'Carbon reduction at community scale', *Energy Policy*, 38(12): 7541–5.

Murphy, P. (2008) *Plan C: Community survival strategies for peak oil and climate change*, Gabriola Island: New Society Publishers.

Neustatter, A. (2012) *A home for the heart: Home as the key to happiness*, London: Gibson Square.

New Economics Foundation (2003) *Common ground – for mutual home ownership*, London: New Economics Foundation.

—— (2010) *Good foundations: Towards a low carbon, high well-being built environment*, London: New Economics Foundation.

Newman, P. (2008) *Cities as sustainable ecosystems: Principles and practices*, New York: Island Press.

Newman, P., Beatley, T. and Boyer, H. (2009) *Resilience cities: Responding to peak oil and climate change*, New York: Island Press.

North, P. (2010) 'Eco-localisation as a progressive response to peak oil and climate change – a sympathetic critique', *Geoforum*, 41(4): 585–94.

Notes from Nowhere (ed.) (2003) *We are everywhere: The irresistible rise of global anti-capitalism*, London: Verso.

O'Neill, D. (2012) 'Measuring progress in the degrowth transition to a steady state economy', *Ecological Economics*, 84: 221–31.

Osmani, M. and O'Reilly, A. (2009) 'Feasibility of zero carbon homes in England by 2016: A house builder's perspective', *Building and Environment*, 44(9): 1917–24.

Partnoy, F. (2012) *Wait: The useful art of procrastination*, New York: Profile Books.

Pavel, P. (ed.) (2009) *Breakthrough communities: Sustainability and justice in the next American metropolis*, Cambridge, MA: MIT Press.

Pearce, F. (2006) *The last generation: How nature will take her revenge for climate change*, London: Eden Project.

Peters, M., Fudge, S. and Jackson, T. (eds) (2010) *Low carbon communities: Imaginative approaches to combating climate change locally*, Cheltenham: Edward Elgar.

Phillips, R., Seifer, B. and Antczak, E. (2013) *Sustainable communities: Creating a durable local economy*, London: Earthscan.

Pickerill, J. and Maxey, L. (2009) 'Geographies of sustainability: Low impact developments and spaces of innovation', *Geography Compass*, 3(4): 1515–39.

Pittini, A. and Laino, E. (2012) *Housing Europe review 2012, the nuts and bolts of European social housing systems*, Brussels: ECODHAS Housing Europe's Observatory.

Plumwood, V. (2002) *Environmental culture: The ecological crisis of reason*, London: Routledge.

Pullen, T. (2011) *The sustainable building bible: An insiders' guide to eco-renovation & newbuilding*, London: Ovolo.

Register, R. (2006) *EcoCities: Rebuilding cities in balance with nature*, Gabriola Island: New Society Publishers.

Rodgers, D. (2009) *New Foundations – unlocking the potential for affordable homes*, London: The Co-operative Party.

Rosenberg, M. (2003) *Nonviolent communication: A language of life*, Encinitas: Puddledancer Press.

—— (2005) *Speak peace in a world of conflict: What you say next will change your world*, Encinitas: Puddledancer Press

Rydin, Y. (2010) *Governing for sustainable urban development*, London: Earthscan.

Santini, C. and Zilafro, D. (2009) *Green is beautiful: The eco-friendly house*, London: Image Publishing.

Sargisson, L. (2007) 'Imperfect utopias: Green intentional communities', *Ecopolitics*, 1(1): 1–24.

—— (2009) 'Sustainability and the intentional community: Green intentional communities', in Leonard, L. and Barry, J. (eds) *The transition to sustainable living and practice*, Bingley: Emerald Management Research Publishing.

—— (2012) 'Second wave cohousing: A modern utopia?', *Utopian Studies*, 21(1): 28–57.

Satterthwaite, D. (ed.) (1999) *The Earthscan reader in sustainable cities*, London: Earthscan.

Schlosberg, D. (2007) *Defining environmental justice: Theories, movements and nature*, Oxford: Oxford University Press.

Schor, J. (2010) *Plenitude: The new economics of true wealth*, London: Penguin Books.

Scotthanson, C. and Scotthanson, K. (2005) *The cohousing handbook. Building a place for community*, Gabriola Island: New Society Publishers.

Sennett, R. (2012) *Together: The rituals, pleasures and the politics of cooperation*, London: Yale University Press.

Seyfang, G. (2009) 'Community action for sustainable housing: Building a low carbon future', *Energy Policy*, 38(12): 7624–33.

Seyfang, G. and Smith, A. (2007) 'Grassroots innovations for sustainable development: Towards a new research and policy agenda', *Environmental Politics*, 16(4): 584–603.

Simms, A., Johnson, V. and Chowla, P. (2010) *Growth isn't possible: Why rich countries need a new economic direction*, London: Earthscan.

Smith, S., Searle, B.A. and Cook, N. (2009) 'Rethinking the risks of home ownership', *Journal of Social Policy*, 38(1): 83–102.

Solnit, D. (2004) *Globalise liberation: How to uproot the system and build a better world*, San Francisco, CA: City Lights Books.

Spratt, S. and Simms, A. (2009) *The great transition*, London: New Economics Foundation.

starhawk (2011) *The empowerment manual: A guide for collaborative groups*, Gabriola Island: New Society Publishers.

Thorpe, A. (2012) *Architecture and design versus consumerism: How design activism confronts growth*, London: Earthscan.

Tormey, S. (2004) *Anti-capitalism: A beginner's guide*, London: One World Books.

Trapese Collective (2008) *Do it yourself. A handbook for changing our world*, London: Pluto Press.

Tuckman, B.W. (1965) 'Developmental sequence in small groups', *Psychological Bulletin*, 63 (6), reprinted in *Group Facilitation: A Research and Applications Journal*, 3(spring 2001): 66–82.

Vanderbilt, T. (2010) 'The new urbanism: In future, what will our cities look like?', *World Policy Journal*, 27(4): 3–7.

Victor, P. (2008) *Managing without growth: Slower by design, not disaster*, London: Edward Elgar.

Wackernagel, M., Kitzes, J., Moran, D., Goldfinger, S. and Thomas, M. (2006) 'The ecological footprint of cities and regions: Comparing resource availability with resource demand', *Environment and Urbanization*, 18(1): 103–12.

Wainwright, H. (2003) *Reclaim the state: Experiments in popular democracy*, London: Verso.

Walker, B. and Salt, D. (2006) *Resilience thinking*, New York: Island Press.

Ward, C. (1985) *When we build again, let's have housing that works*, London: Pluto Press.

While, A., Jonas, A.E.G. and Gibbs, D. (2010) 'From sustainable development to carbon control: Eco-state restructuring and the politics of urban and regional development', *Transactions of the Institute of British Geographers*, 35(1): 76–93.

Wilcox, S. (2006) *The geography of affordable and unaffordable housing*, York: Joseph Rowntree Foundation.

Wilkinson, R. and Pickett, K. (2009) *The spirit level: Why more equal societies almost always do better*, London: Allen Lane.

Williams, J. (2005) 'Designing neighbourhoods for social interaction – the case of cohousing', *Journal of Urban Design*, 10(3): 195–227.

—— (2012) *Zero carbon homes: A roadmap*, London: Earthscan.

Woodin, T., Crook D. and Carpentier, V. (2010) *Community and mutual ownership: A historical review*, York: Joseph Rowntree Foundation.

Woolley, T. (2006) *Natural building: A guide to materials and techniques*, London: Crowood Press.

Worrell, E., Lynn Price, C., Hendricks, L. and Ozawa, M. (2001) 'Carbon dioxide emissions from the global cement industry', *Annual Review of Energy and Environment*, 26: 303–29.

WEB RESOURCES

General resources

http://gen.ecovillage.org (Gobal Ecovillage Network)
http://www.communitylandtrusts.org.uk (UK Community Land Trust Network)
http://mutualhousinggroup.coop (Mutual Housing Group, UK)
http://www.cch.coop (Confederation of Cooperative Housing, UK)
http://www.uk.coop (Co-operatives UK)
http://www.cds.coop (CDS Co-operatives)
http://www.lowimpact.org (Low Impact Living Initiative, UK)
http://www.cohousing.org.uk (Co-housing Network, UK)
http://www.cohousing.org (Cohousing Network, USA)
http://www.cohousingco.com (the Cohousing Company, USA)
http://cohousing.ca (Canadian Cohousing Network)
http://cohousing.it (Italian Cohousing Network)
http://www.communityselfbuildagency.org.uk (the Community Self Build Agency, UK)
http://locality.org.uk (Locality, UK)
http://www.nasba.org.uk (National Self Build Association, UK)
http://www.diggersanddreamers.org.uk (Guide to Communal Living, UK)
http://fic.ic.org (Fellowship for Intentional Community, USA)

Web resources specific to Lilac

www.lilac.coop (Lilac MHOS Ltd)
http://www.leeds.gov.uk (Leeds City Council)
http://www.coho-ltd.co.uk (Coho Ltd)
http://lindumgroup.com (Lindum Group)

www.modcell.com (Modcell)
http://white-design.com (White Design Associates)
http://integral-engineering.co.uk (Integral Engineering)
http://www.maldaba.co.uk (Maldaba Ltd)
http://www.triodos.co.uk (Triodos Bank)
http://www.dwf.co.uk (DWF LLP)
http://www.homesandcommunities.co.uk (Homes and Communities Agency)
https://www.gov.uk/government/organisations/department-of-energy-climate-change
 (Department of Energy and Climate Change)

INDEX